THE MONSTROUS-FEMININE

In almost all critical writings on the horror film, woman is conceptualized only as victim. In *The Monstrous-Feminine* Barbara Creed challenges this patriarchal view by arguing that the prototype of all definitions of the monstrous is the female reproductive body.

Woman as castrator constitutes the most significant face of the monstrous-feminine in film, and Creed challenges the mythical patriarchal view that woman terrifies because she is castrated by arguing that woman primarily terrifies because of a fear that she might *castrate*. With close reference to a number of classic horror films including *Alien*, *The Brood*, *The Hunger*, *The Exorcist*, *Sisters*, *I Spit on Your Grave* and *Psycho*, she presents the first sustained analysis of the seven 'faces' of the monstrous-feminine from a feminist and psychoanalytic perspective, discussing woman as monster in relation to woman as archaic mother, monstrous womb, vampire, witch, possessed body, monstrous mother and castrator.

Her argument disrupts Freudian and Lacanian theories of sexual difference as well as existing theories of spectatorship and fetishism in relation to the male and female gaze in the cinema to provide a challenging and provocative rereading of classical and contemporary film and theoretical texts of interest to all teachers and students of film, feminist theory and cultural studies.

Barbara Creed lectures in Cinema Studies at La Trobe University, Melbourne.

POPULAR FICTION SERIES

Series editors:

Tony Bennett
Professor
School of Humanities
Griffith University

Graham Martin
Professor of English Literature
Open University

THE
MONSTROUS-FEMININE

Film

Barbara Creed

Routledge
Taylor & Francis Group

LONDON AND NEW YORK

First published 1993
by Routledge
2 Park Square, Milton Park, Abingdon, Oxon, OX14 4RN

Simultaneously published in the USA and Canada
by Routledge
711 Third Avenue, New York, NY 10017

Reprinted 1994, 1997, 2001, 2006, 2007

Transferred to Digital Printing 2007

*Routledge is an imprint of the Taylor & Francis Group,
an informa business*

© 1993 Barbara Creed

Typeset in 10 on 12 point Times by
Florencetype Ltd, Kewstoke

British Library Cataloguing in Publication Data
Creed, Barbara
The Monstrous – Feminine: Film, Feminism, Psychoanalysis. – (Popular Fiction
Series)
I. Title II. Series
791.43

Library of Congress Cataloguing in Publication Data
is available

ISBN10: 0-415-05258-0 (hbk)
ISBN10: 0-415-05259-9 (pbk)

ISBN13: 978-0-415-05258-0 (hbk)
ISBN13: 978-0-415-05259-7 (pbk)

CONTENTS

LIST OF ILLUSTRATIONS

Plate Section I

Plate Section II

ACKNOWLEDGEMENTS

I am extremely grateful to a large number of people who have helped make
this book possible. My thanks go to Annette Blonski, Freda Freiberg,
Mandy Merck, Merrilee Moss, Jane Selby, Lesley Stern and Lis Stoney for
reading sections of the manuscript and offering important ideas as well as
editorial assistance. In particular I wish to thank William D. Routt, my
colleague at La Trobe, for his invaluable comments, theoretical insights
and inspirational guidance. I also thank all those who offered me their
friendship and support: in particular Sophie Bibrowska, Nanette Creed,
Joyce Edwards, Joanne Finkelstein, Andrea Goldsmith, Pauline Nestor,
Iris O'Loughlin, Noel Purdon, John Slavin and Ishara Wishart.

Thanks also to my colleagues in the Cinema Studies Division of La
Trobe University who all contributed in some way to the intellectual and
social milieu in which the book was written – in particular: Chris Berry,
Rolando Caputo, Anna Dzenis, Dena Gleeson, Lorraine Mortimer,
Beverly Purnell and Rick Thompson. I am particularly grateful to Ted
Gott for his assistance with the illustrative material. Thanks also to the
editorial staff at Routledge – particularly Rebecca Barden, Emma Cotter
and Tamsin Meddings – for their excellent services and support.

The members of the feminist film group, 'Savage Sisters', who watched
countless horror films with me deserve a special thanks: Jo Comerford,
Allayne Davies, Rachelle DiDio and Krys Sykes. I also thank the many
students at La Trobe University who contributed valuable insights in the
horror film course I teach. Sandra Pascuzzi and Tania Rowe, from my local
videostore, deserve a special vote of thanks for cheerfully keeping me up
with the latest in horror.

I am particularly grateful to the Humanities Research Centre at the
Australian National university for a scholarship which enabled me to have
time for research and writing – and in such a congenial atmosphere. I also
thank those universities and institutions which invited me to present
seminars on my research, particularly: Flinders University in Adelaide; the
South Australian Media Resource Centre; the University of Tasmania; the
George Paton Gallery; the Melbourne Writers' Festival; and the Brisbane

Centre for Psychoanalytic Studies. Finally, the La Trobe University Publications Committee deserves a special acknowledgement for providing a grant towards publication of the illustrative material.

I wish to thank the following individuals for their assistance with the illustrative material. Ken Berryman of the *National Film and Sound Archive* of Australia; Tessa Forbes of the *British Film Institute*; Ted Gott of the *Australian National Gallery*; Beverly Partridge of *Films Around the World Inc*; and James Sabine of the *Australian Film Institute*.

Illustrative material has been provided by the *Kobal Collection*; *Design and Artists Copyright Society*; Robert Le Tet of *Entertainment Media*; Michael Leunig of *The Age*, the *National Film and Sound Archive* of Australia; and Robert Tappert of *Renaissance Pictures*.

Part I

FACES OF THE MONSTROUS-FEMININE: ABJECTION AND THE MATERNAL

INTRODUCTION

The horror film is populated by female monsters, many of which seem to have evolved from images that haunted the dreams, myths and artistic practices of our forebears many centuries ago. The female monster, or monstrous-feminine, wears many faces: the amoral primeval mother (*Aliens*, 1986); vampire (*The Hunger*, 1983); witch (*Carrie*, 1976); woman as monstrous womb (*The Brood*, 1979); woman as bleeding wound (*Dressed to Kill*, 1980); woman as possessed body (*The Exorcist*, 1973); the castrating mother (*Psycho*, 1960); woman as beautiful but deadly killer (*Basic Instinct*, 1992); aged psychopath (*Whatever Happened to Baby Jane?*, 1962); the monstrous girl–boy (*A Reflection of Fear*, 1973); woman as non-human animal (*Cat People*, 1942); woman as life-in-death (*Lifeforce*, 1985); woman as the deadly *femme castratrice* (*I Spit On Your Grave*, 1978). Although a great deal has been written about the horror film, very little of that work has discussed the representation of woman-as-monster. Instead, emphasis has been on woman as victim of the (mainly male) monster. Why has woman-as-monster been neglected in feminist theory and in virtually all significant theoretical analyses of the popular horror film? After all, this image is hardly new.

All human societies have a conception of the monstrous-feminine, of what it is about woman that is shocking, terrifying, horrific, abject. Freud linked man's fear of woman to his infantile belief that the mother is castrated. 'Probably no male human being is spared the fright of castration at the sight of a female genital', Freud wrote in his paper, 'Fetishism' in 1927 (p. 154). Joseph Campbell, in *The Masks of God: Primitive Mythology*, drew attention to woman as castrator and witch.

> there is a motif occurring in certain primitive mythologies, as well as in modern surrealist painting and neurotic dream, which is known to folklore as 'the toothed vagina' – the vagina that castrates. And a counterpart, the other way, is the so-called 'phallic mother,' a motif perfectly illustrated in the long fingers and nose of the witch.
>
> (Campbell, 1976, 73)

1

As well as its expression in surrealist art (see illustrations), the myth of the *vagina dentata* is extremely prevalent. Despite local variations, the myth generally states that women are terrifying because they have teeth in their vaginas and that the women must be tamed or the teeth somehow removed or softened – usually by a hero figure – before intercourse can safely take place. The witch, of course, is a familiar female monster; she is invariably represented as an old, ugly crone who is capable of monstrous acts. During the European witch trials of recent history she was accused of the most hideous crimes: cannibalism, murder, castration of male victims, and the advent of natural disasters such as storms, fires and the plague. Most societies also have myths about the female vampire, a creature who sucks the blood of helpless, often willing, victims and transforms them into her own kind.

Classical mythology, too, was populated with gendered monsters, many of which were female. The Sirens of classical mythology were described as enormous birds with the heads of women. They used their magical songs to lure sailors close to shore in order to drive the sailors' ships into hidden reefs. The Sirens then ate their helpless victims. The Medusa and her two sisters also presented a terrifying sight. They had huge heads, their hair consisted of writhing serpents, their teeth were as long as boars' tusks and they flew through the air on golden wings. Men unfortunate enough to look upon the Medusa with her evil eye were immediately turned to stone. In classical times, pendants and other jewellery depicting the Medusa's frightening appearance were frequently worn to ward off evil spirits, and warriors painted the female genitals on their shields in order to terrify the enemy. Freud takes up this point in his short essay, 'Medusa's head':

> If Medusa's head takes the place of a representation of the female genitals, or rather if it isolates their horrifying effects from their pleasure-giving ones, it may be recalled that displaying the genitals is familiar in other connections as an apotropaic act. What arouses horror in oneself will produce the same effect upon the enemy against whom one is seeking to defend oneself. We read in Rabelais of how the Devil took flight when the woman showed him her vulva.
>
> (p. 274)

It is not by accident that Freud linked the sight of the Medusa to the equally horrifying sight of the mother's genitals, for the concept of the monstrous-feminine, as constructed within/by a patriarchal and phallocentric ideology, is related intimately to the problem of sexual difference and castration. If we accept Freud's interpretation that the 'Medusa's head takes the place of a representation of the female genitals', we can see that the Medusan myth is mediated by a narrative about the *difference* of female sexuality as a difference which is grounded in monstrousness and which invokes castration anxiety in the male spectator. 'The sight of the Medusa's head makes the spectator stiff with terror, turns him to stone.' The irony of this was not lost on Freud, who pointed out that becoming stiff also means having an erection. 'Thus in the original situation it offers consolation to the spectator: he is still in possession of a penis, and the stiffening reassures him of the fact' (ibid., 273). One wonders if the experience of horror – of viewing the horror film – causes similar alterations in the body of the modern male spectator. And what of other phrases that are used by both male and female viewers – phrases such as: 'It scared the shit out of me'; 'It made me feel sick'; 'It gave me the creeps'? What is the relationship between physical states, bodily wastes (even if metaphoric ones) and the horrific – in particular, the monstrous-feminine?

I have used the term 'monstrous-feminine' as the term 'female monster' implies a simple reversal of 'male monster'. The reasons why the monstrous-feminine horrifies her audience are quite different from the reasons why the male monster horrifies his audience. A new term is needed to specify these differences. As with all other stereotypes of the feminine, from virgin to whore, she is defined in terms of her sexuality. The phrase 'monstrous-feminine' emphasizes the importance of gender in the construction of her monstrosity.

Before discussing the questions raised above, it is relevant to consider the various ways in which theorists and critics have approached the question of woman as monster in popular film. In general, they have adopted one of the following approaches: simply discussed female monstrosity as part of male monstrosity; argued that woman only terrifies when represented as man's castrated other; referred to her only in passing; or argued that there are no 'great' female monsters in the tradition of Frankenstein's monster or Dracula. One theorist who has contributed a great deal to a critical appreciation of the horror film is Robin Wood; but, although he is interested in gender relations in the horror film, he has not discussed the nature of female monstrosity in any detail. To my knowledge no one has presented a sustained analysis of the different faces of the female monster or 'the monstrous-feminine'.

Gérard Lenne in his article, 'Monster and victim: women in the horror film', is fairly typical of those who find the very idea of a female monster offensive to their rather quaint, but deeply sexist, notions of chivalry. Gérard Lenne argues that there 'are very few monstrous and disfigured women in the fantastic, and so much the better'. He appears to believe that women should be represented only in terms of their 'natural' role in life. 'Is it not reasonable that woman, who, in life, is both mother and lover, should be represented by characters that convey the feeling of a sheltering peace?' (Lenne, 1979, 35). He allows that there are female monsters but then finds reasons why they are not real monsters; for instance he states that the female vampire exists but her role is usually 'secondary'; the schizophrenic female monsters of *Repulsion* and *Sisters* are understandable because 'schizophrenia is readily assimilated to female behaviour' (ibid., 37). Lenne evades the identification of female monsters such as the half-human, half-animal female hybrids of *Island of Lost Souls* and the 'revolting' figure in *The Reptile* by dismissing them as 'problematic'. 'Woman is seldom to be found among the great psychopaths' and there is 'not one single female mad scientist' (ibid., 38). *The Exorcist* is simply the result of a 'prevailing trend for making female versions of the great myths of the fantastic' (ibid.). The only 'indisputably active role in the fantastic that is exclusively female' is that of the witch (ibid., 39). However, Lenne is more interested in the 'attractiveness of the witch' than in her monstrousness. After producing a litany of sexist comments, he concludes that the 'great monsters are all male'. In his view, woman exists in the horror film primarily as victim. 'Perfect as a tearful victim, what she does best is to faint in the arms of a gorilla, or a mummy, or a werewolf, or a Frankensteinian creature' (ibid., 35).

While it is true that there are fewer classic female monsters than male, it does not follow that these creatures are not terrifying or truly monstrous. Lenne does not even mention Paula the Ape-Woman of the 1940s played by Acquanetta in both *Captive Wild Woman* and *Jungle Woman* and by Vicky Lane in *Jungle Captive* – the classic female monster with more than one film to her credit. Lenne's definition of what constitutes the monstrous is questionable on a number of counts, particularly his statement that the horror of schizophrenia is somehow ameliorated not only because it is understandable but because it is supposedly a 'female' illness.

In his book, *Dark Romance*, David J. Hogan examines the sexual aspect of the horror cinema. While he draws attention to those films, within each sub-genre, in which the monster is female, he does not examine the nature of female monstrosity in any depth. Where he does discuss this issue, his response is ambivalent. On the one hand, he states that horror films with female monsters as central characters are 'a relatively new phenomenon, and seem to have developed parallel with the growth of the women's movement in the United States and Europe'. However, he dismisses most of these films as 'obvious and childish' (Hogan, 1986, 19). On the other hand, Hogan does draw attention to a 'fascinating subgenre' that appeared in the early 1950s, which he calls the 'cinema of lost women'. This sub-genre, in which women choose to live apart from men, includes titles such as: *Queen of Outer Space*, *The She-Creature* and *Voodoo Women*. A central feature of these films is 'their insistence upon the adversary aspect of man–woman relationships', which Hogan finds 'disquieting' (ibid., 61–3). Hogan is generally dismissive of films with female monsters. He does, however, acknowledge the contribution of Barbara Steele, known as the 'High Priestess of Horror', to the genre. He argues that her appeal resides in her ability 'to express a tantalizing sort of evil, and a sexual ambivalence that is at once enticing and ghastly'. In his view, Steele represents, more than any other genre star, the connection between sex and death as well as the culture's ambiguous attitude to female sexuality (ibid., 164).

In *Dreadful Pleasures* James B. Twitchell argues that horror films are similar to 'formulaic rituals' which provide the adolescent with social information. 'Modern horror myths prepare the teenager for the anxieties of reproduction . . . they are fables of sexual identity' (Twitchell, 1985, 7). He is primarily interested in the monster as a figure of transformation – the vampire, werewolf, zombie, psychopath. On the one hand, Twitchell draws attention to female monsters who belong to these categories, but on the other hand he does not seriously examine films, such as *Carrie* and *The Exorcist*, that are made from the perspective of a female rite of passage. He dismisses the female psychopath as 'mannish' (ibid., 257) which suggests he believes that 'femininity', by definition, excludes all forms of aggressive, monstrous behaviour.

Only those writers whose analysis of horror draws on recent debates about the nature of sexual difference attempt to come to terms with the nature of monstrosity in relation to gender. In general, these theorists work from the Freudian position that woman horrifies because she is castrated. One of the most substantial analyses of the monster is presented by Stephen Neale in his book, *Genre*. Drawing on Laura Mulvey's theory of the male gaze and male castration anxiety, Neale argues that the classic male horror monster represents castration but only in order to fill the lack, to disavow castration and thereby entertain the male spectator by soothing his castration anxieties. According to Neale, 'most monsters tend, in fact, to be defined as "male," especially in so far as the objects of their desire are almost exclusively women' (Neale, 1980, 61).

> In this respect, it could well be maintained that it is woman's sexuality, that which renders them desirable – but also threatening – to men, which constitutes the real problem that the horror cinema exists to explore, and which constitutes also and ultimately that which is really monstrous.
>
> (ibid., 61)

In Neale's view, there are two ways of interpreting the monster. The first is that the monster signifies the boundary between the human and the non-human. The second is that it is the male fear of castration which ultimately produces and delineates the monstrous. Neale argues that man's fascination with and fear of female sexuality is endlessly reworked within the signifying practices of the horror film. Thus, the horror film offers an abundant display of fetishistic effects whose function is to attest to the perversity of the patriarchal order founded, as it is, on a misconception – the erroneous belief that woman is castrated.

A sustained and important discussion of the monstrous female is presented by Susan Lurie in her article, 'The construction of the "castrated woman" in psychoanalysis and cinema'. Adopting an approach in opposition to Neale's, Lurie challenges the traditional Freudian position by arguing that men fear women, not because women are castrated but because they are *not* castrated. Lurie asserts that the male fears woman because woman *is not* mutilated like a man might be *if he were* castrated; woman is physically whole, intact and in possession of all her sexual powers. The notion of the castrated woman is a phantasy intended to ameliorate man's real fear of what woman might do to him. (I have used the term 'phantasy' rather than 'fantasy' throughout because I wish to emphasize phantasy in the Freudian sense in which the subject is represented as a protagonist engaged in the activity of wish fulfilment. 'Fantasy' sometimes has the connotations of whimsy – a notion I wish to avoid.) Specifically, he fears that woman could castrate him both psychically and in a sense physically. He imagines the latter might take place during intercourse when the penis 'disappears' inside woman's 'devouring mouth' (Lurie, 1981–2, 55). Lurie's analysis is important, particularly her discussion of man's fear of woman as castrating other. It is this aspect of Lurie's argument that I will develop in detail in Part II of my analysis. But, like Neale, Lurie is ultimately concerned only with the representation of woman as *victim*. She argues that man deals with his anxiety that woman is not castrated by constructing her as castrated within the signifying practices of the film text. She analyses this process in relation to Alfred Hitchcock's *The Birds*. She claims that the 'proliferation of efforts' to represent woman as symbolically castrated, particularly in the romance genre of the fiction film, 'argues vigorously against the hypothesis that men regard women as a priori castrated' (ibid., 56).

Drawing on Lurie's work, Linda Williams argues, in her article 'When the woman looks', that it is woman's 'power-in-difference' (1984, 89) that is central to the representation of the monster in horror. She states that classic horror films such as *Nosferatu* and *The Phantom of the Opera* frequently represent 'a surprising (and at times subversive) affinity between monster and woman' in that woman's look acknowledges their 'similar status within patriarchal structures of seeing'. Both are constructed as 'biological freaks' whose bodies represent a fearful and threatening form of sexuality. This has important implications for the female spectator. 'So there is a sense in which the woman's look at the monster . . . is also a recognition of their similar status as potent threats to vulnerable male power' (ibid., 90). Williams's argument challenges the assumption that the monster is identified with masculinity and opens the way for a discussion of woman's 'power-in-difference'. Although Williams's thesis is important, because it challenges conventional approaches to the horror film, it still leaves unanswered questions about the nature of female monstrosity. What exactly is it about woman herself, as a being quite separate from the male monster, that produces definitions of female monstrosity?

Apart from Williams, nearly all of the articles discussed above deal with woman as victim in the horror film. The main reason for this is that most writers adopt Freud's argument that woman terrifies because she is castrated, that is, already constituted as victim. Such a position only serves to reinforce patriarchal definitions of woman which represent and reinforce the essentialist view that woman, *by nature*, is a victim. My intention is to explore the representation of woman in the horror film and to argue that woman *is* represented as monstrous in a significant number of horror films. However, I am not arguing that simply because the monstrous-feminine is constructed as an active rather than passive figure that this image is 'feminist' or 'liberated'. The presence of the monstrous-feminine in the popular horror film speaks to us more about male fears than about female desire or feminine subjectivity. However, this presence does challenge the view that the male spectator is almost always situated in an active, sadistic position and the female spectator in a passive, masochistic one. An analysis of this figure also necessitates a rereading of key aspects of Freudian theory, particularly his theory of the Oedipus complex and castration crisis.

Part I presents a detailed discussion of at least five faces of the monstrous-feminine in relation to Julia Kristeva's theory of the abject and the maternal. (Chapters 1 and 2, with some modifications, were originally published as a journal article: 'Horror and the monstrous-feminine: an imaginary abjection', *Screen* 27.1 (1986): 45–70.) I will argue that when woman is represented as monstrous it is almost always in relation to her mothering and reproductive functions. These faces are: the archaic mother; the monstrous womb; the witch; the vampire; and the possessed woman. In Part II I will discuss the representation of woman as monstrous in relation to Freud's theory of castration. Whereas Freud argued that woman terrifies because she appears to be castrated, man's fear of castration has, in my view, led him to construct another monstrous phantasy – that of woman as castrator. Here woman's monstrousness is linked more directly to questions of sexual desire than to the area of reproduction. The image of woman as castrator takes at least three forms: woman as the deadly *femme castratrice*, the castrating mother and the *vagina dentata*. Freud did not analyse man's fears of woman as castrator; in fact he seems to have repressed this image of woman in his writings about sexual difference and in his case histories. Of necessity, then, this investigation will, through its analysis of popular fictions, entail a critique of some of the main tenets of Freudian theory and contemporary film theory.

1

KRISTEVA, FEMININITY, ABJECTION

We may call it a border; abjection is above all ambiguity. Because, while releasing a hold, it does not radically cut off the subject from what threatens it – on the contrary, abjection acknowledges it to be in perpetual danger.

Julia Kristeva, *Powers of Horror*

Julia Kristeva's *Powers of Horror* provides us with a preliminary hypothesis for an analysis of the representation of woman as monstrous in the horror film. Although her study is concerned with psychoanalysis and literature, it nevertheless suggests a way of situating the monstrous-feminine in the horror film in relation to the maternal figure and what Kristeva terms 'abjection', that which does not 'respect borders, positions, rules', that which 'disturbs identity, system, order' (Kristeva, 1982, 4). In general terms, Kristeva is attempting to explore the different ways in which abjection works within human societies, as a means of separating out the human from the non-human and the fully constituted subject from the partially formed subject. Ritual becomes a means by which societies both renew their initial contact with the abject element and then exclude that element. Through ritual, the demarcation lines between the human and non-human are drawn up anew and presumably made all the stronger for that process. (One of Kristeva's aims in *Powers of Horror* is to present a rewriting of many of the ideas and beliefs put forward by the College of Sociology, specifically those associated with the nature of femininity, abjection and the sacred. For an introduction to the philosophy and writings of the college see *The College of Sociology (1937–39)* edited by Denis Hollier.)

A full examination of this theory is outside the scope of this project; I propose to draw mainly on Kristeva's discussion of the construction of abjection in the human subject in relation to her notion of (a) the 'border' (b) the mother–child relationship and (c) the feminine body. At crucial points, I shall also refer to her writings on the abject in relation to religious discourses. This area cannot be ignored, for what becomes apparent in reading her work is that definitions of the monstrous as constructed in the modern horror text are grounded in ancient religious and historical notions of abjection – particularly in relation to the following religious 'abominations': sexual immorality and perversion; corporeal alteration, decay and death; human sacrifice; murder; the corpse; bodily wastes; the feminine body and incest. These forms of abjection are also central to the construction of the monstrous in the modern horror film.

The place of the abject is 'the place where meaning collapses', the place where 'I' am not. The abject threatens life; it must be 'radically excluded' (Kristeva, 1982, 2) from the place of the living subject, propelled away from the body and deposited on the other side of an imaginary border which separates the self from that which threatens the self. Although the subject must exclude the abject, the abject must, nevertheless, be tolerated for that which threatens to destroy life also helps to define life. Further, the activity of exclusion is necessary to guarantee that the subject take up his/her proper place in relation to the symbolic.

The abject can be experienced in various ways – one of which relates to biological bodily functions, the other of which has been inscribed in a symbolic (religious) economy. For instance, Kristeva claims that food loathing is 'perhaps the most elementary and archaic form of abjection' (ibid.). Food, however, only becomes abject if it signifies a border 'between two distinct entities or territories' (ibid., 75). Kristeva describes how, for her, the skin on the top of milk, which is offered to her by her father and mother, is a 'sign of their desire', a sign separating her world from their world, a sign which she does not want. 'But since the food is not an "other" for "me," who am only in their desire, I expel myself, I spit myself out, I abject myself within the same motion through which "I" claim to establish myself' (ibid., 3). In relation to the horror film, it is relevant to note that food loathing is frequently represented as a major source of abjection, particularly the eating of human flesh (*Blood Feast, Motel Hell, Blood Diner, The Hills Have Eyes, The Corpse Grinders*).

The ultimate in abjection is the corpse. The body protects itself from bodily wastes such as shit, blood, urine and pus by ejecting these things from the body just as it expels food that, for whatever reason, the subject finds loathsome. The body ejects these substances, at the same time extricating itself from them and from the place where they fall, so that it might continue to live:

Such wastes drop so that I might live, until, from loss to loss, nothing remains in me and my entire body falls beyond the limit – *cadere*, cadaver. If dung signifies the other side of the border, the place where I am not and which permits me to be, the corpse, the most sickening of wastes, is a border that has encroached upon everything. It is no longer I who expel. 'I' is expelled.

(ibid., 3–4)

Within a biblical context, the corpse is also utterly abject. It signifies one of the most basic forms of pollution – the body without a soul. As a form of waste it represents the opposite of the spiritual, the religious symbolic. In relation to the horror film, it is relevant to note that several of the most popular horrific figures are 'bodies without souls' (the vampire), the 'living corpse' (the zombie), corpse-eater (the ghoul) and the robot or android. What is also interesting is that such ancient figures of abjection as the vampire, the ghoul, the zombie and the witch (one of her many crimes was that she used corpses for her rites of magic) continue to provide some of the most compelling images of horror in the modern cinema. Were-creatures, whose bodies signify a collapse of the boundaries between human and animal, also belong to this category.

Abjection also occurs where the individual is a hypocrite, a liar. Abject things are those that highlight the 'fragility of the law' and that exist on the other side of the border which separates out the living subject from that which threatens its extinction. But abjection is not something of which the subject can ever feel free – it is always there, beckoning the self to take up the place of abjection, the place where meaning collapses. The subject, constructed in/through language, through a desire for meaning, is also spoken by the abject, the place of meaninglessness – thus, the subject is constantly beset by abjection which fascinates desire but which must be repelled for fear of self-annihilation. A crucial point is that abjection is always ambiguous. Like Bataille, Kristeva emphasizes the attraction, as well as the horror, of the undifferentiated.

ABJECTION AND THE HORROR FILM

The horror film would appear to be, in at least three ways, an illustration of the work of abjection. First, the horror film abounds in images of abjection, foremost of which is the corpse, whole and mutilated, followed by an array of bodily wastes such as blood, vomit, saliva, sweat, tears and putrefying flesh. In terms of Kristeva's notion of the border, when we say such-and-such a horror film 'made me sick' or 'scared the shit out of me', we are actually foregrounding that specific horror film as a 'work of abjection' or 'abjection at work' – almost in a literal sense. Viewing the horror film signifies a desire not only for perverse pleasure (confronting sickening, horrific images/ being filled with terror/desire for the undifferentiated) but also a desire, once having been filled with perversity, taken pleasure in perversity, to throw up, throw out, eject the abject (from the safety of the spectator's seat). In Kristeva's view, woman is specifically related to polluting objects which fall into two categories: excremental and menstrual. This in turn gives woman a special relationship to the abject – a crucial point which I will discuss shortly.

Second, the concept of a border is central to the construction of the monstrous in the horror film; that which crosses or threatens to cross the 'border' is abject. Although the specific nature of the border changes from film to film, the function of the monstrous remains the same – to bring about an encounter between the symbolic order and that which threatens its stability. In some horror films the monstrous is produced at the border between human and inhuman, man and beast (*Dr Jekyll and Mr Hyde*, *Creature from the Black Lagoon, King Kong*); in others the border is between the normal and the supernatural, good and evil (*Carrie, The Exorcist, The Omen, Rosemary's Baby*); or the monstrous is produced at the border which separates those who take up their proper gender roles from those who do not (*Psycho, Dressed to Kill, A Reflection of Fear*); or the border is between normal and abnormal sexual desire (*The Hunger, Cat People*). Most horror films also construct a border between what Kristeva refers to as 'the clean and proper body' and the abject body, or the body which has lost its form and integrity. The fully symbolic body must bear no indication of its debt to nature. In Kristeva's view the image of woman's body, because of its maternal functions, acknowledges its 'debt to nature' and consequently is more likely to signify the abject (ibid., 102). The notion of the material female body is central to the construction of the border in the horror film. I will explore this crucial area fully in the following chapters.

Interestingly, various sub-genres of the horror film seem to correspond to religious categories of abjection. For instance, cannibalism, a religious abomination, is central to the 'meat' movie (*Night of the Living Dead, The Hills Have Eyes*); the corpse as abomination becomes the abject of ghoul and zombie movies (*The Evil Dead; Zombie Flesheaters*); blood is central to the vampire film (*The Hunger*) as well as the horror film in general (*Bloodsucking Freaks*); the corpse is constructed as the abject of virtually all horror films; and bodily disfigurement as a religious abomination is also central to the slasher movie, particularly those in which woman is slashed, the mark a sign of her 'difference', her impurity (*Dressed to Kill, Psycho*).

The third way in which the horror film illustrates the work of abjection is in the construction of the maternal figure as abject. Kristeva argues that all individuals experience abjection at the time of their earliest attempts to break away from the mother. She sees the mother–child relation as one marked by conflict: the child struggles to break free but the mother is reluctant to release it. Because of the 'instability of the symbolic function' in relation to this most crucial area – 'the prohibition placed on the maternal body (as a defense against autoeroticism and incest taboo)', Kristeva argues that the maternal body becomes a site of conflicting desires. 'Here, drives hold sway and constitute a strange space that I shall name, after Plato (*Timaeus*, 48–53), a *chora*, a receptacle' (ibid., 14). The position of the child is rendered even more unstable because, while the mother retains a close hold over the child, it can serve to authenticate her

11

existence – an existence which needs validation because of her problematic relation to the symbolic realm.

In the child's attempts to break away, the mother becomes an 'abject'; thus, in this context, where the child struggles to become a separate subject, abjection becomes *a precondition of narcissism* (ibid.). Once again we can see abjection at work in the horror text where the child struggles to break away from the mother, representative of the archaic maternal figure, in a context in which the father is invariably absent (*Psycho, Carrie, The Birds*). In these films the maternal figure is constructed as the monstrous-feminine. By refusing to relinquish her hold on her child, she prevents it from taking up its proper place in relation to the symbolic. Partly consumed by the desire to remain locked in a blissful relationship with the mother and partly terrified of separation, the child finds it easy to succumb to the comforting pleasure of the dyadic relationship. Kristeva argues that a whole area of religion has assumed the function of tackling this danger:

> This is precisely where we encounter the rituals of defilement and their derivatives, which, based on the feeling of abjection and all converging on the maternal, attempt to symbolize the other threat to the subject: that of being swamped by the dual relationship, thereby risking the loss not of a part (castration) but of the totality of his living being. The function of these religious rituals is to ward off the subject's fear of his very own identity sinking irretrievably into the mother.
>
> (ibid., 64)

How, then, are prohibitions against contact with the mother enacted and enforced? In answering this question, Kristeva links the universal practices of rituals of defilement to the mother. She argues that within the practices of all rituals of defilement, polluting objects fall into two categories: excremental, which threatens identity from the outside; and menstrual, which threatens from within. Both categories of polluting objects relate to the mother. The relation of menstrual blood is self-evident: the association of excremental objects with the maternal figure is brought about because of the mother's role in sphincteral training. Here, Kristeva argues that the subject's first contact with 'authority' is with the maternal authority when the child learns, through interaction with the mother, about its body: the shape of the body, the clean and the unclean, the proper and improper areas of the body. It is the concept of the 'maternal authority' that, in my analysis of the monstrous-feminine in horror, I will expand and extend into the symbolic in relation to castration. Kristeva refers to the processes of toilet training as a 'primal mapping of the body' which she calls 'semiotic'. She distinguishes between maternal 'authority' and 'paternal laws': 'Maternal authority is the trustee of that mapping of the self's clean and proper body; it is distinguished from paternal laws within which, with the phallic phase and acquisition of language, the destiny of man will take shape' (ibid., 72). In her discussion of rituals of defilement in relation to the Indian caste system, Kristeva draws a distinction between maternal authority and paternal law. She argues that the period of the 'mapping of the self's clean and proper body' (ibid.) is characterized by the exercise of 'authority without guilt', a time when there is a 'fusion between mother and nature' (ibid., 74). However, the symbolic ushers in a 'totally different universe of socially signifying performances where embarrassment, shame, guilt, desire etc. come into play – the order of the phallus'. In the Indian context, these two worlds exist harmoniously side by side because of the working of defilement rites. Here Kristeva is referring to the practice of public defecation in India. Kristeva argues that this split between the world of the mother (a universe without shame) and the world of the father (a universe of shame), would in other social contexts produce psychosis; in India it finds a 'perfect socialization': 'This may be because the setting up of the rite of defilement takes on the function of the hyphen, the virgule, allowing the two universes of *filth* and *prohibition* to brush lightly against each other without necessarily being identified as such, as *object* and as *law*' (ibid.).

Virtually all horror texts represent the monstrous-feminine in relation to Kristeva's notion of maternal authority and the mapping of the self's clean and proper body. Images of blood, vomit, pus, shit, etc., are central to our culturally/socially constructed notions of the horrific. They signify a split between two orders: the maternal authority and the law of the father. On the one hand, these images of bodily wastes threaten a subject that is already constituted, in relation to the symbolic, as 'whole and proper'. Consequently, they fill the subject – both the protagonist in the text and the spectator in the cinema – with disgust and loathing. On the other hand they also point back to a time when a 'fusion between mother and nature' existed; when bodily wastes, while set apart from the body, were not seen as objects of embarrassment and shame. Their presence in the horror film may invoke a response of disgust from the audience situated as it is within the social symbolic but at a more archaic level the representation of bodily wastes may invoke pleasure in breaking the taboo on filth – sometimes described as a pleasure in perversity – and a pleasure in returning to that time when the mother–child relationship was marked by an untrammelled pleasure in 'playing' with the body and its wastes.

The modern horror film often 'plays' with its audience, saturating it with scenes of blood and gore, deliberately pointing to the fragility of the symbolic order in the domain of the body where the body never ceases to signal the repressed world of the mother. In *The Exorcist* the world of the symbolic, represented by the priest-as-father, and the world of the pre-symbolic, represented by a pubescent girl aligned with the devil, clashed

13

head on in scenes where the foulness of woman was signified by her putrid, filthy body covered in blood, urine, excrement and bile. Significantly, the possessed girl is also about to menstruate – in one scene, blood from her wounded genitals mingles with menstrual blood to provide one of the film's key images of horror. (See Chapter 3 for a detailed discussion of *The Exorcist*.) In *Carrie*, the film's most monstrous act occurs when the couple are drenched in pig's blood, which symbolizes menstrual blood in the terms set up by the film: women are referred to in the film as 'pigs', women 'bleed like pigs', and the pig's blood runs down Carrie's body at a moment of intense pleasure, just as her own menstrual blood ran down her legs during a similar pleasurable moment when she enjoyed her body in the shower. Here, women's blood and pig's blood flow together, signifying horror, shame and humiliation. In this film, however, the mother speaks for the symbolic, identifying with an order which has defined women's sexuality as the source of all evil and menstruation as the sign of sin. (See Chapter 5 for further elaboration).

Kristeva's semiotic posits a pre-verbal dimension of language which relates to sounds and tone of the voice and to direct expression of the drives and physical contact with the maternal figure: 'it is dependent upon meaning, but in a way that is not that of *linguistic* signs nor of the *symbolic* order they found' (ibid., 72). With the subject's entry into the symbolic, which separates the child from the mother, the maternal figure and the authority she signifies are repressed. Kristeva then argues that it is the function of defilement rites, particularly those relating to menstrual and excremental objects/substances, to point to the 'boundary' between the maternal semiotic authority and the paternal symbolic law.

Kristeva argues that, historically, it has been the function of religion to purify the abject, but with the disintegration of these 'historical forms' of religion, the work of purification now rests solely with 'that catharsis *par excellence* called art' (ibid., 17). This, I would argue, is also the central ideological project of the popular horror film – purification of the abject through a 'descent into the foundations of the symbolic construct'. The horror film attempts to bring about a confrontation with the abject (the corpse, bodily wastes, the monstrous-feminine) in order finally to eject the abject and redraw the boundaries between the human and non-human. As a form of modern defilement rite, the horror film attempts to separate out the symbolic order from all that threatens its stability, particularly the mother and all that her universe signifies. In this sense, signifying horror involves a representation of, and a reconciliation with, the maternal body. Kristeva's theory of abjection provides us with an important theoretical framework for analysing, in the horror film, the representation of the monstrous-feminine, in relation to woman's reproductive and mothering functions. However, abjection by its very nature is ambiguous; it both repels and attracts. Separating out the mother and her universe from the

14

symbolic order is not an easy task – perhaps it is, finally, not even possible. Furthermore, when we begin to examine closely the nature of the monstrous mother we discover she also has a crucial role to play in relation to castration and the child's passage into the symbolic order – issues discussed in Part II in relation to the images of the *vagina dentata* and the castrating mother.

2

HORROR AND THE ARCHAIC
MOTHER: *ALIEN*

Fear of the archaic mother turns out to be essentially fear of her
generative power.

Julia Kristeva, *Powers of Horror*

The science-fiction horror film, *Alien*, presents a complex representation of
the monstrous-feminine as archaic mother. *Alien* begins with a long shot of a
spaceship, the *Nostromo*, hovering in outer space, poised above a set of
subtitles which tells us that the ship has a crew of seven and is returning to
earth with a cargo of 20 million tons of mineral ore. Inside the ship an eerie
atmosphere seems to engulf everything: the dark labyrinthine passages,
storerooms, pipes, machinery. The silence is suddenly pierced by the star-
ship's computer flickering to life as it awakens the crew members, each one
held in a state of suspended animation, lying peacefully in a white sleep pod.

Director Ridley Scott introduces us to the ship and its crew in a matter-
of-fact way, emphasizing the small, practical details of life in outer space.
Awakened by the computer, affectionately called 'Mother', the crew members complain about the cold, their low salaries, and the fact that the only
good thing on board is the coffee. After communicating with 'Mother'
Dallas, the Captain, discovers she has interrupted the voyage because she
has intercepted a transmission from a nearby planet. After some technical
problems three of the crew leave the *Nostromo* for the planet's dark,
inhospitable surface. They enter a derelict space craft where Kane, one of
the crew members, is attacked by an alien life form which attaches itself
with a deadly grip to his face. Kane and the 'thing' are taken back on board
the ship despite strong objections from Ripley (Sigourney Weaver), who
reminds the others that they have broken quarantine orders. But it is too
late; the alien is on board. The remainder of the narrative is concerned
with the creature's deadly attacks on the crew and their attempts to kill it.
The alien is a mysterious, terrifying creature that changes shape as it
metamorphoses into a mature life form. Highly intelligent, secretive,
sadistic, it is impossible to find or kill. Eventually Ripley, the only one left
alive, prepares to do battle with the alien.

16

One of the major concerns of the sci-fi horror film (*Alien*, *The Thing*, *Invasion of the Body Snatchers*, *Altered States*) is the reworking of the primal scene, the scene of birth, in relation to the representation of other forms of copulation and procreation. *Invasion of the Body Snatchers* explores the themes of bodily invasion and paranoia. The invading creature first exists as a giant egg/pod, which has come to Earth from another galaxy. As the pod silently hatches the creature simultaneously creates a replica of the human it wishes to become. In *The Thing* the primal scene is also presented as a series of grotesque bodily invasions; here the creature is able to take over both the human and animal body and clone itself into an exact replica of the invaded being. In both these films conception and birth are presented as a form of cloning; the sexual act becomes an act of vampirism. In *Altered States* a male scientist is able to take himself back to more primitive stages of existence through the agency of hallucinogenic drugs. He takes these while enfolded in a womb-like bath of special fluids. Eventually he gives birth to himself as an ape-creature. Procreation and birth take place without the agency of the opposite sex; and the creature born is primitive rather than civilized suggesting that a thin line separates the human animal from its ancestors. Central to all of these films are scenes which explore different forms of birth.

The primal scene is also crucial to *Alien* as is the figure of the mother, in the guise of the archaic mother. The archaic mother is the parthenogenetic mother, the mother as primordial abyss, the point of origin and of end. Although the archaic mother, the creature who laid the eggs, is never seen in *Alien*, her presence is signalled in a number of ways. She is there in the text's various representations of the primal scene, and in its depiction of birth and death. She is there in the film's images of blood, darkness and death. She is also there in the chameleon figure of the alien, the monster as fetish-object of and for the archaic mother. Signs of the archaic mother are particularly evident in the film's first section, with its emphasis on at least four different representations of the primal scene. Before discussing the archaic mother in detail, it is important to consider Freud's theory of the primal phantasies and the various representations of this scene in the text.

According to Freud, every child either watches its parents in the act of sexual intercourse or has phantasies about that act. These phantasies are about origins: the primal scene represents to the child its own origins in its parents' lovemaking; the seduction phantasy is about the origin of sexual desire; and the phantasy of castration pictures the origins of sexual differ- ence. In 'From the history of an infantile neurosis' Freud left open the question of the cause of the phantasy but suggested that it may initially be aroused by 'an observation of the sexual intercourse of animals' (p. 59). In situations where the child actually witnesses sexual intercourse between its parents, Freud argued that all children arrive at the same conclusion. In 'The sexual theories of children' he stated that children may 'adopt what may be called a *sadistic view of coition*' (p. 220). If the child perceives, whether in reality or phantasy, the primal scene as a monstrous act it may phantasize animals or mythical creatures as taking part in the scenario. Possibly the many mythological stories in which people copulate with animals and other creatures (Europa and Zeus, Leda and the Swan) are reworkings of the primal scene narrative. The Sphinx, with her lion's body and woman's face, is an interesting figure in this context. Freud suggested that the Riddle of the Sphinx was probably a distorted version of the great riddle that faces all children – Where do babies come from? In *Introductory Lectures on Psychoanalysis*, Freud stated that an extreme form of the primal phantasy is that of 'observing parental intercourse while one is still an unborn baby in the womb' (p. 370).

Alien presents various representations of the primal scene. Behind each of these lurks the figure of the archaic mother, that is, the image of the mother as sole origin of all life. The first primal scenario, which takes the form of a birthing scene, occurs in *Alien* at the beginning, when the camera/spectator explores the inner space of the mother-ship. This exploratory sequence of the inner body of the 'Mother' culminates in a long tracking shot down one of the corridors which leads to a womb-like chamber where the crew of seven are woken up from their protracted sleep by Mother's voice. The seven astronauts emerge slowly from their sleep pods in what amounts to a rebirthing scene which is marked by a fresh, antiseptic atmosphere. In outer space, birth is a well controlled, clean, painless affair. There is no blood, trauma or terror. This scene could be interpreted as a primal phantasy in which the human subject is born fully developed – even copulation is redundant. The first birth scene could be viewed as a representation of incestuous desire *par excellence*, for the father is completely absent; here the mother is sole parent and sole life-support.

The second representation of the primal scene takes place when three of the crew approach the body of the unknown spaceship. They enter through a 'vaginal' opening which is shaped like a horseshoe, its curved sides like two long legs spread apart at the entrance. They travel along a corridor which seems to be made of a combination of inorganic and organic material – as if the inner space of this ship were alive. Compared to the atmosphere of the *Nostromo*, however, this ship is dark, dank and mysterious. A ghostly light glimmers and the sounds of their movements echo throughout the caverns. In the first chamber, the three explorers find a huge alien life form which appears to have been dead for a long time. Its bones are bent outward as if it exploded from the inside. One of the trio, Kane (John Hurt) is lowered down a shaft into the gigantic womb-like chamber in which rows of eggs are hatching. Kane approaches one of the eggs; as he touches it with his gloved hand it opens out, revealing a mass of pulsating flesh. Suddenly, the monstrous thing inside leaps up and attaches itself to

Kane's helmet, its tail penetrating Kane's mouth in order to fertilize itself inside his stomach.

This representation of the primal scene recalls Freud's reference to an extreme primal scene phantasy where the subject imagines travelling back inside the womb to watch her/his parents having sexual intercourse, perhaps to watch themselves being conceived. Here, three astronauts explore the gigantic, cavernous, malevolent womb of the mother. Two members of the group watch an enactment of the primal scene in which Kane is violated in an act of phallic penetration. Kane himself is guilty of the strongest transgression; he actually peers into the egg/womb in order to investigate its mysteries. In so doing, he becomes a 'part' of the primal scene, taking up the place of the mother, the one who is penetrated, the one who bears the offspring of the union. When male bodies become grotesque, they tend to take on characteristics associated with female bodies; in this instance man's body becomes grotesque because it is capable of being penetrated. From this union, the monstrous creature is born. But man, not woman, is the 'mother' and Kane dies in agony as the alien gnaws its way through his stomach. The birth of the alien from Kane's stomach recalls Freud's description of a common misunderstanding that many children have about birth, that is, that the mother is somehow 'impregnated' through the mouth – she may eat a special food – and the baby grows in her stomach, from which it is also born. Here, we have a version of the primal scene in which the infant is conceived orally.

Another version of the primal scene – Daniel Dervin argues it is a convention of the science fiction film (Dervin, 1980, 102) – occurs when smaller crafts or bodies are ejected from the mother-ship into outer space; although sometimes the ejected body remains attached to the mother-ship by a long lifeline or umbilical chord. This scene is presented in two separate ways: (1) when Kane's body, wrapped in a white shroud, is ejected from the mother-ship; and (2) when the small space capsule, in which Ripley is trying to escape from the alien, is expelled from the underbelly of the mother-ship. In the former, the mother's body has become hostile; it contains the alien whose one purpose is to kill and devour all of Mother's children who, in terms of normal burial procedures, would be ejected from the ship to float away into a more friendly environment – outer space rather than inner space. In the second birth scene the living infant is ejected from the malevolent body of the mother before the infant is destroyed; in this scenario, the 'mother's' body explodes at the moment of giving birth.

Although the archaic mother as a visible figure does not appear in *Alien*, her presence forms a vast backdrop for the enactment of all the events. She is there in the images of birth, the representations of the primal scene, the womb-like imagery, the long winding tunnels leading to inner chambers, the rows of hatching eggs, the body of the mother-ship, the voice of the life-support system, and the birth of the alien. She is the generative mother, the pre-phallic mother, the being who exists prior to knowledge of the phallus. This archaic figure is somewhat different from the mother of the semiotic chora, posed by Kristeva, in that the latter is the pre-Oedipal mother who exists in relation to the family and the symbolic order. The concept of the parthenogenetic, archaic mother adds another dimension to the maternal figure and presents us with a new way of understanding how patriarchal ideology works to deny the 'difference' of woman in her cinematic representation.

In 'Fetishism in the horror film' Roger Dadoun also refers to this archaic maternal figure. Dadoun's discussion of fetishism and the mother is worth considering here as it helps us to understand the workings of fetishism in relation to the creature in *Alien*. He describes the archaic mother as:

> a mother-thing situated beyond good and evil, beyond all organized forms and all events. This is a totalizing and oceanic mother, a 'shadowy and deep unity', evoking in the subject the anxiety of fusion and of dissolution; a mother who comes before the discovery of the essential *béance*, that of the phallus. This mother is nothing but a fantasy inasmuch as she is only ever established as an omnipresent and all-powerful totality, an absolute being, by the very intuition – she has no phallus – that deposes her . . .
>
> (Dadoun, 1989, 53–4)

In his discussion of the Dracula variant of the vampire film, Dadoun argues that the archaic mother exists as a 'non-presence' which should be 'understood as a very archaic mode of presence'. Signs of the archaic mother in the Dracula film are: the small, enclosed village; the pathway through the forest that leads like an umbilical cord to the castle; the central place of enclosure with its winding stairways, spider webs, dark vaults, worm-eaten staircases, dust and damp earth – 'elements which all relate back to the *imago* of the bad archaic mother'. At the centre of this, Dracula himself materializes. With his black cape, pointed teeth, rigid body – carried 'like an erect phallus' – piercing eyes and 'penetrating look', he is the fetish form, a 'substitute for the mother's penis' (ibid., 52–5):

> It is clear, however, since the threat comes from the mother's absent phallus, that the principal defense is sex. The vampire, marked and fascinated by the mother's missing penis and identifying with the archaic mother, doesn't have a phallus but becomes one instead. He moves from what he does not *have* to what he can *be*, if only in illusion.
>
> (ibid., 57)

Roger Dadoun argues very convincingly that the Dracula figure symbolizes an attempt to deny the totalizing power of the archaic mother, to build a fortress against her imagined omnipotence:

> against primitive identification with the mother, a phallus; against the anxiety of psychotic collapse, sexuality; against spatio-temporal disorganization, a ritual – and that completes the construction, on the positive side of fetishism, as it were, of a sexualized phallic object, all the more rigid and impressive for being fragile and threatened. In this object, one may perhaps have the pleasure of recognizing a familiar figure of the horror film, Count Dracula.
>
> (ibid., 41)

As he emerges in Dadoun's argument, the Dracula figure is very much acting on behalf of the mother – he desires to be the phallus for the mother, not understanding, or forgetting in his fear, that she is the mother who exists prior to the uncovering of 'the essential *béance*', the mother who is 'nothing but a fantasy inasmuch as she is only ever established as an omnipresent and all-powerful totality' (ibid., 54). Identifying with the archaic mother, Dracula attributes to her the phallus she never had and does not need because she exists prior to knowledge of the phallus. She is all-powerful and absolute unto herself. Dracula, however, becomes her fantasized phallus, attributes to her a shape, a clearly defined, erect form in order to combat the threat of her formlessness, her totalizing, oceanic presence. When he is finally penetrated by the stake, his heart is revealed 'to be hollow, a gaping wound. This is castration made flesh and blood and absence' (ibid., 57). In this way, according to Dadoun, the large 'omnipresent mother' is displaced on to the small 'occulted mother' (ibid., 43). In other words, the figure of the archaic mother is collapsed into that of the pre-symbolic or dyadic mother, the mother who is thought to possess a phallus. In the process, the monster comes to represent the mother's 'missing' phallus. This act of displacement would appear to be particularly relevant to *Alien* because of the phallic nature of the alien itself as well as its origin in the womb/cave of the archaic mother. But before relating Dadoun's theory to *Alien*, it is important to bring in Freud's views on the possibility of a female fetishist.

In general, the fetishist is usually assumed to be male, although in 'An outline of psycho-analysis' Freud did allow that female fetishism was a possibility. 'This abnormality, which may be counted as one of the perversions, is, as is well known, based on the patient (who is *almost always* male) not recognizing the fact that females have no penis' (p. 202; emphasis added). The notion of female fetishism is much neglected although it is present in various patriarchal discourses.

In her article, 'Woman–desire–image', Mary Kelly argues that 'it would be a mistake to confine women to the realm of repression, excluding the possibility, for example, of female fetishism':

When Freud describes castration fears for the woman, this imaginary scenario takes the form of losing her loved objects, especially her children; the child is going to grow up, leave her, reject her, perhaps die. In order to delay, disavow, that separation she has already in a way acknowledged, the woman tends to fetishise the child: by dressing him up, by continuing to feed him no matter how old he gets, or simply by having another 'little one'.

(Kelly, 1984, 31)

In *The Interpretation of Dreams*, Freud discusses the way in which the doubling of a penis symbol indicates an attempt to stave off castration anxieties. Juliet Mitchell refers to doubling as a sign of a female castration complex. 'We can see the significance of this for women, as dreams of repeated number of children – "little ones" – are given the same import' (Mitchell, 1985, 84). In this context, one aspect of female fetishism can be interpreted as an attempt by the female subject to continue to 'have' the phallus, to take up a 'positive' place in relation to the symbolic.

Both aspects of female fetishism are, of course, constructions of a patriarchal ideology unable to deal with the threat of sexual difference as it is embodied in the images of the feminine as archaic mother and as castrated other. Both of these notions of female fetishism are present in *Alien*: the monster as fetishized phallus of the archaic mother is represented through the chameleon figure of the alien and the phallus as a fetishized child or 'little one' is present in the dynamic between the heroine and her cat. However, the Freudian theory of the fetish is inadequate because it does not take into account the possibility that woman also terrifies because she threatens to castrate.

Like Count Dracula, the monstrous creature of *Alien* is constructed as the agent of the archaic mother but in my view the mother's phallus-fetish covers over, not her lack – as Freud argued – but rather, her castrating *vagina dentata*. (See Part II for a full explication of this view.) Mother Alien is primarily a terrifying figure not because she is castrated but because she castrates. Her all-consuming, incorporating powers are concretized in the figure of her alien offspring; the creature whose deadly mission is represented as the same as that of the archaic mother – to tear apart and reincorporate all life. I would also argue that the archaic mother of the Dracula films terrifies primarily because she threatens to castrate. Dadoun argues that Dracula represents her fetishized phallus; in my view he also represents, through his fanged mouth, her castrating *dentata*. Kristeva points to this aspect of the mother in her analysis of abjection: 'Fear of the uncontrollable generative mother repels me from the body; I give up cannibalism because abjection (of the mother) leads me toward respect for the body of the other, my fellow man, my brother' (Kristeva, 1982, 78–9). Discussions of the archaic mother in her all-devouring cannibalistic aspect, as distinct from her originating aspect, tend to blur her image with that of the oral-sadistic mother of the pre-Oedipal. It is in relation to incorporation that the archaic and pre-symbolic forms of the mother are most likely to coalesce. In her role as the cannibalistic parent, the mother is represented as completely abject. In *Alien*, each of the crew members comes face to face with the alien in a scene where the *mise-en-scène* is coded to suggest a monstrous, cannibalistic maternal figure which also represents the threat of the *vagina dentata*. Dallas, the captain, encounters the alien after he has crawled along the ship's enclosed, womb-like air ducts; and the other three members are cannibalized in a frenzy of blood in scenes which place emphasis on the alien's huge razor-sharp teeth, signifying the all-incorporating mother. Other scenes suggest her malevolent presence in different ways. Apart from the scene of Kane's death, when the creature gnaws its way through his stomach, all of the other death sequences occur in dimly lit, enclosed, threatening spaces which are reminiscent of the giant hatchery where Kane first encounters the pulsating egg. In these death sequences the terror of being abandoned is matched only by the fear of reincorporation and death. Ironically, these scenarios of death are staged within the body of the mother-ship, the vessel which the space travellers initially trust until 'Mother' herself is revealed as a treacherous figure who has been programmed to sacrifice the lives of the crew in the interests of the Company.

Alien supports the general principle of fetishization but it suggests that the origin of the process of denial is fear not of the castrated mother but of the castrating mother. If we consider *Alien* in the light of a theory of fetishism, then the nature of the alien begins to make sense. Its changing appearance represents a form of doubling or multiplication of the 'phallus' pointing to the workings of the fetish project. The alien's ever-changing shape, its chameleon nature also points to the maternal fetish object as an 'alien' or foreign shape. This is why the body of the heroine becomes so important at the end of the film.

Various critics (Greenberg, 1986; Kavanaugh, 1980) have debated the potential voyeurism of the final scene, where Ripley undresses before the camera. There has also been considerable discussion of the cat. Why does she rescue the cat and thereby risk her life, and the lives of Parker and Lambert, when she has previously been so careful about quarantine regulations? Again, satisfactory answers to these questions are provided by a phallocentric concept of female fetishism. Compared to the horrific sight of the alien as fetish object of the monstrous archaic mother, Ripley's body is pleasurable and reassuring to look at. She signifies the 'acceptable' form and shape of woman. The unacceptable, monstrous aspect of woman is represented in two ways: Mother as an omnipresent archaic force linked to death and Mother as the cannibalistic creature represented through the alien as fetish-object. The visually horrifying aspects of the Mother are offset through the display of woman as reassuring and pleasurable sign. The image of the cat functions in the same way; it signifies an acceptable, and in this context, a reassuring, fetish-object for the 'normal' woman. The double bird image in Hitchcock's *The Birds* functions in a similar way: the love birds signify an acceptable fetish, the death birds a fetish of the monstrous woman. Thus, Ripley holds the cat to her, stroking it as if it were her 'baby', her 'little one'. Finally, Ripley enters her sleep pod, assuming a virgin-like repose. The nightmare is over and we are returned to the opening sequence of the film where birth was a clean, pristine affair. The final sequence works, not only to dispose of the alien, but also to repress the nightmare image of the archaic mother, constructed as a sign of abjection, within the text's patriarchal discourses. *Alien* presents a fascinating study of the archaic mother and of the fear her image generates.

THE ARCHAIC MOTHER

Freudian psychoanalytic theory is primarily concerned with the pre-Oedipal mother, the mother of infancy, weaning and toilet training who is responsible for the early socialization of the child. I think it is possible to open up the mother question still further and posit an even more archaic maternal figure, by going back to mythological narratives of the generative, parthenogenetic mother – that ancient archaic figure who gives birth to all living things. She exists in the mythology of all human cultures as the Mother-Goddess who alone created the heavens and earth. In China she was known as Nu Kwa, in Mexico as Coatlicue, in Greece as Gaia (literally meaning 'earth') and in Sumer as Nammu. In 'Moses and monotheism' Freud attempts to explain the origin of the archaic mother; he argues that the great mother-goddesses are not mythical but belong to the matriarchal period of human history:

> It is likely that the mother-goddesses originated at the time of the curtailment of the matriarchy, as a compensation for the slight upon the mothers. The male deities appear first as sons beside the great mothers and only later clearly assume the features of father-figures. These male gods of polytheism reflect the conditions during the patriarchal age.
>
> (p. 83)

Freud proposed that human society developed through stages from patriarchy to matriarchy and finally back to patriarchy. During the first, primitive people lived in small groups, each dominated by a jealous, powerful father who possessed all the females of the group. One day the sons, who had been banished to the outskirts of the group, overthrew the father – whose body they devoured – in order to secure his power and to take his women for themselves. Overcome by guilt, they later set up a totem as a substitute for the father and also renounced the women whom they had liberated from the father. The sons voluntarily gave up the women, whom they all wanted to possess, in order to preserve the group which otherwise would have been destroyed as the sons fought amongst themselves. In 'Totem and taboo' Freud suggests that here 'the germ of the institution of matriarchy' (p. 144) may have originated. Eventually, however, this new form of social organization, constructed upon the taboo against murder and incest, was replaced by the re-establishment of a patriarchal order. He pointed out that the sons had 'thus created out of their filial sense of guilt the two fundamental taboos of totemism, which for that very reason inevitably corresponded to the two repressed wishes of the Oedipus complex' (ibid., 143). Freud's account of the origins of patriarchal civilization is generally regarded as pure speculation. In *The Elementary Structures of Kinship*, Lévi-Strauss points out that it is a fair explanation 'not for the beginning of civilisation, but for its present state' in that it expresses in symbolic form an 'ancient and lasting dream' – the desire to murder the father and possess the mother (Lévi-Strauss, 1969, 491). In my view, Freud's theory also attempts to demystify myths concerning the archaic mother and her terrifying powers of creation.

From the above, it is clear that the figure of the mother in both the history of human imagination and in the history of the individual subject poses immense problems. Both Freud and Lacan conflate the archaic mother with the mother of the dyadic and triadic relationship. Freud refers to the archaic mother as a 'shadowy' figure ('Female sexuality', p. 226); and Lacan refers to her as the 'abyss of the female organ from which all life comes forth' (quoted in Heath, 1978, 54). They make no clear attempt to distinguish this aspect of the maternal figure from what they see as the protective/suffocating mother of the pre-Oedipal, or the mother as object of sexual jealousy and desire as she is represented in the Oedipal configuration.

Kristeva extends the notion of the Freudian Oedipal mother to include two other faces of the mother: the fecund mother and the phantasmatic mother who constitutes the abyss which is so crucial in the formation of subjectivity. It is the notion of the fecund mother-as-abyss that is central to *Alien*; it is the abyss, the cannibalizing black hole from which all life comes and to which all life returns that is represented in the film as a source of deepest terror. Kristeva discusses the way in which the fertile female body is constructed as an 'abject' in order to keep the subject separate from the phantasmatic power of the mother, a power which threatens to obliterate the subject. An opposition is drawn between the impure fertile (female) body and pure speech associated with the symbolic (male) body.

Kristeva argues that a boundary is drawn between feminine and masculine as a means of establishing an order that is 'clean and proper'. In her discussion of the archaic mother, Kristeva stresses her double signifying function as both source of life and abyss. In both aspects she is constructed as abject to ensure the constitution of subjectivity and the law. Kristeva draws attention to the phantasmatic power of the archaic mother and to the power of the mother in general whether 'historical or phantasmatic, natural or reproductive' (Kristeva, 1982, 91). She is specifically interested in how the processes of abjection are used to subordinate maternal power to symbolic law. Her central interest, however, lies with the mother of the pre-symbolic. Nevertheless, we can draw on her theory of abjection to analyse the way in which the phantasized figure of the archaic mother – particularly in relation to birth and death – is constructed as an abject within the signifying practices of the horror film.

The maternal figure constructed within/by the writings of Freud and Lacan is inevitably the mother of the dyadic or triadic relationship. Even when she is represented as the mother of the imaginary, of the dyadic relationship, she is still constructed as the pre-Oedipal mother, that is, as a figure about to 'take up a place' in the symbolic – as a figure always in relation to the father, the representative of the phallus. Without her 'lack', he cannot signify its opposite – lack of a 'lack' or presence. But if we posit a more archaic dimension to the mother – the mother as originating womb – we can at least begin to talk about the maternal figure as *outside* the patriarchal family constellation. In this context, the mother-goddess narratives can be read as primal scene narratives in which the mother is the sole parent. She is also the subject, not the object, of narrativity.

For instance, in the Spider Woman myth of the North American Indians, there was only the Spider Woman, who spun the universe into existence and then created two daughters from whom all life flowed. She is also the Thought Woman or Wise Woman who knows the secrets of the universe. Within the Oedipus narrative, however, she becomes the Sphinx, who also knows the answers to the secret of life but, no longer the subject of the narrative, has become the object of the narrative of the male hero. After he has solved her riddle, she will destroy herself. The Sphinx is an ambiguous figure; her name, derived from 'sphincter', suggests she is the mother of sphincteral training, the pre-Oedipal mother who must be repudiated by the son so that he can take up his proper place in the symbolic. Oedipus has always been seen to have committed two horrific crimes: patricide and incest. But his encounter with the Sphinx, which leads to her death, suggests another horrific crime – that of matricide. For the Sphinx, like the Medusa, is a mother-goddess figure; they are both variants of the same mythological mother who gave birth to all life. In *Structural Anthropology*, Lévi-Strauss has argued that the major issue at stake in the Oedipus myth is the problem of whether or not man is born from woman. This myth is also central to *Alien*: 'Although the problem obviously cannot be solved, the Oedipus myth provides a kind of logical tool which relates the original problem – born from one or born from two? – to the derivative problem:

born from different or born from same?' (Lévi-Strauss, 1963, 216). What is most interesting about the mythological figure of woman as the source of all life is that, within patriarchal signifying practices, particularly the horror film, she is reconstructed and re-presented as a *negative* figure, one associated with the dread of the generative mother seen only as the abyss, the all-incorporating black hole which threatens to reabsorb what it once birthed.

The central characteristic of the archaic mother is her total dedication to the generative, procreative principle. She is the mother who conceives all by herself, the original parent, the godhead of all fertility and the origin of procreation. She is outside morality and the law. Ash, the Science Officer who is also a cyborg, delivers a eulogy to the eponymous alien of the film which could be a description of this mother: 'I admire its purity; a survivor unclouded by conscience, remorse or delusions of morality.' Clearly, it is difficult to separate out completely the figure of the archaic mother, as defined above, from other aspects of the maternal figure – the maternal authority of Kristeva's semiotic, the mother of Lacan's imaginary, the phallic woman, the castrated and castrating woman. While the different figures signify separate aspects of the monstrous-feminine, as constructed in the horror film, each one is also only part of the whole. At times the horrific nature of the monstrous-feminine results from the merging of all aspects of the maternal figure into one – the horrifying image of woman as archaic mother, phallic woman, castrated body and castrating parent represented as a single figure within the horror film. However, the archaic mother is clearly present in two distinct ways in the horror film.

Constructed as a negative force, she is represented in her phantasmagoric aspect in many horror texts, particularly the sci-fi horror film. We see her as the gaping, cannibalistic bird's mouth in *The Giant Claw*; the terrifying spider of *The Incredible Shrinking Man*; the toothed vagina/womb of *Jaws*; and the fleshy, pulsating, womb of *The Thing* and *Poltergeist*. What is common to all of these images of horror is the voracious maw, the mysterious black hole that signifies female genitalia which threatens to give birth to equally horrific offspring as well as threatening to incorporate everything in its path. This is the generative archaic mother, constructed within patriarchal ideology, as the primeval 'black hole', the originating womb which gives birth to all life.

In the horror films mentioned above, it is the suggested presence of the gestating, all-devouring womb of the archaic mother which generates the horror. Nor are these images of the womb constructed in relation to the penis of the father. Unlike the female genitalia, the womb cannot be constructed as a 'lack' in relation to the penis. The womb is not the site of castration anxiety. Rather, the womb signifies 'fullness' or 'emptiness' but always it is its *own point of reference*. This is why we need to posit a more archaic dimension to the mother. For the concept of the archaic mother allows for a notion of the feminine which does not depend for its definition

27

on a concept of the masculine. In contrast, the maternal figure of the pre-Oedipal is almost always represented in relation to the penis – the phallic mother who later becomes the castrated mother. Significantly, there is an attempt in *Alien* to appropriate the procreative function of the archaic mother, to represent a man giving birth, to deny the mother as signifier of sexual difference – but here birth can exist only as the other face of death. When one of the alien creatures orally rapes Kane, one of the male astronauts, it implants its embryo in Kane's stomach. But the primeval mother does not need the male as a 'father', only as a host body, and the alien creature murderously gnaws its way through Kane's belly. Its birth leads to the male mother's death.

The archaic mother is present in all horror films as the blackness of extinction – death. The desires and fears invoked by the image of the archaic mother, as a force that threatens to reincorporate what it once gave birth to, are always there in the horror text – all pervasive, all encompassing – because of the constant presence of death. The desire to return to the original oneness of things, to return to the mother/womb, is primarily a desire for non-differentiation. If, as George Bataille argues in *Death and Sensuality*, life signifies discontinuity and separateness, and death signifies continuity and non-differentiation, then the desire for and attraction of death suggests also a desire to return to the state of original oneness with the mother. As this desire to merge occurs after differentiation, that is after the subject has developed as separate, autonomous self, it is experienced as a form of psychic death. In this sense, the confrontation with death as represented in the horror film gives rise to a terror of self-disintegration, of losing one's self or ego – often represented cinematically by a screen which becomes black, signifying the obliteration of self, the self of the protagonist in the film and the spectator in the cinema. This has important consequences for the positioning of the spectator in the cinema.

One of the most interesting structures operating in the screen–spectator relationship relates to the sight/site of the monstrous within the horror text. In contrast with the conventional viewing structures working within other variants of the classic text, the horror film does not work to encourage the spectator to identify continually with the narrative action. Instead, an unusual situation arises whereby the filmic processes designed to encourage spectatorial identification are momentarily undermined as horrific images on the screen challenge the viewer to run the risk of continuing to look. Here I refer to those moments in the horror film when the spectator, unable to stand the images of horror unfolding before his/her eyes, is forced to look away, to not-look, to look anywhere but at the screen – particularly when the monster is engaged in the act of killing. Strategies of identification are temporarily broken and pleasure in looking is transformed into pain as the spectator is punished for his/her voyeuristic desires. For instance, the scene in *Alien* where the alien creature gnaws its way out of the stomach of one of the astronauts is designed to command our attention while simultaneously punishing us for looking. We watch in horrified fascination as we see blood spatter up from underneath his shirt as something tries to push its way up from under. When we realize that the movement is actually coming from inside his stomach it is too late to disavow what we know. Even if we do look away – as do many spectators – we still have a fair idea of what is about to happen. Such scenes satisfy a morbid desire to see *as much as possible* of the unimaginable, such as graphic horrifying images of a man giving birth to a monster, of the human body torn apart before our disbelieving eyes, before we are forced to look away. Graphic displays of gore and bodily dismemberment are repeated each time the alien strikes.

The three main 'looks' which have been theorized in relation to the screen–spectator relationship are: the camera's look at the pro-filmic event; the look of the character(s) in the diegesis; and the look of the spectator at the events on the screen. In his discussion of pornography Paul Willemen (1980) has specified a fourth look, the possibility of the viewer being overlooked while engaged in the act of looking at something he or she is not supposed to look at. The act of 'looking away' when viewing horror films is such a common occurrence that it should be seen as a fifth look that distinguishes the screen–spectator relationship.

Confronted by the sight of the monstrous, the viewing subject is put into crisis – boundaries, designed to keep the abject at bay, threaten to disintegrate, collapse. According to Lacan, the self is constituted in a process which he called the 'mirror-phase' in which the child perceives its own body as a unified whole in an image it receives from outside itself. Identity is an imaginary construct, formed in a state of alienation, grounded in misrecognition. In 'Some reflections on the ego' Lacan argues that the self, because it is constructed on an illusion, is always in danger of regressing. The horror film puts the viewing subject's sense of a unified self into crisis, specifically in those moments when the image on the screen becomes too threatening or too horrific to watch, when the abject threatens to draw the viewing subject to the place 'where meaning collapses', the place of death. By not-looking, the spectator is able momentarily to withdraw identification from the image on the screen in order to reconstruct the boundary between self and screen and reconstitute the 'self' which is threatened with disintegration. This process of reconstitution of the self, via the fifth look, is also reaffirmed by the conventional ending of some horror narratives in which the monster is 'named' and destroyed.

Fear of losing oneself and one's boundaries is made more acute in a society which values boundaries over continuity, and separateness over sameness. Given that death is represented in the horror film as a threat to the self's boundaries, symbolized by the threat of the monster, death images are most likely to cause the spectator to look away, to not-look.

Because the archaic mother is closely associated with death in its negative aspects – death seen as a desire for continuity and the loss of boundaries – her presence is marked negatively within the project of the horror film. Both the mother and death signify a monstrous obliteration of the self and both are linked to the demonic, as *Alien* so terrifyingly demonstrates.

3

WOMAN AS POSSESSED
MONSTER: *THE EXORCIST*

> Why does corporeal waste, menstrual blood and excrement, or every-
> thing that is assimilated to them, from nail-parings to decay, rep-
> resent – like a metaphor that would have become incarnate – the
> objective frailty of symbolic order?
>
> Julia Kristeva, *Powers of Horror*

Regan, the young female protagonist of *The Exorcist*, is a truly monstrous
figure. She spews green bile, utters foul obscenities, tries to fuck her
mother, causes inanimate objects to fly, rotates her head full circle on her
neck, knocks men to the floor with one punch, tries to castrate a priest,
murders two men, and in her spare time masturbates with a crucifix.
Connections drawn in the film between feminine desire, sexuality and
abjection suggest that more is at stake than a simple case of demonic
possession. Possession becomes the excuse for legitimizing a display of
aberrant feminine behaviour which is depicted as depraved, monstrous,
abject – and perversely appealing. The enormous popularity of *The
Exorcist*, one of the horror genre's biggest box-office successes, led to a
series of second-rate imitations including: *The Devil Within Her*, *Abby*,
Cathy's Curse, *Lisa and the Devil*, *To The Devil – A Daughter*, *Audrey
Rose* and *The Sexorcist*. All of these portray a girl/woman possessed by the
devil. Central to these imitations was a strong sense of the vulnerability of
the body and its susceptibility to possession. They also focused attention on
the graphic detailed representation of bodily destruction. In general, however, these imitations lacked the power and horror of the original.

The Devil Within Her (1975), tells the story of Lucy, a young woman
who gives birth to a baby that is possessed. The mother had previously
been involved in a sexual relationship with the owner of a nightclub where
she was employed as a stripper. She fears he may be the father. Lucy also
encouraged and then rejected the invitations of a dwarf who murders her
husband and then herself; thus Lucy is punished for her sexual transgressions. The film depicts a number of gruesome scenes including the dwarf's
death and exorcism of the baby but it lacks suspense and drive. *Audrey*

31

Rose (1977), which does not rely on special effects for its strong sense of suspense, presents the story of Ivy, a young girl who appears to be a reincarnation of another girl, Audrey Rose, who was burnt to death in a car accident. The dead girl's father, a rather sinister figure, befriends the family. When Ivy is traumatized by screaming fits and when her hands catch fire only Audrey Rose's father is able to soothe her. During these scenes he addresses her as his dead daughter. After a court case, in which an Indian religious figure explains the nature of reincarnation, an exorcism is conducted and the dead girl's soul is put to rest. The film is marred by the inclusion of some unconvincing material about reincarnation. *Cathy's Curse* (1976) is a completely impoverished reworking of *The Exorcist*. Young Laura is killed with her father in a car accident. Thirty years later, when her brother and his wife and daughter, Cathy, return to the family home Laura begins to possess Cathy. All of the special effects that made *The Exorcist* so terrifying to watch – telekinesis, scenes of familial destruction, speaking in weird voices – are exploited in this film but to no avail; the acting is poor, direction uninspired and special effects clichéd. No attempt is made to explore the film's theme of possession. Eventually Laura's doll, which survived the accident and which has weird eyes, is located as the source of the horror. When its eyes are torn out the horror ceases.

None of the above films explores the nature of possession in any depth or successfully generates the horror of *The Exorcist*. As a possessed figure, Regan belongs to that lineage of dual personality horror figures such as the split personality (*Sisters*), werewolf (*The Wolf Man*) and invaded subject (*Invasion of the Body Snatchers*). The possessed or invaded being is a figure of abjection in that the boundary between self and other has been transgressed. When the subject is invaded by a personality of another sex the transgression is even more abject because gender boundaries are violated. In this case, the invasion usually takes the form of a female taking over the personality of a male (*Psycho*, *Dressed to Kill*, *A Reflection of Fear*). Not many horror films deal with the opposite situation (*Deadly Blessing* is one example). In films depicting invasion by the devil, the victim is almost always a young girl, the invader the male devil. One of the major boundaries traversed is that between innocence and corruption, purity and impurity. *The Exorcist* is usually seen as involving a case of possession by the male devil. However, I will argue that the devil, in this case, may well be female.

The central conflict in *The Exorcist* is ostensibly between Christ and the devil. The opening scenes take place at an archaeological site in northern Iraq where a famous exorcist, Father Merrin (Max von Sydow) is supervising an excavation. The opening image is of an enormous red sun glowing in the sky over a barren desert. The workers uncover a medallion, the sight of which fills Father Merrin with fear. The events that take place in the Iraqi desert are filmed in such a way as to create a foreboding atmosphere fraught with eerie tension. The soundtrack is filled with sounds of hammering, voices babbling, the chanting of prayers. A sense of foreboding also fills the nearby village.

Tension is heightened by the sudden appearance of a woman wearing black and hurrying through the streets; at the moment of her appearance the noisy sounds fade away. A second black-garbed female figure peers menacingly at Father Merrin from her position on a rooftop. Two more female figures, also in black, cross his path. Another old woman, her face creased in a toothless grin, stares at him from a carriage which nearly runs him down. The sense of foreboding seems to be particularly linked to the sinister, robed figures of these women who, in this context, take on the stereotypical features associated with the witch as hag or post-menopausal woman (Greer, 1991, 411) – black dress, hump, wrinkled face, toothless grin.

Father Merrin, aware of some impending disaster, returns to the site and climbs a rocky hill, from where he looks at a large, menacing statue of the Babylonian deity, Pazuzu, a relatively minor Mesopotamian deity who possessed a snake-like penis and was consort of the serpent-mother, Lamia. Pazuzu's gaping mouth and sinister appearance recall the toothed grin of the old woman in the carriage. Father Merrin's adversary is linked mythologically and visually to woman as witch. The setting changes abruptly. Another sun fills the screen, superimposed over a wide-angle shot of Washington, DC. The camera zooms slowly in on a particular house. A woman is writing; a bed lamp glows beside her. Suddenly she hears strange, snarling noises coming from the attic. She thinks the sounds are made by rats. Iraq and Georgetown are linked by common images and sounds: the sun, a glowing lamp, disturbing sounds. The motif of the old women is later developed in relation to the elderly mother of the priest, Father Damien.

The opening sequence of *The Exorcist* sets the scene for the story of demonic possession which follows. The house is the home of Regan MacNeil (Linda Blair) an apparently normal happy twelve-year-old who lives with her mother Chris MacNeil (Ellen Burstyn), a well-known film star. Together with various household employees, mother and daughter exist in what appears to be a happy family situation. Whatever tension exists in the family emanates from the figure of the mother, who has clearly not resolved her relationship with her estranged husband; she quarrels constantly with him during long-distance telephone calls. The most disquieting thing about Regan is her namesake, Regan, who was one of King Lear's monstrous daughters, 'sharper than a serpent's tooth'. Through her name, Regan is associated with the snake, Christian symbol of woman's disobedience, unbridled sexual appetite and treachery. It is the body of this serpentine child that is possessed by Pazuzu, the devil and consort of the snake goddess.

At one level, *The Exorcist* appears to be arguing that the modern world, like Sodom and Gomorrah, has sold itself to the devil (Derry, 1987, 169; Kinder and Houston, 1987, 52); hence, the moral climate is so corrupt that the devil is able to take possession of the young with the greatest of ease. Life in the modern city is marked by a sense of decay associated with poverty, overcrowding, alienation, loneliness, neglect of the old, divorce, alcoholism and violence. Central to this modern wasteland is the growing decline of religious belief. This theme of moral and spiritual decline is played out in relation to the figure of Father Damien (Jason Miller). An intense, despairing young man, he is torn between devotion to two mothers: his spiritual mother, the Church, and his earthly mother who is alone and dying in pain. When he is unable to prevent the latter from being forcibly taken from her home and moved into a ward in an asylum (he can't afford a hospital), she turns her back on him in disgust and despair. The betrayal of mother by child is highlighted in a pathetic scene in which Father Damien walks through the psychiatric ward to reach his mother's bed. His passage is like a journey through hell: women in various stages of dementia reach out to him, wanting comfort or help from a man they see as a priest. These women recall the Iraqi women dressed in black who set an ominous tone in the film's opening scenes. When his mother dies, she returns to haunt his nightmares.

The theme of urban and spiritual decay is linked to a decline in proper familial values through the MacNeil family. What better ground for the forces of evil to take root than the household of a family in which the father is absent and where the mother continually utters profanities, particularly in relation to her husband? 'He doesn't give a shit. I've been on this fucking line for twenty minutes! Jesus Christ!' Chris MacNeil is currently acting in a film about student rebellion – a phenomenon which many would see as a sign of impending social collapse. But while the theme of spiritual decline is central to *The Exorcist*, it is secondary to the film's exploration of female monstrousness and the inability of the male order to control the woman whose perversity is expressed through her rebellious body.

The film's middle section focuses on various signs of Regan's gradual possession, the final section on her exorcism. Initially, signs of Regan's transformation are not openly sexual. First, she begins to draw figures of winged lions and sculptures which suggest the figure of Pazuzu. Through her ouija board she communicates with a spirit friend, Captain Howdy. At night she complains that she cannot sleep because her bed is shaking. One night when her mother is entertaining guests, Regan comes downstairs and in front of the dismayed group urinates on the carpet. She tells one of the guests, an astronaut, that he is going 'to die up there'. Regan's mother rushes into her daughter's room to see the bed jumping violently up and down. Chris takes her to a doctor, who recommends various medical tests –

all of which are more terrifying than the symptoms. Regan deteriorates further. The doctors are unable to help.

A new development terrifies Chris even more. Regan's body is pulled up and slapped violently down on the bed as if by an outside force. Chris brings in a number of doctors. In the middle of these gymnastics, Regan suddenly stops, rolls the whites of her eyes and utters a savage snarl. A doctor approaches. Regan knocks him to the floor with one punch as she commands in a deep mannish voice, 'Keep away! The sow is mine! Fuck me! Fuck me! Fuck me!' Chaos grips the room as the doctors forcibly inject her. 'Pathological states can induce abnormal strength,' says one doctor. Regan is subjected to another round of horrifying examinations. They can find nothing wrong with her and recommend a psychiatrist. When Chris returns home she finds that Burke, who was minding Regan, is dead. The explanation is that he fell from the upstairs window and broke his neck. Later we learn that his head was turned completely around and facing backwards.

A psychiatrist is brought in; he hypnotizes Regan and 'the person inside her' in order to find out the identity of Regan's other 'self'. Suddenly Regan, who has acquired supernatural strength, grabs his genitals. He falls to the floor, screaming in agony. Regan leaps on top of him as if to bite his genitals but is dragged off by two other doctors and forcibly sedated. The doctors at the psychiatric clinic tell Regan's mother that her daughter appears to be suffering from a form of possession which is usually only seen in primitive cultures. One of the doctors suggests an exorcism – a stylized ritual in which a priest or rabbi drives out the 'spirit' which the patient believes has taken over her or his body.

Regan's possession now takes a new form as she tries to force a sexual encounter with her mother. Chris hears noises coming from her daughter's room; she rushes inside to see objects and bedroom furniture whizzing through the air. Regan, her face covered in blood, is stabbing her genitals with a cross, screaming in a deep voice, 'Let Jesus fuck you!' Chris tries to hold her. Regan grabs her mother and pushes her face into her bloody genitals. It is not clear if the blood is menstrual or caused by self-mutilation although we do know that Regan has just entered puberty. 'Lick me! Lick me!' she orders. She then punches her mother in the face. Chris tries to scramble from the room but Regan uses telekinetic powers to move pieces of furniture to bar her mother's way. Next, Regan's head starts to turn round in a circle as she asks with a grin, 'Do you know what she did? Your cunting daughter?' This is one of the most confronting scenes in the film. Regan's transformation from angel into devil is clearly a sexual one; it suggests that the family home, bastion of all the right virtues and laudable moral values, is built on a foundation of repressed sexual desires including those which flow between mother and daughter – a theme explored in *Carrie*.

In *The Exorcist* the sexual dimension of the mother–daughter relationship is made more explicit. Desire, disguised as possession, is not expressed through a symbolic exchange of objects (the knife/rape in *Carrie*) but is spoken out loud in the daughter's bedroom. After the scene of sexual confrontation between mother and daughter, the film moves in a different direction. Until now Regan's display of powers has been limited to telekinesis, voice distortion and feats requiring enormous strength. After her verbal violation of the incest taboo, Regan's actions become even more monstrous and she commits a physically impossible act – with her head. The film seeks to exonerate Regan of this terrible deed by making it clear she is possessed – the devil is to blame for the utterance of incestuous desire. It seems clear that explanations drawn from physics or psychoanalysis are now out of the question. The suggestion that the devil is really at large is reinforced in the scene of the Virgin's phallus. In a nearby church a priest discovers to his horror that a statue of the Virgin Mother has sprouted two large phallic breasts and an extremely large penis. The Virgin is linked visually to Pazuzu, who also sported a giant phallus.

Convinced that Regan must be possessed, Chris seeks help from Father Damien. Although rejecting her plea for an exorcism, he agrees to see Regan, who is now strapped to the bed. Regan's face is white, puffy and covered in sores; she looks almost half-human, half-animal, like a dirty sow. 'Where's Regan?' he asks. The witch replies: 'In here. With us! Your mother is in here with us, Father Damien. Would you like to leave a message? I'll see that she gets it.' Father Damien bends forward as Regan vomits green bile over him. That night Chris calls Father Damien back to the house. Regan's room is freezing. Chris unbuttons Regan's nightgown to reveal a message that seems to be written on the inside of her stomach. The words 'Help Me' appear through the skin, indicating that the 'real' Regan is trapped inside her own body. At this point, shortly after the suggestion of incestuous desire on Regan's part, the narrative makes another attempt to distinguish between Regan and the devil. Regan did not violate the incest taboo, it was the devil. The film seeks to cover over the explosive issue it has laid bare. The question of mother–daughter incest has rarely been explored in the cinema, even in the horror film.

Father Merrin, a well-known exorcist, is brought in at Father Damien's request. Regan greets them with: 'Stick your cock up her ass. You motherfucking worthless cock-sucker.' Her taunts are now directed at the taboo sexual desires of men, particularly homosexual desire. Regan sits up, indicating another devilish performance is about to take place. Again her head slowly turns a full circle on her neck. She accuses Father Damien: 'You killed your mother. You left her alone to die!' In the final confrontation Father Merrin dies of a heart attack. Father Damien takes over; he drags Regan to the floor and punches her repeatedly. 'Take me,' he screams to the devil. As the devil enters his body he throws himself out of the window, falls down the long flight of steps and dies. In the last scene, we see Regan and her mother – both dressed in black – about to leave for good. Mother and daughter are reunited. The image of the two women dressed in black echoes the opening images of the sinister old hags also robed in black.

Various patterns and conflicts in *The Exorcist* suggest that the central struggle is between men and women, the 'fathers' and the 'mothers'. This struggle is played out in relation to the black-garbed crones/witches and Father Merrin; Chris MacNeil and her husband; Father Damien and his mother; Father Damien and the abandoned women in the hospital; Regan and the fathers of the Church as well as the men of the medical profession. The wider struggle is played out or concentrated in the relationship between Regan and Father Damien. Both are linked in a pattern of similarities and oppositions. Whereas Regan-as-devil is powerful, Father Damien as a representative of God is weak and impotent. Not only has he lost his faith, he is thinking of leaving the Church.

WOMAN'S ABJECT BODY

One of the most interesting aspects of *The Exorcist* is the way in which it uses woman's body to represent this conflict. The rebellion is presented as monstrous yet immensely appealing; in this way the film presents the ambiguous aspect of abjection. Abjection 'fascinates desire' but must in the interests of self-preservation be repelled. Regan's behaviour is outrageous yet compelling. The monster is an alluring but confronting figure: the 'very act of constituting another is ultimately a refusal to recognize something about the self' (Polan, 1984, 203). It takes us to the limits of what is permissible, thinkable, and then draws back. *The Exorcist* is not unlike a 'ritual' of purification in that it permits the spectator to wallow vicariously in normally taboo forms of behaviour before restoring order. This, of course, is a central appeal of the horror film; what is different about *The Exorcist* is its graphic association of the monstrous with the feminine body. Before exploring this aspect of the film, I would first like to consider in greater detail the relationship between abjection and ritual as this provides us with a particularly helpful way of understanding the representation of Regan as monstrous.

As discussed in Chapter 1, the abject is placed on the side of the feminine: it exists in opposition to the paternal symbolic, which is governed by rules and laws. The abject represents that which 'disturbs identity, system, order' (Kristeva, 1982, 4). Analysis of the abject centres on ways in which the 'clean and proper self' is constructed. The abject is that which must be expelled or excluded in the construction of that self. In order to enter the symbolic order, the subject must reject or repress all forms of behaviour, speech and modes of being regarded as unacceptable, improper or unclean. A crucial area of the subject's personal history which must be rejected relates to infantile bodily experiences and toilet training. All signs of bodily excretions – bile, urine, shit, mucus, spittle, blood – must be treated as abject, cleaned up and removed from sight. It is this aspect of abjection which is central to *The Exorcist*, its graphic display of bodily excretions – bile, blood, spit, urine, vomit.

The 'maternal authority is the trustee of that mapping of the self's clean and proper body'. This mapping of the body is 'semiotic' because the way in which the mother teaches the infant about its body is similar to the experience of learning language. 'Through frustrations and prohibitions, this authority shapes the body into a *territory* having areas, orifices, points and lines, surfaces and hollows' (ibid., 71–2).

The semiotic is 'the precondition of language' (ibid., 72). The repressed semiotic chora of language which finds expression in non-rational discourses such as poetry and art – here I would include the horror film – challenges the rational discourse of the symbolic order and the seeming stability of the rational subject. Kristeva places semiotic language on the side of femininity and symbolic language on the side of masculinity although both aspects of language, the semiotic/feminine and the symbolic/masculine are open to all individuals regardless of their biological sex.

The semiotic chora is brought into being with the entry of the subject into the symbolic order and the various forms of repression that this entails. Specifically, this entry involves the repression of the maternal authority and the period of her training when the mother controls the body of the infant. 'If language, like culture, sets up a separation and, starting with discrete elements, concatenates an order, it does so precisely by repressing maternal authority and the corporeal mapping that abuts them' (ibid., 72). The mother is gradually rejected because she comes to represent, to signify, the period of the semiotic which the paternal symbolic constructs as 'abject'. Because the mother is seen as effacing the boundary between herself and her child, the function of ritual becomes that of reinforcing separation. The ideological project of horror films such as *Psycho*, *Carrie*, *The Brood* and *The Hunger*, all of which feature the monster as female, appears to be precisely this – constructing monstrosity's source as the failure of paternal order to ensure the break, the separation of mother and child. This failure, which can also be viewed as a *refusal* of the mother and child to recognize the paternal order, is what produces the monstrous. The possessed female subject is one who refuses to take up her proper place in the symbolic order. Her protest is represented as a return to the pre-Oedipal, to the period of the semiotic chora. The normal state of affairs, however, is reversed; the dyadic relationship is distinguished not by the marking out of the child's 'clean and proper body' but by a return of the unclean, untrained, unsymbolized body. Abjection is constructed as a rebellion of filthy, lustful, carnal, female flesh.

Most critical articles either never question the identity of the devil that possesses Regan or assume that it is male, that is, the traditional devil of Christianity. Such critics tend to interpret the film as a struggle between the forces of good and evil, God and the devil, rather than a struggle between man and woman. The following comment is fairly typical: '*The Exorcist*, which deals with the balance between good and evil, perfectly reflected the concerns of its audience: if we could not find God reflected in the modern world, perhaps we could at least find the devil' (Derry, 1987, 169). According to Andrew Tudor in his study of major changes in the horror genre, *The Exorcist* marked an important transition in the modern horror film in that it introduced possession of a young innocent as its central theme (Tudor, 1989, 176). In my view the devil of *The Exorcist*, the monster who possesses Regan, is female and far from 'innocent'. The film supports this view in its construction of the 'devil's voice'.

Most critics have drawn attention to the voice that speaks through Regan. It has been described variously as 'the deep and aged voice of the demon' (Carroll, 1990, 23); as a 'masculine/bass voice' (Britton, 1979, 27), 'a hoarsely mocking voice' (Hardy, 1986, 28); and a 'guttural . . . terrifying' voice (Kinder and Houston, 1987, 46). The voice actually belongs to Mercedes McCambridge. In her study of the horror film, S. S. Prawer even states that 'the real "star" of this crude and unpleasant movie was the unseen Mercedes McCambridge, who lent the demon her voice' (1980, 172). Most writers, although aware that the voice belonged to a female actor, nevertheless assume that the voice is intended as the voice of the male devil *as spoken by a young girl* – hence the voice is 'masculinized'. Yet the voice makes more sense if we interpret it as that of a 'female' devil. Furthermore, when Father Damien plays backwards a tape of the devil's voice speaking through Regan, he discovers the voice does, in fact, belong to Regan.

A major cause of Regan's possession is related to the mother–daughter relationship. Regan's relationship with her mother is represented, in the opening scenes, as happy, caring and intimate. After her possession Regan's feelings for her mother become perverse and crudely sexual. Like Father Damien's relationship with his mother, Regan's relationship with hers is also problematic – although for vastly different reasons. Where Father Damien's emotional and spiritual journey takes him further and further away from his mother, Regan's journey ultimately cements her bond with her mother. The deep bond between mother and daughter is reinforced in the text at a number of different levels: Mother's swearing becomes Regan's obscenities; Mother's sexual frustrations become Regan's lewd suggestions; Mother's anger becomes Regan's power.

One reason for Regan's possession/rebellion appears to be her desire to remain locked in a close dyadic relationship with the mother. Regan's parents are divorced. Regan expresses jealous feelings towards Burke, whom she thinks her mother wants to marry; later, when possessed by the devil, Regan murders Burke. She hurls him through the upstairs window and down the long flight of steps. He is found at the bottom with his head turned backwards on his neck – he has been literally forced to 'look the other way'. Without a father or a father-figure present, Regan and her mother live together, almost like lovers. They share an unusual physical intimacy, holding and caressing each other as they plan the daily details of their lives. It is clearly significant that Regan is possessed when she is about to reach her thirteenth year, which marks the commencement of puberty, the threshold between girlhood and womanhood, the time when adolescent sexual desires find shape and expression.

Given this context, it is not surprising that Regan's possession is aggressively sexual. She is possessed by or linked to a serpent-devil who is the consort of Lamia, the snake goddess. Her voice changes – as is customary for pubescent boys – becoming deep and guttural, giving her gender an ambiguous character. Eschewing all forms of ladylike behaviour, she utters obscene blasphemies; makes lewd sexual suggestions to her mother; and attacks a doctor by grabbing his testicles. She becomes the castrating girl/woman, a figure designed to strike terror into the hearts of men. She also becomes a figure of extreme abjection as her body is transformed into a playground for bodily wastes. Her skin erupts in oozing sores, her hair hangs in a tangled filthy mat, she urinates on the carpet, spews green bile, and bleeds from her genitals. She masturbates with a crucifix and refers to herself as her mother's 'cunting daughter'. Regan's body is represented as a body in revolt. The film's rhythms and use of sounds and language, particularly Regan's snarling, grunting voice, exert a disturbing and powerful effect almost as if the film's semiotic voice had overpowered its symbolic one.

What Regan does is take us back to the period of the infant's early relationship with the mother and allow us, vicariously, to wallow in the forms of abjection, or bodily wastes, most closely associated with the mother and the period of toilet training. Regan is monstrous because she breaks the major taboos, set down by the laws of the symbolic order, which help to establish and maintain the self's 'clean and proper body'. More importantly, she demonstrates the *fragility* of those laws and taboos. Regan's possession demonstrates that those abject substances can never be successfully obliterated but lie in wait at the threshold of the subject's identity, threatening it with possible breakdown. What is most interesting about Regan's journey is the way in which it is represented as a struggle between the subject and the abject. It is Regan's body which becomes the site of this struggle – a struggle which literally takes place within the interior of and across the body. Slime, bile, pus, vomit, urine, blood – all of these abject forms of excrement are part of Regan's weaponry. Regan is possessed not by the devil but by her own unsocialized body.

One of the most bizarre scenes occurs when the words 'Help Me' appear on Regan's stomach. The scene makes it clear that Regan is trapped inside her own body, a prisoner of her own carnality. The daughter's desire to remain always close to her mother, perhaps to become her mother's lover, is central to our understanding of her possession. Regan is 'possessed' with an incestuous longing. Regan's descent into the realm of abjection enables her to *speak* her desires but her mother remains *physically* out of reach as long as Regan is marked by abjection. Unlike the mother of some horror films, Regan's mother is physically upright, clean, proper – one of her most popular films was appropriately called *Angel* – although, like her daughter, her language is coarse. In *Psycho*, Norman Bates's desire for his mother is also represented as a breakdown of bodily relations but there the mother's body does become accessible – the price, however, is death. There, the mother's body, taboo object of the son's desire, is represented as a disgusting vile thing yet the son still clings to her mummified corpse, continues to desire only a maternal embrace. In *Carrie*, mother and daughter spill each other's blood in a mutual knife/rape attack; the daughter then drags her mother's body into a womb-like closet where they die locked together like the fated lovers of Buñuel's *The Exterminating Angel*.

The Exorcist clearly demonstrates the argument that a reconciliation with the maternal body, the body of our origins, is only possible through an encounter with horror, the abject of our culture. Woman is constructed as possessed when she attacks the symbolic order, highlights its weaknesses, plays on its vulnerabilities; specifically, she demonstrates that the symbolic order is a sham built on sexual repression and the sacrifice of the mother. In the end Regan and her mother are reunited; the two 'fathers' are dead. The symbolic order is restored, but in name only.

There is another aspect of abjection which is relevant to our discussion. Kristeva argues that after the advent of Christ the nature of abjection changes. In her discussion of abjection in relation to the Old Testament, Kristeva examines the nature of biblical abomination and defilement. As we have seen, the feminine, particularly the maternal, is constructed as unclean specifically in relation to menstruation and childbirth. Judaic laws, based on a series of corporeal prohibitions, work to separate out those things which signify the maternal and to construct them as abject. Biblical abominations established a symbolic order that excluded women, through a structure that defined a polluting object as that which threatens identity from 'outside'. Christ's radically different message involved the abolition of these taboos – for instance Christ ate with pagans, associated with the prostitute and established contact with lepers. After the advent of Christ, pollution is redefined as 'sin' which comes from *within* and is spoken by the subject. Christ's role is to drive out sin from within the individual. Abjection is no longer exterior. Emphasis 'is henceforth placed on the inside/outside boundary, and . . . the threat comes no longer from outside but from within' (Kristeva, 1982, 114). In the New Testament, sin is associated with the spoken word. To confess one's sins is to create 'a wholly different speaking subject'. Abjection becomes internalized but, because it can be spoken, the subject can come to terms with it. But rather than encourage the possibility of speaking the abject, of transcending sin by articulating it, the Church adopted a brutal policy of 'the fiercest censorship, and punishment' towards those who advocated such a path. It has been left to the artist and writer to give voice to the abject. This also appears to be the project of films such as *The Exorcist*, in which Regan's blasphemies could be interpreted as speaking the abject.

What position does woman come to hold in relation to the definition of abjection as an inside/outside conflict? There are two ways of interpreting sin. One is in relation to God's will: the other in relation to the desire of the flesh: 'the brimming flesh of sin belongs, of course, to both sexes; but its root and basic representation is nothing other than feminine temptation' (ibid., 126). The story of the Garden of Eden and man's fall from grace sets up 'a diabolical otherness in relation to the divine' (ibid., 127). Man desires woman but he 'must protect himself from that sinful food that consumes him and that he craves' (ibid.). In my view, the definition of sin/abjection as something which comes from *within* opens up the way to position woman as deceptively treacherous. She may appear pure and beautiful on the outside but evil may, nevertheless, reside within. It is this stereotype of feminine evil – beautiful on the outside/corrupt within – that is so popular within patriarchal discourses about woman's evil nature. This dichotomous view of woman is central to the representation of the female killers in the vampire film and other horror texts such as *Cat People*, *Repulsion*, *Sisters* and *Fatal Attraction*. This is one reason why Regan's possession is so horrifying. When we first see Regan she appears to be so chaste and innocent; no wonder her gradual possession, with its emphasis on filthy utterances and depraved acts, seems so shocking. Regan's mockery of all established forms of propriety, of the clean and proper body and of the law itself define her as abject. Yet, despite her monstrous appearance and shocking utterances, she remains a strongly ambiguous figure. Regan's carnivalesque display of her body reminds us quite clearly of the immense appeal of the abject. Horror emerges from the fact that woman has broken with her proper feminine role – she has 'made a spectacle of herself' – put her unsocialized body on display. And to make matters worse, she has done all of this before the shocked eyes of two male clerics.

4

WOMAN AS MONSTROUS WOMB: *THE BROOD*

But devotees of the abject, she as well as he, do not cease looking, within what flows from the other's 'innermost being,' for the desirable and terrifying, nourishing and murderous, fascinating and abject inside of the maternal body.

Julia Kristeva, *Powers of Horror*

From classical to Renaissance times the uterus was frequently drawn with horns to demonstrate its supposed association with the devil. 'Fear of the archaic mother turns out to be essentially fear of her generative power. It is this power, a dreaded one, that patrilineal filiation has the burden of subduing' (Kristeva, 1982, 77). Margaret Miles argues in her study of the grotesque that 'the most concentrated sense of the grotesque' comes from the image of woman because of her associations with natural events such as sex and birth which were seen as 'quintessentially grotesque'. She points out that in Christian art, hell was often represented as a womb, 'a lurid and rotting uterus' where sinners were perpetually tortured for their crimes (Miles, 1989, 147). In the horror film the ancient connection drawn between woman, womb and the monstrous is frequently invoked. As virtually nothing, to my knowledge, has been written about this subject, I will briefly discuss the narratives of several of these films before analysing *The Brood* in some detail.

In *Demon Seed*, Susan (Julie Christie) is raped by the household computer, Proteus IV, a new super-computer designed by her husband, Alex. Proteus IV wants to create a superior human being who will replace ordinary human beings in order to save the world from certain destruction. Proteus takes over the house via a computer terminal in the basement. Through the agency of a robotic 'henchman', he extracts an egg from Susan, later fertilizes it, removes it from her womb and implants it in an incubator where it grows to full term in twenty-eight days.

The film's horrific impact centres on the scenes of rape and birth. As much as Proteus, woman is positioned as 'other' – a human capable of mating with a machine. Our sense of her monstrousness is reinforced by

43

the ending when we confront her offspring – a daughter who is both female and 'other'. The representation of woman, however, is not entirely monstrous. *Demon Seed* presents an interesting critique of male intelligence as a destructive force. Proteus says to Susan: 'Our child will learn from you what it is to be human.' Woman is represented as the one who has the potential to save the planet from destruction, to pass on the human qualities that are worth preserving.

In *Xtro* a young boy sees his father abducted by a spaceship; the father is later returned to earth as an alien disguised as a human. The most horrifying sequence takes place when the missing man's wife is raped by the alien. Her stomach swells to huge proportions in a remarkably short period. As her womb pushes outward, pregnant with the alien creature, her outer skin stretches taut across her stomach. A fully-grown man, covered in blood, emerges from between her legs. He bites the umbilical cord, cleans off the foetal blood and leaves. The birth is a bizarre primal phantasy in which man is born fully grown and therefore completely independent of the mother.

In *The Incubus* a woman space traveller is raped by an alien creature. Again her period of gestation is brief. During this period she develops a hunger for raw meat and begins to murder and cannibalize the crew. Eventually, she gives birth to twin boys. The film ends as she heads for earth with her alien sons. In the 1986 remake of *The Fly* the question of the heroine's pregnancy haunts the latter part of the film once we know that her scientist/lover is metamorphosing into a fly. These fears are expressed in a hideous nightmare in which the heroine sees herself giving birth to a giant maggot; it slithers from between her legs, emphasizing that woman, because of her reproductive capabilities, is not far removed from the world of nature. Her generative functions position her on the side of the abject. In *The Manitou* the heroine grows a mysterious tumour on her neck. Eventually, it is discovered that the growth is actually the foetus of a witch-doctor, the manitou, who is able to control his own reincarnations. The most horrifying sequences of the film are centred on her mysterious womb/tumour and the birth of the manitou.

Cronenberg has described *The Brood* as his own version of *Kramer versus Kramer* – both films deal with the dark side of family life and with the break-up of a marriage (Handling, 1983, 93). Nola Carveth (Samantha Eggar), is attending the controversial Somafree Institute of Psychoplasmics, a therapy clinic, which is run by Dr Hal Raglan (Oliver Reed) who teaches his patients to purge themselves of their anxieties and neuroses. Their pent-up emotions are manifested as physical changes to their bodies such as sores and welts. Raglan keeps Nola in isolation from her husband, Frank (Art Hindle) but insists she have weekend visits from Candy (Cindy Hinds), her young daughter. Frank gradually comes to realize that anyone who threatens Nola is murdered by strange midget-like creatures. When one dies an autopsy reveals that it is a child without teeth, speech, retinas, sex or a navel. According to the doctor, the 'creature has never really been born'.

Frank discovers that the creatures are part of a 'brood'; its members are 'children' born of Nola's rage. They are physical manifestations of her enraged psyche who have been born directly from her body. They are connected to her mentally and carry out her unconscious desires, but because her rage is short-lived, so too are the creatures. Frank searches the Institute and finds Nola sitting on a raised platform, looking very much like a 'Queen Bee' – the name she has been given by a patient jealous of Raglan's devotion to her. She asks Frank if he is sure he really loves her and everything about her. He says he does. With a regal sweep of her arms, Nola lifts up her white nightgown. At this point the film's mood changes abruptly: mystery and suspense give way to pure horror.

A hideous sac is hanging from the side of Nola's stomach. Smiling, she bends over, bites open the sac and takes out a misshapen foetus complete with bloody placenta which drips on to her legs. She then bends over to lick away the blood and afterbirth. Realising Frank is filled with disgust, Nola accuses him of lying to her about his feelings of love. 'I disgust you!' she says in amazement. Nola is like a creature in the wild, completely at home with her bodily instincts and reproductive functions. Frank's response is first to gag and then to leap at his wife and strangle her. Nola and her brood die. Frank and Candy drive away into the night. Candy, however, has not really been 'saved'; we notice a lump beginning to form on her arm. The disease has been passed from mother to daughter, from one generation of women to the next.

The final scenes help us to understand the possible origins of Nola's rage – her husband's disgust at her maternal, mothering functions. Nola as archetypal Queen Bee, as woman in her reproductive role, repulses man. The difference here of course is that Nola, compared to other women, conceives and gives birth to her brood alone. Her parthenogenetic offspring are like zombies; without a mind of their own they are completely at their mother's bidding. They are, in fact, the mother. The father, it appears, has retreated from the family scene altogether. The implication is that without man, woman can only give birth to a race of mutant, murderous offspring. While it is true that the film presents Nola as a victim of her upbringing, she is also mainly a victim of her mother and the latter is a victim of her own mother, and so on. Woman's destructive emotions, it seems, are inherited.

From the time of Hippocrates to Ambrose Pare, it was generally believed that monstrous offspring were created by the maternal imagination. According to Marie-Hélène Huet the belief that mothers create monstrosities through the power of their imagination has a long tradition:

Heliodorus of Emusa tells of a queen of Ethiopia who reputedly bore a white child after seeing, on the wall of her bedchamber, a picture of the pale Andromeda. Ambrose Pare reports the birth of a fur-covered girl whose mother had spied from her bed a picture of John the Baptist in animal skins. There is a long tradition of such stories; they explain monstrous births as the effect produced on pregnant women by lengthy contemplation of a desired object.

(Huet, 1983, 73)

In other words, the child is transformed into a visible image of its mother's desire. The 'monster publicly signals all aberrant desire, reproves all excessive passion and all illegitimate phantasy' (ibid., 74). Monsters were also thought to be sterile. Huet suggests this was to remove the possibility of granting legitimacy to the mother's illegitimate desire (ibid., 84). Not until the nineteenth century, when monstrosities were classified, was the cause of monstrosity attributed elsewhere – although, of course, some would have continued to believe that birth deformities were the result of a curse or copulation with the devil. By the nineteenth century, however, categories of normal and abnormal replaced that of the monstrous, and the monster in general was seen as a variation from the norm. *The Brood* ignores the modern explanation of the birth of monsters and returns to a more ancient notion in which the maternal desire was held as the origin of monstrosity. In *The Brood* woman's desire is represented as a form of internal rage – a rage against the mother which is shown to stretch back in time, passing from one generation to the next.

What kind of maternal desire, then, does *The Brood* posit as illegitimate? First, the desire – conscious or otherwise – for woman to give birth without the agency of the male; and second, woman's desire to *express* her desires, specifically her anger. Parthenogenetic birth is represented as bestial and the offspring have only short lives. Whereas Dr Raglan's patients usually erupt in boils and skin lesions when they express their rage, Nola's body gives birth to a different type of growth – a brood of deformed infants. The idea that woman should give physical expression to her anger is represented as an inherently destructive process. The film suggests two possible reasons for the origin of woman's rage: child abuse, which is enacted not by the fathers but by the mothers; and the failure of the fathers to protect their daughters. Nola's mother attacked her: now Nola attacks Candy. But the film makes no attempt to explore the origins of woman's desire to harm her daughter physically; rather it suggests that this rage is passed down through the female generations as if it were some kind of inherited disease. Similarly, the fathers appear weak – as if by nature.

Kristeva's theory of the abject provides us with at least three ways of understanding the nature of Nola's monstrousness. First, Nola has the power to deny her offspring an autonomous identity. She controls her children even before their birth; they are literally 'her creatures'. The brood's offspring are without gender, incapable of articulate speech, unable to reason, seeing the world only in black and white. They are born with a hump, filled with nutrients which keep them alive but only for a short time. The brood is also completely under the sway of the mother's emotions. The brood members do not have any identity of their own and are directed to act by the unconscious feelings of the mother. When she is calm, they are calm; when she is angry, they become enraged, murdering anyone who attracts her hostility. It is not that their identity has sunk irretrievably into the mother's; their identity *is* the mother's. It is interesting to note that when Candy is captured, Raglan says she is, 'in a way, one of them'. The disease which is passed from mother to daughter is the disease of being female – an abject creature not far removed from the animal world and one dominated totally by her feelings and reproductive functions. The mother's offspring in *The Brood* represent symbolically the horrifying results of permitting the mother too much power. An extreme, impossible situation – parthenogenetic birth – is used to demonstrate the horrors of unbridled maternal power. Parthenogenesis is impossible, but if it could happen, the film seems to be arguing, woman could give birth only to deformed manifestations of herself.

The second reason why woman's maternal function is constructed as abject is equally horrifying. Her ability to give birth links her directly to the animal world and to the great cycle of birth, decay and death. Awareness of his links to nature reminds man of his mortality and of the fragility of the symbolic order. The idea that woman in her mothering role is transformed into a human/animal figure is represented very strongly in *The Brood*, and in other horror films, such as *Aliens* where the generative mother *is* literally a creature and the 'human' mother is a surrogate who does not actually give birth. The scene where Nola tears open the sac with her teeth and pulls out the bloody infant suggests quite clearly that woman is like an animal. The torn and bleeding birth sac which functions as an external womb clearly points to woman's special relationship to the animal world.

Kristeva traces the representation of the birthing woman as unclean back to the representation of impurity in the Bible. Leviticus draws a parallel between the unclean maternal body and the decaying body. The two are associated through childbirth. 'Evocation of the maternal body and childbirth induces the image of birth as a violent act of expulsion through which the nascent body tears itself away from the matter of maternal insides' (Kristeva, 1982, 101). In order for the body to represent the symbolic order it must be unmarked. 'The body must bear no trace of its debt to nature: it must be clean and proper in order to be fully symbolic' (ibid., 102). Woman's reproductive functions place her on the side of nature rather than the symbolic order. In this way woman is again linked to the abject through her body.

In *The Brood*, the symbolic function of the sores that grow on the skin of Dr Raglan's patients takes on new significance in the light of a discussion of birth and abjection. Dr Raglan actually teaches his patients to manifest their inner hostilities as open sores and lesions on the skin. When Frank visits Jan Hartog, a former patient, the sick man reveals a hideous growth on his neck. He tells Frank that Raglan has taught his body 'to revolt against' him. Expression of anger becomes synonymous with the opening of a wound – literally. A wound is something which violates the integrity of the skin. As mentioned above, the act of birth tears at the mother's skin and transforms her body into an open wound. A wound or leprous sore on the skin reminds the subject of its origins, of having been born of woman. In a sense, then, the subject's rage – manifested as sores on the skin – is a rage at having been born of woman, of having a 'debt to nature'. This is why leprosy, which ruptures the surface of the skin, is represented as an impurity in Leviticus. Interestingly, Kristeva even relates this rage to a form of parthenogenesis. The subject who phantasizes about giving birth to himself does so in order to cut his tie to the mother. 'The obsession of the leprous and decaying body would thus be the phantasy of a self-rebirth on the part of a subject who has not introjected his mother but has incorporated a devouring mother' (ibid.).

The third way in which the womb suggests the monstrous relates to the definition of abjection in terms of inside/outside. In her analysis of the way in which woman is constructed as abject in religious discourses, Kristeva examines the crucial change that occurred in the theorization of abjection with the advent of Christianity. Central to Christ's teachings are a set of actions which challenge earlier prohibitions and categories of the unclean. These include partaking of meals with pagans, mixing with lepers, and the abolition of dietary taboos. How does this affect the theorization of abjection? Whereas abjection was formulated in Judaism as a series of abominations external to the human subject, in Christianity abjection is interiorized. 'An essential trait of those evangelical attitudes or narratives is that abjection is no longer exterior. It is permanent and comes from within' (ibid., 113). An individual who appears clean on the outside may be corrupt on the inside. The dichotomy of pure/impure is transformed into one of inside/outside. Both forms of abjection exist within the horror film. In their respective articles on horror and the body, Philip Brophy and Pete Boss generally agree that one of the major changes in the representation of the monstrous is that it has increasingly been represented as coming from within. The latter view appears to represent a more sophisticated perspective in that categories of pure/impure are no longer seen as a simple opposition exterior to the individual.

THE ABJECT WOMB

Horror films that depict monstrous births play on the inside/outside distinction in order to point to the inherently monstrous nature of the womb as well as the impossibility of ever completely banishing the abject from the human domain. The concept of inside/outside suggests two surfaces that fold in on each other; the task of separating inside from outside seems impossible as each surface constitutes the 'other' side of its opposite. The implication is that the abject can never be completely banished; if 'inside', the abject substance forms a lining for the outside; if 'outside', it forms a skin for the inside. The womb represents the utmost in abjection for it contains a new life form which will pass from inside to outside bringing with it traces of its contamination – blood, afterbirth, faeces. The abject nature of the womb and the birth process caused the Church fathers to recoil in horror at the very idea that man should be born of woman. The horror film exploits the abject nature of the womb by depicting the human, female and male, giving birth to the monstrous.

In *The Brood* the womb, which looks like a cancerous growth, is placed on the outside of woman's body; the viewer is thereby confronted directly with the scene of horror. Critical response to Nola's external womb is interesting. In Robin Wood's view, 'the unborn child, a huge excrescence on Nola's body, has the appearance of an enormous penis' (Wood, 1983, 131). Paul Sammon sees her womb as a malignant growth: Nola 'majestically spreads out her arm to lift up her gown and reveal the brood fetuses growing in cancerous sacs on her body' (Sammon, 1981, 30). In my view, woman's womb is viewed as horrifying, not because it is made to look like a penis or a cancerous growth, but because of its essential functions – it houses an alien life form, it causes alterations in the body, it leads to the act of birth. The womb is horrifying *per se* and within patriarchal discourses it has been used to represent woman's body as marked, impure and a part of the natural/animal world. Not only is Nola impure because she gives birth, she also immerses her lips in foetal blood – a further sign of her debased state. Nola is monstrous not simply because she has created a brood of mutant, murderous children; the other source of her monstrousness is her alliance with mother nature symbolized by her grotesque external uterus.

Representations of the birth scenario in these films point to the split between the natural world of the mother and the paternal symbolic which is regulated by a completely different set of rules, rules that reinforce proper civilized codes of behaviour and the clean and proper body. Miles points to the centrality of woman's body, particularly the pregnant body, in Rabelais's categorization of the grotesque. The conclusion which Miles draws supports Kristeva's theory of the female body as a central source of abjection. While the male body signifies form and integrity, and is clearly differentiated from the world, woman's body possesses none of these characteristics. The mutable nature of women's bodies is made most clear during pregnancy.

There is certainly a strong element of the grotesque in the horror film which deals with the pregnant womb particularly where horror is related to *alterations* in the womb. In *Xtro* the impregnated womb swells to monstrous proportions; *The Brood* presents woman's womb sac as a disgusting growth; in *Aliens* the creature's birth chamber, complete with rows of newly-laid pulsating egg sacs, is like a gaping black maw; while *The Manitou* depicts the womb as a displaced tumour growing on woman's neck – presumably the 'neck' stands in for the cervix or neck of the womb. In these texts, emphasis is on becoming, change, expansion, growth, alteration. Menstruation and childbirth are seen as the two events in woman's life which have placed her on the side of the abject. It is woman's fertilizable body which aligns her with nature and threatens the integrity of the patriarchal symbolic order.

Woman's birth-giving function has provided the horror film with an important source of many of its most horrific images – its intra-uterine iconography, the parthenogenetic mother, evocations of the uncanny and images of alien births. A recent film which plays throughout on all of these associations is *Aliens*. After the phenomenal success of *Alien* a sequel was made. In the sequel, *Aliens*, the heroine of the first part, Ripley (Sigourney Weaver), is found asleep in her capsule which has been travelling in outer space for over fifty years. The Company sends her to a planet to investigate the apparent disappearance of the people stationed there. Ripley discovers that this is the home of Mother Alien whose offspring have seized the settlers to use as host bodies for the hatchery. Only one small girl remains alive.

Like Nola in *The Brood*, Mother Alien is the primal mother who gives birth, without the agency of a male, to a brood of deadly creatures. These infant aliens metamorphose into a number of different life forms before reaching maturity; one of these forms, which resembles a crab complete with a long phallic tail, rapes its victims orally – as we first saw in *Alien* when the creature attached itself to Kane's face. A phallic organ emerges from a slit in the creature's vagina-like underbelly; the organ then enters through the mouth and implants its embryo inside the human body. *Aliens* presents a graphic representation of the sexual organs of the female monster capable of self-generation. David Cronenberg depicts a similar vagina/penis in *Rabid*; here we see a penis-like organ protrude from the heroine's armpit, poised and ready to penetrate its victim. John Carpenter's *The Thing* also portrays an alien monster, which is capable of cloning itself in the exact image of other life forms, as a gigantic organ with a large vaginal opening whose lips are peeled back to reveal a phallic-shaped bony structure hidden inside. These films provide a graphic representation of the infantile phantasy of the phallic mother who takes at least two forms (Laplanche and Pontalis, 1985, 311). She is thought either to possess an external penis or to have a penis hidden inside her body.

These films appear to explore the latter phantasy. To my knowledge the horror film rarely presents a graphic display of the opposite phantasy – the male thought to possess a vagina – although the theme of couvade, that is, of man giving birth, is explored in many texts.

A scene of most abject horror occurs in *Aliens* when the heroine, Ripley (Sigourney Weaver), enters Mother Alien's birth chamber in order to rescue Newt, the little girl held prisoner in the monster's external hatchery/womb. Everything about the *mise-en-scène* suggests a nightmare vision of what Kristeva describes as 'the fascinating and abject inside of the maternal body' (1982, 54). The interior is dark and slimy and the floor alive with rows of follicles and eggs. A long tube extends from Mother Alien's belly; like a conveyor belt it drops eggs on to the ground already covered with rows of eggs waiting to hatch. An enormous figure, Mother Alien hisses in the dark, her teeth glistening as her double set of jaws drip with venom, erect and ready to rip apart anyone who threatens her brood. Ripley has only fifteen minutes to save Newt before a nuclear reactor explodes. This explosion is paralleled with the idea of birth as an explosion, a bursting forth from the inside to the outside. Early in the film we experienced one of Ripley's recurring nightmares, in which she imagined her stomach exploding from within as she gave birth to one of the aliens. Throughout, *Aliens* opposes two forms of mothering: Ripley's surrogate mothering in which there is no conception or birth and where the female body is unmarked; and Mother Alien's biological, animalistic, instinctual mothering where the maternal body is open and gaping. As Bundtzen rightly points out: 'The Marines feel at home with plastic metal, glass, but are utterly bewildered when they arrive at this womb-tomb, an organic and female interior' (1987, 14). However, it is not so much that Ripley is an 'antifertility mother' and that she and Mother Alien represent diametrically opposed principles of reproduction – instinctual and cultural – as Bundtzen suggests (ibid., 17) but rather that Mother Alien represents Ripley's other self, that is, *woman's*, alien, inner, mysterious powers of reproduction. It is the latter, the female reproductive/mothering capacity *per se*, which is deemed monstrous, horrifying, abject. Like Mother Alien, Ripley also transforms into an indestructible killing machine when her child – even though a surrogate offspring – is threatened.

Alien[3] develops parallels between Ripley (Sigourney Weaver) and the alien in even more depth. When Ripley's space craft crashes on Fury 161, a maximum security prison for rapists and murderers, she becomes the human 'alien', a lone woman forced to cohabit with a group of hostile, desperate men. When Ripley questions Dillon, the priest, about the response of the men to her presence, he replies: 'Well, we've never had any before but we tolerate anybody – even the intolerable'. Other parallels are drawn between

Ripley and the alien: they are the only survivors of the crash; their combined presence brings disaster to the planet; they are the only forms on Fury 161 capable of reproduction; and both are fighting to save their own species.

Alien³ is completely different in style and tone from its predecessors – and this difference is also used to align woman and alien – both 'bitches' in their respective ways. (Advertising material for the film used the logo – 'The Bitch is Back'.) The men of Fury 161 have voluntarily given up women and adopted a form of apocalyptic, millenarian, Christian funda-mentalism. Wearing brown sack-cloth robes and sporting shaved heads, they look like a band of monks. The *mise-en-scène* suggests a medieval fortress, a place left behind by the industrial, technological and communi-cations revolutions of later centuries; there is no hi-tech weaponry or technology of any kind. The heart of Fury 161 is a gigantic fiery furnace, a visible reminder of the Christian vision of hell. It casts a red glow over the planet, suffusing the dark landscape with shadowy light. *Alien³* is set in the past which is also the future; this is the end of the world, the death of civilization, the Apocalypse heralded by the arrival of the alien/woman.

It is not surprising that in this 'rat's ass end of space' the only life form woman is able to carry represents death for the morally decrepit male/human race. In an opening sequence of *Aliens*, Ripley wakes from a nightmare in which she watches in horror as an infant alien births itself from her stomach by tearing its way through flesh and bone to the surface. In the final sequence of *Alien³*, the dream becomes reality. While in hyper-sleep on the space craft, Ripley has been raped and impregnated by the alien. She is now a vessel of Mother Alien's seed, her body/womb contami-nated by what the neuroscanner describes as 'foreign tissue'. While it rips apart the men, the alien will not touch Ripley; it is protecting its unborn offspring which Ripley discovers is a 'queen' and therefore capable of giving birth to thousands of other aliens. In one terrifying scene, the alien presses its bared jaws and dripping mouth against Ripley's trembling cheeks; the image suggests both death and desire.

Aware that she is carrying the monstrous infant, Ripley decides to sacrifice herself. In possibly the most stunning sequence in the *Alien* trilogy, Ripley throws herself backwards into the fiery furnace. A close-up shot reveals an expression of ecstasy on her face as she plummets back-wards into the void. At the same time, the alien bursts forth. Ripley brings her arms forward, enclosing the infant queen in an embrace both maternal and murderous – an embrace that ensures the alien will die alongside its surrogate mother. Ripley's death is represented as if it were a holy sacri-fice. The close-up shot of Ripley's face, with shaven head and expression of blissful resignation, bears a striking resemblance to the face of Falconetti in Carl Dreyer's *The Passion of Joan of Arc*, as she, too, is consumed by the flames. The medieval surroundings of *Alien³* thereby assume a new signifi-cance; Ripley's death is represented as a supreme sacrifice akin to that of an ancient androgynous god or religious saint. As Ripley plummets into the flames, the screen is filled with an image of the rising sun and we recall Dillon's words about rebirth when he earlier presided over the consignment to the furnace of Ripley's crew and surrogate daughter, Newt. Despite her integrity and courage, Ripley/woman is betrayed by her body, unable finally to preserve her own flesh from contamination by the abject, alien other – the monstrous fecund mother.

THE WOMB IN HORROR FILMS

From the above discussion we can see that the womb is represented in the horror film in at least two main ways: symbolically in terms of intra-uterine settings and literally in relation to the female body. In many films the monster commits her or his dreadful acts in a location which resembles the womb. These intra-uterine settings consist of dark, narrow, winding passages leading to a central room, cellar or other symbolic place of birth. In other horror films the monstrous womb belongs to woman or a female creature who is usually about to give birth to an alien being or brood of terrifying creatures. Her womb is depicted as grotesque thus giving concrete expression to its monstrous nature. The women who give birth to aliens or possess mutated wombs are not all active monsters like the witch or vampire. Some are active (*The Brood*) in that they control their evil offspring; some are raped by an alien (*Inseminoid*) or even by a computer (*Demon Seed*) and give birth to non-human offspring; in a recent film (*Dead Ringers*) the heroine was represented as a freak because she possessed a triple uterus – a medical impossibility.

Freud's discussion of the uncanny (*unheimlich*) is relevant to the depiction of uterine imagery in the horror film. He defines the uncanny as that which 'is undoubtedly related to what is frightening – to what arouses dread and horror' ('The uncanny', 219). Throughout his discussion, Freud refers to those things which are frequently called uncanny: they fall into three main categories.

(i)   – those things which relate to the notion of a double: a cyborg; twin; doppelganger; a multiplied object; a ghost or spirit; an involuntary repetition of an act.
(ii)   – castration anxieties expressed as a fear of the female genitals or of dismembered limbs, a severed head or hand, loss of the eyes, fear of going blind.
(iii) – a feeling associated with a familiar/unfamiliar place, losing one's way, womb phantasies, a haunted house.

All of these fears are explored in the horror film. The horror presented within each category can be defined in relation to a loss of clear boundaries. The double disturbs the boundary which establishes each human

53

being as a discrete entity; castration fear plays on a collapse of gender boundaries and the uncanny feeling associated with a familiar/unfamiliar place disturbs the boundary which marks out the known and the knowable. It would appear that the uncanny and the abject share common features for the uncanny also disturbs identity and order. Freud states that the 'uncanny is that class of the frightening which leads back to what is known of old and long familiar' (ibid., 220). This suggests that the notion common to all aspects of the uncanny is that of origins. 'This uncanny is in reality nothing new or alien, but something which is familiar and old-established in the mind and which has become alienated from it if only through the process of repression' (ibid., 241).

The womb, of course, relates not only to the literal origin of the subject but also to the subject's first experience of separation. What is this thing which is 'known of old and long familiar?'

> It often happens that neurotic men declare that they feel there is something uncanny about the female genital organs. This *unheimlich* place, however, is the entrance to the former *Heim* [home] of all human beings, to the place where each one of us lived once upon a time and in the beginning. There is a joking saying that 'Love is home-sickness'; and whenever a man dreams of a place or a country and says to himself, while he is still dreaming: 'this place is familiar to me, I've been here before,' we may interpret the place as being his mother's genitals or her body. In this case too, then, the *unheimlich* is what was once *heimisch*, familiar; the prefix '*un*' ['un-'] is the token of repression.
>
> (ibid., 245)

Generally, critical writings emphasise the fear aroused by castration anxiety in Freud's theory of the uncanny. But Freud did not refer simply to the *external* genitals of woman; he allocates a central place to the subject's 'former home', the womb. The uncanny is that place which is 'known of old, and long familiar', the place from which the individual has become alienated through repression. It is in fact this feeling of something 'known of old' that is central to the uncanny. Freud points out that in some languages the German term 'an *unheimlich* house' is only translatable as 'a *haunted* house' (ibid., 241). The house is haunted by the ghost or trace of a memory which takes the individual back to the early, perhaps foetal, relation with the mother. This theme is central to the Gothic horror film in which the heroine is haunted by the memory of another woman, usually the husband's former wife, the symbolic mother. We see this dynamic at play in *Rebecca*, *Gaslight*, *Secret Beyond the Door* and *Dragonwyck*. Apart from Gothic horror, exploration of the uncanny in other horror films is more violent, the monsters more monstrous. If the pull is particularly strong the individual may find her/himself literally haunted by the ghost, even pulled into another dimension as in *Poltergeist*, where the ghost is represented as a huge sucking uterus.

The symbolization of the womb as house/room/cellar or any other enclosed space is central to the iconography of the horror film. Representation of the womb as a place that is familiar and unfamiliar is acted out in the horror film through the presentation of monstrous acts which are only half glimpsed or initially hidden from sight until revealed in their full horror. In her discussion of the woman's film, Mary Ann Doane argues that there is also a relation between the uncanny and the house which 'becomes the analogue of the human body, its parts fetishized by textual operations, its erotogenous zones metamorphosed by a morbid anxiety attached to sexuality' (Doane, 1987, 72–3). The haunted house is horrifying precisely because it contains cruel secrets and has witnessed terrible deeds, usually committed by family members against each other. Almost always the origin of these deeds takes us back to the individual's quest for her or his own origins which are linked to the three primal scenes – conception, sexual difference, desire. The house becomes the symbolic space – the place of beginnings, the womb – where these three dramas are played out. Norman Bates's murdered mother dies in her bed and Norman hides her mummified corpse in the cellar; Carrie washes away her menstrual blood in her mother's bath before the entire house sinks into the ground; the alienated father of *The Amityville Horror* baptizes himself in blood, which fills the cellar before he can rejoin his family. Behind the quest for identity in these films lies the body of the mother represented through intra-uterine symbols and devices. Here the body/house is literally the body of horror, the place of the uncanny where desire is always marked by the shadowy presence of the mother.

When the house is the central location, the narrative usually leads us back to some terrible crime committed by or against a family that once lived there. These include matricide (*Psycho*); cannibalism (*The Texas Chainsaw Massacre*); incest (*Dr Jekyll and Sister Hyde*, *Shivers*); necrophilia (*The Black Cat*); family slaughter (*The Stepfather*, *The Shining*), dismemberment (*The House That Screamed*), witchcraft and torture (*The House That Dripped Blood*), suicide (*House*). In these films, the house is horrifying not simply because of its appearance (dark, dank, empty, slimy, mysterious, foreboding) but also because of the crimes committed within a familial context. Blood is one of the most common images of horror associated with the house. Blood drips from walls, fills cellars (*The Amityville Horror*) and gushes in waves along corridors (*The Shining*). The significance of the house to the horror genre can be seen in the number of films which link house and horror in their titles: *House of Dark Shadows*, *House of Evil*, *House of Exorcism*, *House of Freaks*, *House of the Damned*, *House of Usher*, *House on Sorority Row*, *House of Fear*.

In many films, the house is initially depicted as a place of refuge. The monster either shelters or the victim seeks safety in a house. Inevitably, the situation is reversed and the house that offered a solace ultimately becomes a trap, the place where the monster is destroyed and/or the victim murdered. Almost a cliché of the contemporary horror film is the scene where the hunted locks her/himself inside the room, trunk or cupboard and waits, hardly daring to breathe, as the killer tries to force an entry. The victim huddles in a foetal position as if trying to disappear into the walls. Then he or she will burst forth unexpectedly in order to catch the assailant off guard. These scenes tend to utilize similar actions or movements, all of which suggest a reworking of the birth scenario which is represented as fearful experience: enclosure in a safe place followed by a bursting forth into the unknown.

The second way in which the horror film represents the womb as monstrous occurs in films in which women give birth to inhuman offspring as we saw in *The Brood*. These films have much in common with those that depict the mad, male scientist (*Dr Jekyll and Mr Hyde*, *Frankenstein*, *The Nutty Professor*, *The Fly*) attempting to create new life forms but succeeding only in constructing monsters. According to Sharon Russell: 'Females seldom create monsters or control them (except perhaps as a variant of the mother/son relationship, as in *Trog*, or through the act of giving birth to a monster)' (Russell, 1984, 117). Gérard Lenne even argues that there are no female mad scientists in the horror film (1979, 38). This is not correct – *The Wasp Woman* and *The Kindred* both have female scientists who tamper with nature. However, it is true that female scientists rarely create monsters in an artificial environment. Why should they? Woman possesses her own womb. Interestingly, the theme of woman giving birth to (physical) monsters from her own body has been explored by a number of recent horror films – possibly in response to recent debates about scientific experiments in cloning and reproductive technology. Horror films that represent woman as womb monster include: *The Brood*, *Xtro*, *Demon Seed*, *Alien Seed*, *The Fly*, *The Manitou* and *Dead Ringers*. Some horror films present the monstrous female womb or nest as a part of nature as in *Alien*, *Aliens*, *Arachnophobia* and *The Giant Claw*. What all of these films have in common is that they define woman as monstrous in relation to her womb, that is, her reproductive capacity.

Theories about the womb have also linked it to another discourse related to the monstrous – the occurrence of hysteria in woman. The earliest known medical reference to hysteria comes from Egypt and dates from about 1900 BC. It was believed that the womb could wander around the woman's body, thus leading to certain illnesses. The Greeks believed that the womb began to travel around the body if the woman was sexually frustrated; deprivation caused her bodily fluids to dry up and this caused the womb to move around seeking moisture. According to Vern Bullough

56

medieval doctors believed that changes in the womb's position caused certain illnesses. This view persisted for centuries:

> If the organ came to rest in this position [near the hypochondrium] it would cause convulsions similar to those of epilepsy. If it mounted higher and attached itself to the heart, the patient would feel anxiety and oppression and begin to vomit. If it fastened to her liver, the woman would lose her voice and grit her teeth and her complexion would turn ashen. If it lodged in the loins, she would feel a hard ball or lump in her side. If it mounted as high as her head, it would bring pain around her eyes and nose, make the head to feel heavy, and cause drowsiness and lethargy to set in.
>
> (Bullough, 1973, 493–4)

The fact that the womb is still represented in cultural discourses as an object of horror tends to contradict the argument that the reason for this is ignorance. A more probable explanation is that woman's womb – as with her other reproductive organs – signifies sexual difference and as such has the power to horrify woman's sexual other. It is interesting that psycho-analytic theory tends to concentrate on woman's outer genitalia, her so-called castrated organ, as the most horrifying sign of her sexual difference. Yet woman's ability to give birth clearly does constitute a major area of difference giving rise to a number of contradictory responses on the part of men, such as awe, jealousy and horror. The practice of couvade in 'primi-tive' societies in which men simulate the act of giving birth (they experi-ence pains, go through labour, squat in a birthing position) indicates the extent to which men may see woman's birth-giving powers as significant. The practice of couvade also poses problems for conventional approaches to debates on the issue of sexual difference which refer only to woman's castrated state as the main signifier of difference, as Sneja Gunew makes clear in her discussion of the issue (Gunew, 1983, 156–7). But, according to Freud, it is specifically woman's castrated appearance that fills man with terror. Yet even a cursory glance at these films suggests that woman's pregnant womb, whose outer sign appears to be a grotesquely swelling stomach, also awakens man's attraction to and fear of woman as sexual 'other'. Man's desire to create life – to give birth – suggests a more profound desire at work – to become woman. Insofar as these horror films explore this yearning it is possible to argue that this represents in the male an hysterical rejection of his ordained gender role. The hysterical symptom surfaces in the male body in the form of a female reproductive organ or act such as a vaginal opening (*Videodrome*), a pregnancy (*Alien*), a birth (*Total Recall*).

In his work on Rabelais, Mikhail Bakhtin isolated three instances/ examples of the grotesque body; they are 'sexual intercourse, death throes (in their comic presentation – hanging tongue, expressionless popping

57

eyes, suffocation, death rattle), and the act of birth' (Bakhtin, 1984, 353). According to Bakhtin the 'artistic logic of the grotesque image ignores the closed, smooth, and impenetrable surface of the body and retains only its excrescences (sprouts, buds) and orifices, only that which leads beyond the body's limited space or into the body's depths' (ibid., 318). The act of birth is represented as grotesque through its 'gaping mouth, the protruding eyes, sweat, trembling, suffocation, the swollen face . . .' (ibid., 308). In other words, the act of birth is grotesque because the body's surface is no longer closed, smooth and intact – rather the body looks as if it may tear apart, open out, reveal its innermost depths. It is this aspect of the pregnant body – loss of boundaries – that the horror film emphasizes in its representation of the monstrous.

5

WOMAN AS VAMPIRE: *THE HUNGER*

> But blood, as a vital element, also refers to women, fertility, and the assurance of fecundation. It thus becomes a fascinating semantic crossroads, the propitious place for abjection.
>
> Julia Kristeva, *Powers of Horror*

The female vampire is a figure who came to prominence in vampire films of the 1970s. During this period, the vampire film began to explore openly the explicit relationship between sex, violence and death. According to Andrew Tudor, the 1970s vampire films conflated the female vampire with voracious sexual desire and placed the two 'at the heart of the vampire narrative' in films such as *Sex and the Vampire* and *Shadow of the Werewolf* (Tudor, 1989, 64–5). Tudor suggests there might be a connection between this and the rise of the women's liberation movement, which also led to public fears about a more aggressive expression of female sexuality. In her pioneering article on the lesbian vampire, Bonnie Zimmerman (1984) draws a similar connection. The representation of women in the vampire film opens up a number of areas for study: woman as lesbian vampire; woman as victim; woman as creature; gender and metamorphosis; abjection and the maternal.

Although Count Dracula represents the archetypal cinema vampire, one of the most interesting and compelling of monsters is the female vampire, frequently represented as a lesbian. In one sense, her lesbianism arises from the nature of the vampiric act itself. Sucking blood from a victim's neck places the vampire and victim in an intimate relationship. Unlike other horror-film monsters, the vampire enfolds the victim in an apparent or real erotic embrace. This is as true for the female vampire as the male. She embraces her female victims, using all the power of her seductive wiles to soothe and placate anxieties before striking. Of necessity, then, the female vampire's seduction exploits images of lesbian desire. In some films this is incidental, in others the female Dracula is clearly a lesbian. The combination of 'lesbian' and 'vampire' is a happy one since both figures are represented in popular culture as sexually aggressive women. For these reasons I will discuss the female vampire in her popular guise as a lesbian. In the pre-1970s vampire film, lesbian encounters were suggested rather than explicit. The vampire of Carl Dreyer's *Vampyr* was an old woman, hinting at lesbian desire, and *Dracula's Daughter* contains a relatively low-key encounter which also suggests lesbian desire. Since the 1970s, however, vampire films have dealt openly with the lesbianism of the vampire.

According to James Ursini and Alain Silver in their book *The Vampire Film*, most lesbian vampire films draw on one of two sources. One source is Sheridan Le Fanu's novella 'Carmilla', which tells the story of the Countess Millarca Karnstein, who has lived for centuries by vampirizing young women. The other is an historical figure, the sixteenth-century Hungarian noblewoman, the Countess Elizabeth Bathory, who was accused of torturing to death over 600 young virgins and bathing in their blood in order to maintain her youth and beauty. Horror films which deal exclusively with the lesbian vampire include: *The Vampire Lovers*, *Lust for a Vampire*, *Twins of Evil*, *Blood and Roses*, *Vampyres*, *Vampyros Lesbos*, *The Velvet Vampire*, *The Hunger*, *Daughters of Darkness*, and Walerian Borowczyk's *Immoral Tales*, which employs the Countess Elizabeth Bathory as the subject of one sequence. The first three above-mentioned films, sometimes referred to as the Karnstein trilogy, adopt Sheridan Le Fanu's 'Carmilla' as their source. Of these, *The Vampire Lovers* takes extra care to emphasize the deadly nature of the female vampire by associating her with the Medusa.

In *The Vampire Lovers*, Ingrid Pitt plays Mircalla, the beautiful daughter of the Karnstein family who escaped death at the hands of Baron Hartog, the famous vampire hunter. Mircalla, who earns a living as a female companion to the daughters of the wealthy, first seduces and vampirizes Laura, daughter of General Spielsdorf. She then vampirizes another young girl, Emma, her male doctor, governess and butler. Mircalla is finally hunted down and killed by Laura's father. He insists that she must be decapitated and we see him hold her head up high, just as Perseus is often depicted holding the Medusa's decapitated head. Spielsdorf leads the fathers of the neighbouring families on the vampire hunt. He is depicted as a cold, cruel and puritanical figure in opposition to the values represented by the sensual, erotic, female vampire.

The reason why Carmilla as the lesbian vampire is doubly terrifying is made fairly clear during Emma's seduction. Emma's delirious response suggests that anyone else, particularly her fiancé who is similar to the puritanical fathers, would have a difficult time equalling Carmilla's erotic, sensual embrace. The film clearly contrasts the passionate sexuality of the women with the cold, withdrawn repressed sexuality of the men, particularly the father. Because of Carmilla's death, the film does not have to explore this contrast any further. The implication, however, is that – given a choice – women might prefer the embrace of their own sex. Zimmerman argues that by depicting the lesbian as 'a vampire–rapist who violates and destroys her victim, men alleviate their fears that lesbian love could create an alternate model' (1984, 156). In my view, the female vampire is monstrous – and also attractive – precisely because she does threaten to undermine the formal and highly symbolic relations of men and women essential to the continuation of patriarchal society. In *The Vampire Lovers* this threat is visibly reinforced through the comparison of the stiff, unbending postures of the fathers and the sensual, eroticized bodies of the women. Because female, and – like Count Dracula – a seducer *par excellence*, the lesbian vampire is doubly dangerous. As well as transforming her victims into blood-sucking creatures of the night (she does not necessarily destroy her victims), she also threatens to seduce the daughters of patriarchy away from their proper gender roles.

The horror film consistently places the monster in conflict with the family, the couple and the institutions of patriarchal capitalism, as Robin Wood has so clearly demonstrated in his essay, 'The American nightmare: horror in the 70s' (in Wood, 1986, 70–94). It does not, however, usually challenge the *gender* basis of the heterosexual couple. The couple, threatened by the monster, is almost always heterosexual; the monster who desires the woman is usually male. While there have been some attempts to create gay male vampires (*The Fearless Vampire Killers*), these have been infrequent and are usually made as comedy–vampire films – sometimes with homophobic undertones (Russo, 1981, 53–4). The most persistent threat to the institution of heterosexuality represented in the horror film comes from the female vampire who preys on other women. Once bitten, the victim is never shy. She happily joins her female seducer, lost to the real world for ever.

The female vampire is abject because she disrupts identity and order; driven by her lust for blood, she does not respect the dictates of the law which set down the rules of proper sexual conduct. Like the male, the female vampire also represents abjection because she crosses the boundary between the living and dead, the human and animal.

The vampire's animalism is made explicit in her bloodlust and the growth of her two pointed fangs. Because she is not completely animal or human, because she hovers on the boundary between these two states, she represents abjection.

The lesbian vampire is monstrous for another reason, one which is directly related to her sexuality and which offers a threat of a more abject nature. Like the male, the lesbian vampire also causes woman's blood to flow. Given the abject status of woman's blood within religious and cultural discourses, bloodletting alone constitutes a prime case of abjection. Lesbian vampirism, however, is doubly abject because woman, already more abject than man, releases the blood of another woman. In this reworking of the primal scene, abjection is everywhere.

61

Secretions mark the body, present it as imperfect, not fully symbolic, part of the natural world. Blood, as a bodily emission, is itself an abject substance. 'Any secretion or discharge, anything that leaks out of the feminine or masculine body defiles' (Kristeva, 1982, 102). There is no doubt that the horror film, in its confrontation with the abject, is fascinated with blood. Film titles alone point to this obsession: *Blood Bath*, *Blood Brides*, *Blood Drinkers*, *Blood Feast*, *Blood for Dracula*, *Blood Orgy*, *Bloodbath at the House of Death*, *Bloody Birthday*, *A Bucket of Blood*, *The House That Dripped Blood* and so on. According to Kristeva, woman's blood has been represented within patriarchal discourses as more abject than man's for at least three reasons. First, woman's menstrual blood threatens 'the identity of each sex in the face of sexual difference' (ibid.). Second, woman's blood points to the fertile nature of the female body and bears witness to woman's alliance with the natural world. Third, woman's blood, which symbolizes birth and life, reminds man of his capacity, even willingness, to shed blood, to murder.

> Blood, indicating the impure, takes on the 'animal' seme of the previous opposition and inherits the propensity for murder of which man must cleanse himself. But blood, as a vital element, also refers to women, fertility, and the assurance of fecundation. It thus becomes a fascinating semantic crossroads, the propitious place for abjection, where *death* and *femininity*, *murder* and *procreation*, *cessation of life* and *vitality* all come together.
>
> (Kristeva, 1982, 96)

As mentioned before, the lesbian is associated with a number of forms of abjection. She signifies sexual difference and the threat of castration, she causes woman's blood to flow and she crosses gender boundaries. There is, however, another reason why the lesbian vampire is a truly monstrous figure. In my view, this relates to the mythical meaning of the vampire legend as a symbolic story about woman's menstrual flow.

THE VAMPIRE AS MENSTRUAL MONSTER

The vampire story contains many symbolic elements which have persisted over the centuries. The vampire is one of the undead, a figure who rises from the grave on the full moon in search of young virgins, almost always female. The vampire's resting place is usually a coffin secreted in a dark, cobweb-filled cellar or crypt, which is reached by a long flight of stairs. The vampire sinks his/her two sharp fangs into the victim's neck in order to suck blood. Visual emphasis is usually placed on the two marks, like a snake bite, left by the vampire's fangs. After the attack the victim is transformed into a member of the undead. It is interesting to note that frequently the female victims shed their state of languid torpor and emerge from their ordeal filled with an active, predatory desire. Common symbolic elements in this narrative are: womb-like coffins, the full moon, snake-like fangs, two bite marks, dripping blood, transformation.

In their study of menstruation, *The Wise Wound*, Penelope Shuttle and Peter Redgrove point out that in filmic versions of the vampire narrative the Dracula figure is a sexually ambiguous character (1978, 267). The male Dracula is feminized: he is a sensual, elegant, aristocratic figure who wears a black satin cloak, speaks with a seductive accent, is clearly evil and yet immensely attractive to women. In his death he is 'feminized' in that his body is usually penetrated by a phallic stake. The female Dracula is masculinized; she is an active, predatory seducer.

In *Dracula was a Woman*, Raymond T. McNally argues, quite convincingly, that Bram Stoker's Dracula was, to a significant extent, based not on a male but a female figure – the Transylvanian Countess, Elisabeth Bathory. Not only do Stoker's unpublished papers contain copious notes about the Elisabeth Bathory case; he also incorporated aspects of her story into the published novel. For instance, the idea that after drinking blood Count Dracula begins to look younger comes from the legend of Countess Bathory. In *Idols of Perversity*, a fascinating analysis of the representation of woman in European art, Bram Dijkstra points out that a popular belief of the time was that woman became a vampire in order to replace the blood she lost during menstruation.

What is the relationship between the vampire and blood? Shuttle and Redgrove interpret the vampire myth as a rite of passage which is used to explain the phenomenon of menarche, or the first menstruation, in young girls. They argue that the neck, which is almost always the place that is bitten, represents the neck of the uterus. They place great emphasis on the altered state of the vampire's victims – after being bitten, that is, after menstruation begins, the women are filled with new energy:

> After their blood has been shed for the vampire, though (and it is always from the *neck*; as we say neck or cervix of the womb), and they had suffered their first death into their new lives as vampires – why, what creatures they became! . . . Their eyes shone, their gait was swift and vigorous, they spoke energy with every glance, and their smiles, full of bright teeth with handsome canines, like neat panthers, were flashing and free, like Keats' 'La Belle Dame Sans Merci.' At last there seemed some point in becoming a vampire!
>
> (Shuttle and Redgrove, 1978, 267–8)

Given this interpretation, what meanings can we give to the various symbolic elements of the vampire narrative, particularly the moon, fangs, bite marks and blood? According to Barbara Walker (1983, 635), the belief that blood could bring back the dead influenced the thinking of Western nations from the time of Homer. Why was blood associated with the moon? Walker argues that it was believed that the moon was responsible for rebirth. The moon's rays not only caused blood – one of the body's four humours or fluids – to rise in the veins of the living but the rays also called forth the blood of the dead. This belief, of course, has some factual basis; the full moon does exert an influence on the earth's tides and, according to some people, on the fluids within many living bodies including both animal and plant life (Brown, 1972, 756–66; Shuttle and Redgrove, 1978, 163). The perfect time for one of the undead to suck blood from the living was on the night of a full moon. The undead, such as the vampire, could live temporarily by drinking blood, the source of life. The Greek word for vampire was *sarcomens*, 'flesh made by the moon' (Walker, 1983, 1040).

The association between blood and the moon is, however, more complex than this. In *The Roots of Civilization*, Alexander Marshack argues that the lunar calendar, which consists of thirteen months of twenty-eight days each, was originally based on woman's menstrual cycle. Robert Graves makes a related point in *The White Goddess* when he argues that 'twenty-eight is a true lunar month not only in the astronomical sense . . . but in the mystic sense that the Moon, being a woman, has a woman's normal menstrual period ("menstruation" is connected with the word "moon") of twenty-eight days' (Graves, 1966, 166). Some ancient cultures also associated the full moon and woman's monthly bleeding with the snake. All three – the moon, snake and woman's cycle – move through stages in which the old is shed and the new reborn: the moon moves through its cycle from the old to the new moon; the snake sheds and renews its skin; woman sheds and renews her blood. Many early myths state that the young girl begins to bleed when the snake-goddess, or god which lives in the moon, bites her. In his book, *The Beginnings*, H. R. Hays states that Cretan religious vessels were represented as a vagina with a snake crawling inside. They thought of the garden of paradise as the Goddess's womb in which a serpent dwelt (Hays, 1963, 101). Not all people believed that a snake bite brought on menstruation. Bats were also cited as bringing on the blood flow. Vampires were thought to be able to transform into bats. In *From Honey to Ashes*, Lévi-Strauss discusses the links drawn by the Aztecs and Columbians between the onset of menstruation and vampire bats (Lévi-Strauss, 1973, 382). They believed that once a girl was bitten she would begin to menstruate.

Given the above myths and symbolic associations, Shuttle and Redgrove's interpretation of the vampire story seems plausible. The vampire's biting teeth are like the fangs of a snake; significantly these fangs always leave behind two round puncture marks which resemble those of a snake bite. In some vampire films the puncture marks on the victim's body are placed much closer together than the fangs in the vampire's mouth would indicate was logical. In some films (*The Vampire Lovers*, *The Brides of Dracula*, *Son of Dracula*) the holes are also round and neat – not the kind of bloody tear one would expect long fangs to make. This would suggest that the convention of making the puncture marks resemble a snake bite is more important, in terms of the vampire myth, than cinematic verisimilitude. The link between the vampire and snake is made clear in *The Reptile*, in which the monstrous mouth of the snake-woman could also be that of a vampire (see illustration). The factors discussed above suggest that the vampire is symbolically the snake of myth and legend who first draws the menstrual blood from the uterus through the neck of the cervix and into the vagina. He/she strikes at night but particularly when the moon is full, that is, in accordance with a twenty-eight-day cycle, which is also the average length of the woman's menstrual cycle. There are close mythological associations between the vampire and the werewolf. In *Horrors* Drake Douglas points to the ancient belief that the vampire could transform into a werewolf and the latter, on its death, could become a vampire. The werewolf's blood lust is more closely tied to the twenty-eight-day cycle as it only strikes on the night of the full moon. Walter Evans states that 'the werewolf's bloody attacks – which occur regularly every month – are certainly related to the menstrual cycle which suddenly and mysteriously commands the body of every adolescent girl' (Evans, 1973, 357) – but he does not develop this notion.

The vampire is the sexual initiator *par excellence*. Critical articles on the vampire film almost always point to the unusual state of the female victim. Tudor writes that the female victims of Tod Browning's *Dracula* lie in bed, 'throats bare, arms lying languidly on the bedclothes, unable and unwilling to resist' (Tudor, 1989, 164). After the victim has been bitten she rises and, filled with sexual energy, she seeks out her own victims/partners. According to Shuttle and Redgrove, with the onset of menarche sexual desire is aroused and the clitoris is particularly energized (1978, 59). This would help to explain the sudden transformation that takes place in the vampire's female victims. They also point out that it is quite common in life for a girl to commence masturbating with her first menstruation (ibid., 244). This occurs in *Carrie*, where the female protagonist is shown masturbating with the onset of bleeding. Tudor also notes that the vampire's victims 'are always, in some sense, willing victims' (1989, 165) and that the scene is marked with an expectant and sensual air. The unusual change in the victim – from a state of passivity to one of activity – makes sense if explained in terms of a rite of passage for the pubescent girl. Western societies, of course, no longer have puberty rituals for menarche but perhaps popular culture in the form of the vampire film provides teenagers with a seductive but terrifying view of this important threshold event.

A vampire can be killed only in specific ways. A stake through the heart and decapitation are two of the better known methods. The female vampire is sometimes decapitated (e.g., *The Vampire Lovers*). In this context, it is worth noting that there are some mythical connections between the

Medusa and the female vampire. According to Philip Slater, the glance of a menstruating woman, like the glance of the Medusa or Gorgon, was once thought to turn men to stone. The origin of the word 'Gorgon' is from the phrase 'the moon as it is terrible to behold' (Shuttle and Redgrove, 1978, 262). The moon was associated with snakes and vampires for the reasons discussed above. Freud argued that the Medusa's head represented the terrifying genitals of the mother. How much more terrifying would the Medusa's head appear when her two long boar's tusks were covered with blood! Her face would take on the appearance of the bleeding female genitals; in its horrifying aspect this would resemble not the castrated female genitals but the castrating genitals, the terrifying *vagina dentata*.

While the vampire narrative appears to be closely tied to myths associated with menarche, it can also be related to another important threshold event in a woman's life, an event which also involves a sudden blood flow – defloration. In his essay, 'The taboo of virginity', Freud discusses the taboo placed by 'primitive' cultures on sexual intercourse with a virgin. Although I discuss this essay in detail in Chapter 8, it is relevant to mention it briefly in this context. Defloration was regarded as terrifying because it resulted in a mysterious flow of blood from the woman's vagina. According to Freud, these people believed the blood flow was caused by the bite of a 'spirit animal' which lived in the vagina ('Taboo', p. 197). Consequently, sexual intercourse is first enacted with the girl by someone experienced and able to withstand the threat. The young bridegroom is always protected from woman's terrifying blood. It is possible to interpret the vampire myth as a story about defloration. The vampire bites the woman, the teeth penetrate her neck, blood flows. She is transformed from an innocent into a creature of the night who, because she has been sexually awakened, is now a threatening female figure. She is the deadly vampire who desires to suck men's blood, which in this context could be seen as a metaphor for semen. Ernst Jones proposes this interpretation in his essay, 'On the nightmare of bloodsucking'. The female vampire was certainly viewed in this way in *fin-de-siècle* culture (Dijkstra, 1986, 334) where she is represented as a sexual predator *par excellence*. It is possible that these two explanations of the vampire myth – it symbolizes the menstrual and hymenal flow – were once an explanation of a single phenomenon, that is, woman's blood flow. In ancient societies, people would have had no way of distinguishing between the two occurrences – both were seen as related to the deadly nature of woman's womb. Woman's womb is a site of terror because it bleeds; it is the blood which flows from the inside to the outside of woman's body that is viewed as abject. The vampire is a creature of evil because she/he lives on blood drawn from a wound that marks the surface of the skin. Like all abject figures, the vampire is both terrifying and seductive.

THE LESBIAN VAMPIRE

In *The Hunger*, directed by Tony Scott, the vampire is represented as a particularly abject figure because it is female and therefore associated more closely with woman's blood. The film has been criticized for its 'glossy top dressing' and 'modish trappings' (Hardy, 1986, 387) but its smooth, opulent surface is used to great effect in scenes of contrast, particularly those dealing with physical decay and blood. *The Hunger* draws on the stories of both Carmilla and the Countess Bathory. Catherine Deneuve plays Miriam Blaylock, a woman who, like Carmilla, is an expert in the art of seduction and who, like Bathory, seeks immortality through blood. She appears to have achieved immortality and is represented as an eternally beautiful rather enigmatic figure, a bisexual vampire who has apparently lived for at least 2000 years. A blood-sucking, meat-eating, ageless beauty, she seduces her partners, male and female, with the promise of immortality. The addition of cannibalism associates her vampirism with the meat-lust of the werewolf which, as I explained earlier, only hunts on the full moon and is therefore linked more closely to the menstrual cycle. Ironically, Miriam's mysterious beauty also suggests the glamour of death – something her lovers eventually yearn for but can never attain.

When the film opens, Miriam (Catherine Deneuve) is living with her current partner John (David Bowie), who has been with her for two centuries. Two beautiful, chic figures, they have no trouble luring their young victims, whom they pick up at nightclubs and discotheques, back to their lavish apartment. Unlike conventional vampires, they do not possess fangs. Instead each wears a small, sharp blade in a sheath which hangs around their necks. With this they cut the throats of their victims and later dispose of the carcasses in the basement furnace. Miriam and John have been together for centuries; they appear to be deeply in love. One morning John wakes up to discover that Miriam's promise of immortality is false; he has begun to grow old. Although Miriam promises immortality, she knows that none of her lovers will live for ever. John seeks the help of Sarah Roberts (Susan Sarandon), a scientist who is researching the ageing process. All his attempts fail and he begins to age rapidly. When he turns into an old, decrepit man, Miriam carries his crumbling body upstairs to the attic where she keeps the coffins of her undead lovers.

Meanwhile Miriam has already decided to make Sarah her next lover. She seduces and vampirizes the willing Sarah, who develops a mysterious but ravenous hunger for meat. When Miriam finally explains, Sarah embraces her and then attempts suicide by cutting her own throat. Miriam carries Sarah's dying body upstairs to the attic/bell tower. In the tower, however, Miriam is attacked by her aged lovers. She falls backwards over the balcony to the floor below. As Miriam dies, her face and body crumbling into a grotesque mask, the power of life and death that she holds over her lovers is broken. The final scene shows Sarah in Miriam's place. She is now the reigning vampire queen. We see her with a male partner and a young girl whose appearance reminds us of Miriam. They seem to duplicate the trio of Miriam/John and a young girl who came to them for music lessons. The final shot is of Miriam's coffin, locked and stored in Sarah's special graveyard.

The Hunger deliberately sets out to update the vampire movie. The word 'vampire' is never used and most of the imagery and conventions associated with the vampire film are absent. There are no fangs, bats, wan virgins, or gliding predatory vampires in black silk capes. The opening scenes suggest a blend of video-clip conventions and fashion photography. The *mise-en-scène* for each shot appears to have been meticulously arranged. Interior scenes are bathed in soft shadows, creating a sense of timelessness. Dominating all of this is the superbly elegant and implacable beauty of Catherine Deneuve. The film's discourse on the transitory nature of glamour is ironically offset by its other discourse on the permanence of ageing and death. It is against this surface impression of smooth, coherent perfection that the film explores the forces of abjection associated with blood, wounds and the decaying, crumbling body.

In terms of abjection, Miriam is monstrous because she promises everlasting life, which means her lovers never age, their bodies remain strong, healthy and flawless. This is the bodily perfection sanctioned by the symbolic order. However, she also knows that in the end there is only decay and death. Miriam is fully aware of the fate of her lovers. She is the cruel mother, the parent who nurtures her lovers/children in life and then keeps them in a state of living death. She represents the suffocating mother – the mother who refuses to let go. When John finally becomes a grotesque old man, he begs her to let him die. Miriam tells him that there is no release, no rest. Carrying him upstairs to the attic, she places him in a coffin with her other past lovers, now members of the undead. The attic is the antithesis of the conventional vampire's crypt in the cellar. Whereas the cellar is dank and cold, the attic of *The Hunger* is dry and dusty. Miriam represents the dead face of the archaic mother, the maternal figure whose fertility has dried up. She has no nourishment to offer. Miriam's vampire lovers exist in a limbo of decay. Blood can no longer keep them alive. The horror of such a state, which has no boundaries, no end, is forcefully represented in the scene where the undead begin to crumble. In one instance, a male and female vampire fall over, the male's head then drops off on to his chest and crumbles into his legs, finally becoming dust. The most horrific sequence focuses on Miriam's collapse. As she falls on to the floor below, her body and face seem to crumble backwards in time until her face is a grinning, crumbling female death's head not unlike the grinning skull of Mrs Bates in *Psycho*.

Woman's association with blood as an abject substance is graphically represented in the scene of Sarah's attempted suicide. Because the two women are kissing at the time, Sarah's blood spurts up and out from her mouth into Miriam's open mouth. The sudden explosion of blood in this scene relates specifically to the representation of the vampire as female. The two women, both vampires, appear to be drinking each other's blood. It is impossible to tell if the blood signals life or death. The film deliberately plays on this ambiguity, reinforcing the notion that lesbian desire is deadly. Throughout the narrative, short flashback scenes suddenly interrupt the flow of events. These show Miriam in various poses as she crouches over the bodies of her victims. Blood covers her lips and trickles down her face. In these scenes she is represented as the devouring mother whose cannibalistic, incorporating desires are the other side of her possessive, smothering urges. When she is placed in a sexual embrace with another female vampire, the predatory/lesbian energies released lead to a fountain of blood. It is difficult to imagine two male vampires embracing in such a context, their abject nature defined in terms of an oral exchange of blood.

In her discussion of biblical abomination, Kristeva lists three major categories of the taboo: food taboos; bodily change and its end in death; the female body and incest. These taboos, she argues, are ultimately designed to perform 'the tremendous forcing that consists in subordinating maternal power (whether historical or phantasmatic, natural or reproductive) to symbolic order' (Kristeva, 1982, 91). In other words, by constructing the maternal figure as an abject being, the symbolic order forces a separation of mother and infant that is necessary to guarantee its power and legitimacy. When Miriam and Sarah become lovers, a series of boundaries are crossed, violating taboos that appear to be specific to the lesbian vampire film: a symbolic mixing of blood and milk; a collapse of boundaries between self and other; a possible retreat into narcissism; and the representation of lesbian desire. All of these are in addition to the usual boundaries crossed in the male Dracula film (life and death, human and creature, pagan and Christian) as well as a breaking of the taboos on murder and cannibalism. The female Dracula is a particularly abject figure.

One of the strongest of food taboos relates to the ancient imperative that blood and milk should be kept separate. According to Exodus: 'Thou shalt not seethe a kid in his mother's milk.' In *The Hunger* there is a sense in which blood is equivalent to the mother's milk. In the classic vampire film (*Dracula, Vampire Lovers*), the vampire sleeps in her/his coffin like an unborn baby nestled in the dark comfort of the mother's womb. After feeding, the vampire must return to the 'womb' or die. Blood of course is the first food of the foetus/vampire. The connection between the vampire and a foetus is drawn even more strongly in those texts where Dracula is female. According to Ernst Jones, the female vampire's blood-sucking is equivalent to oral sex. She sucks the innocent male's blood as if she were sucking the semen from his penis. Semen is sometimes referred to as milk, as in *Moby Dick* where Herman Melville has Ishmael refer to the whale's spermaceti as 'the very milk and sperm of kindness'. Insofar as the act of vampirism mixes the idea of blood/semen/milk, it becomes a particularly abject act in relation to the biblical taboos on mixing blood and milk. The penis also takes the place of the breast in that it is suckled and it gives forth a milky substance. In a sense, the male victim is placed in the position of the suckling mother; the vampire becomes his child. But the vampire also threatens to bite, to draw blood and sever the penis. Vampirism combines a number of abject activities: the mixing of blood and milk; the threat of castration; the feminization of the male victim.

In texts where the vampire is female, we are made more aware of the dependent relationship between the vampire as mother and her lover as child. In *The Hunger*, Miriam lives with her current lover in her darkly lit, opulent home which is like a vast womb-like mausoleum. When her lovers 'die' she places them in individual coffins in the attic, symbolically returning them to the womb. She is the vampire/mother who gives birth to her vampire/lover with the promise of eternal life and it is she who teaches the vampire/child how to feed. Only she knows how to appease 'the hunger' for blood. This parallel between blood and milk is made clear in the seduction scene. Here Miriam transforms Sarah into her lover/child by sucking and biting open a wound in Sarah's skin. She then injects her own blood/milk into Sarah's veins. When the metamorphosis is complete Miriam then teaches her offspring how to feed. Blood is the vampire's milk.

When Miriam and Sarah become lovers, the violation of the taboos associated with incest and decay becomes more marked. In the bloodletting spectacle we are at first unable to tell which of the women has been cut. This scene draws attention to the taboo of incest in that the female vampire is the mother; her lover, to whom she gives eternal life, is also symbolically her child. Furthermore, because the two vampires are female, and both are capable of mothering, and feeding their offspring, we are made more aware of the vampire's blood as woman's blood, a special blood which gives life/birth to the lover/child. But this is also a death scene in which the blood spurt is in excess. Thus the relationship between Miriam and Sarah is abject in a number of ways: it violates not only the incest taboo but also the interdiction against homosexual love or love of the same. In some lesbian vampire films (*Twins of Evil*, *Vampyres*) the female vampires even look alike, further reinforcing the suggestion of narcissistic desire.

Abjection is also present because the vampire's union is brought about by the opening up of a wound, a form of abjection discussed earlier in relation to *The Brood*. Wounds, particularly leprous sores, point to the imperfection of the bodily surface and the opening of the maternal body during childbirth. The mark of Sarah's transformation is the wound on her wrist that Miriam makes with her teeth. With its repeated emphasis on marking the skin, opening up a wound, the vampire narrative points continually to the imperfection of the body and the particularly abject nature of the maternal body. In the lesbian vampire film, *Vampyres*, the vampire keeps her male victim alive for a longer period of time by sucking his wound slowly and spasmodically. Gradually the wound grows larger and larger until it constitutes one of the most grotesque sights in the film.

The lesbian vampire relationship as represented in *The Hunger* emphasizes those three areas – orality, death, incest – which work to cement the mother/child relationship rather than bring about the separation which is necessary for the institution of sociality and the law:

> In other words, the place and law of the One do not exist without
> *a series of separations* that are oral, corporeal, or even more gener-
> ally material, and in the last analysis relating to fusion with the
> mother.
>
> (Kristeva, 1982, 94)

The figure of the mother vampire refuses the separation necessary for the introduction of the father or the third term as it is described in Freud and Lacan. As the oral sadistic mother, she keeps her lover/child by her side in a relationship which symbolically collapses the boundaries between milk and blood as well as violating the taboo on incest. Vampires are members of the undead who feed off the flesh of the living. In *The Hunger*, the abject nature of this relationship is even more pronounced because the boundary between heterosexual and homosexual love is also transgressed. Significantly, the final scene re-establishes the vampire as a heterosexual, although the embrace between Sarah and the young blonde girl who looks remarkably like Miriam suggests that the desire to violate that taboo is always at hand.

Significantly, a number of vampire films oppose the world of the vampire to that of the human through a series of oppositions which take on maternal and paternal characteristics. The female vampire's world signifies darkness, the undead, moon, the tomb/womb, blood, oral sadism, bodily wounds and violation of the law. The world of the living, frequently represented by a patriarchal figure (Van Helsing in Dracula films) versed in vampire lore, signifies light, life, the sun, destruction of the tomb, blood taboos, the stake/phallus, the unviolated body, and enforcement of the law. Through an interplay of these oppositions, the vampire myth becomes a narrative about the construction of the maternal world as pagan and abject. In many vampire films (*Dracula*, *The Vampire Lovers*) the figure of Dracula is represented as pagan and the avenging fathers as Christian. Given that the pagan religions celebrated fertility and the power of the maternal body (Frazer, 1922; Stone, 1976) it would appear that this conflict

71

is between these two opposing domains – the worlds of the mother and the father.

In most vampire films, particularly those featuring Dracula, the archaic mother is there only as a shadowy presence. Roger Dadoun argues that those 'elements' which relate to the presence of the mother include the dark, enveloping uterine space of the crypt, creaking sounds, hidden doors, cobwebs and dust (Dadoun, 1989, 52–3). In the conventional scenario, Dracula, with his erect body and penetrating look, becomes 'the phallus-fetish' of the omnipresent mother (ibid., 55). In *The Hunger* where the chief vampire is female we are brought face to face with the archaic mother; there is no need to infer her shadowy presence through the intermediary and fetishized figure of the male vampire. The vampire *is* the archaic mother. Furthermore, if the male vampire is a fetish figure of the mother, it seems clear that he does not represent the imaginary phallus of the mother, as Dadoun argues, but rather her terrifying, imaginary *vagina dentata*. This image is presented very clearly when the vampire is female; in these texts one of the most frequent images is that of woman's open mouth, sharp pointed teeth and blood-covered lips. As we have seen, *The Hunger* represents the figure of the archaic mother in two forms – as a beautiful, ageless woman and as an ancient, crumbling figure whose ubiquitous presence is attested to by the final shot of her coffin where she lies for ever as one of the undead. A new vampire/mother has taken her place; the line cannot be broken. In the final sequence we see her mothering her new family, its members bound to her by ties of blood/milk, cannibalism, death and desire. But it is the sexual desires of the lesbian vampire that render her the most abject of all vampire monsters.

6

WOMAN AS WITCH: *CARRIE*

> One of them, the masculine, apparently victorious, confesses through
> its very relentlessness against the other, the feminine, that it is
> threatened by an asymmetrical, irrational, wily, uncontrollable power.
>
> Julia Kristeva, *Powers of Horror*

There is one incontestably monstrous role in the horror film that belongs to
woman – that of the witch. The witch was not always a figure of monstrosity, as Sharon Russell points out in her excellent discussion of the changing image of the witch in film. Early silent films, such as those of Georges
Méliès (*The Witch's Revenge*, *The Witch*) were primarily interested in using
this topic in order to exploit the trick properties of the cinema. Several
films (such as *Witchcraft through the Ages*) presented a serious exploration
of the subject by adopting a documentary form. This approach also
influenced Dreyer's *Day of Wrath*. Universal did not deal at all with the
witch in its horror films of the 1930s. One of the first films to present a
terrifying picture of the witch was a children's film, *The Wizard of Oz*
(1939). In the 1940s the subject of 'woman as witch' was made the topic of
humour in some Hollywood comedies, such as *I Married a Witch*. Not until
1943, with the appearance of *The Seventh Victim*, did the witch clearly
become a figure of terror. By the 1960s the witch had joined the ranks of
popular horror film monsters with *Black Sunday* and *Witchcraft*. Emphasis,
however, tended to be more on the witch-hunt or the male leader of the
coven rather than on the witch as a monster in her own right. This was
certainly true of the few Hammer horror films which dealt with this subject.
Burn Witch Burn!, released in 1962, is probably the first horror film with a
witch as the central monster. Barbara Steele, who became known as the
'High Priestess of Horror', played a witch in both *The She-Beast* and *Black
Sunday*. Today the witch, as a figure of horror in her own right, has
become central to films such as *Seizure*, *Suspiria*, *Inferno*, *Carrie*, *A
Stranger in Our House* and *Witches*. In postmodern horror films such as
The Evil Dead and *Evil Dead II* the abject nature of the witch's appearance
(see illustration) has even become a source of grim humour.

Historically and mythologically, the witch has inspired both awe and dread. In ancient societies all magical powers, whether used for good or evil purposes, inspired the deepest dread amongst the members of the community. One of the most interesting aspects of the witch in earlier centuries was her role as healer. Barbara Walker points out (1983, 1076–7) that in many cultures witches had metaphoric names such as 'herberia' (one who gathers herbs), 'pixidria' (keeper of an ointment box), and 'femina saga' (wise-woman). In her role as mother, woman no doubt was the one responsible for developing early forms of herbal medicine. Joseph Campbell (1976) argues that women were the first witches and associated with the powers of magic long before men because of their mysterious ability to create new life. During her periods of pregnancy, woman was seen as the source of a particularly powerful form of magic (Walker, 1983, 315). The earliest known witches were feared not as agents of the devil – as the Christian Church later argued – but because they were thought to possess magical, terrifying powers.

In some cultures, a young girl who had prophetic dreams at the time of her menarche was frequently singled out as a future shaman or witch. Again we see the association between woman's blood and the supernatural. Menstruation was also linked to the witch's curse – a theme explored in *Carrie*. Witches were feared because it was thought they could cast terrible spells and bring death to those they cursed. Historically, the curse of a woman, particularly if she were pregnant or menstruating, was considered far more potent than a man's curse. A 'mother's curse', as it was known, meant certain death. The curse of a woman who also practised as a witch was even more deadly than that of an ordinary woman.

When witchcraft was deemed heresy by the Catholic Church in the fourteenth century, the services witches had previously performed were labelled as crimes – particularly midwifery. The crime that ensured that witches would be burnt at the stake was, as Walker points out, a crime of which they were actually innocent because it was impossible to commit – this was the crime of collaborating literally with the devil (Walker, 1983, 1084). The most common form of collaboration of which they were accused was that of having intercourse with the devil. Detailed information contained in *The Malleus Maleficarum* (1484), an inquisitor's manual for witch prosecution which was commissioned by the Catholic Church and written by two Dominicans, Heinrich Kramer and James Sprenger, makes it clear that a central reason for the persecution of witches was morbid interest in the witch as 'other' and a fear of the witch/woman as an agent of castration.

The Malleus Maleficarum, in use for nearly three centuries, lists in exacting detail the various ways an official could identify a witch. A telling sign was the presence of an extra nipple somewhere on the body, ostensibly used by witches to suckle their familiars or even the devil himself. Consequently, when women were arrested they were stripped, shaved and searched (often publicly) for this tell-tale nipple. (Some people actually do have a small raised nipple – known medically as a supernumerary nipple – on their bodies. Frequently, it is located near the aureole.) Many of the witches' alleged crimes were of a sexual nature; it is this aspect of witchcraft which is central to *The Exorcist*. Witches were accused, among other things, of copulating with the devil, causing male impotence, causing the penis to disappear and of stealing men's penises – the latter crimes no doubt exemplify male fears of castration.

> And what, then, is to be thought of those witches who in this way sometimes collect male organs in great numbers, as many as twenty or thirty members together, and put them in a bird's nest, or shut them up in a box, where they move themselves like living members, and eat oats and corn, as has been seen by many and is a matter of common report?
>
> (*Malleus Maleficarum*, 121)

The Malleus Maleficarum also supplies a series of supposedly logical reasons why women are more inclined to witchcraft than men. The reasons all relate to the classic and phallocentric definition of woman as the 'other', the weaker but dangerous complement of man. 'What else is woman but a foe to friendship, an unescapable punishment, a necessary evil, a natural temptation, a desirable calamity, a domestic danger, a delectable detriment, an evil of nature, painted with fair colours!' (ibid., 43). The major reason given for woman's 'otherness' is her carnal nature. Women are less intelligent, less spiritual, more like children. 'But the natural reason is that she is more carnal than a man, as is clear from her many carnal abominations' (ibid., 44). *The Malleus Maleficarum* is permeated by an extreme hatred of women and fear of their imaginary powers of castration. It is alarming to note that the Introduction to an edition printed in 1948 by the Reverend Montague Summers praises the two Dominican authors as men of 'extraordinary genius' and the book itself as 'supreme' from the point of view of jurisprudence, history and psychology (Summers, 1948, viii–ix).

No doubt women and men accused of witchcraft eventually confessed to all kinds of absurd and impossible 'crimes' in order to bring an end to their torture. In general, the accused were tortured until they confessed the names of other witches in the community. Burning on a funeral pyre was most likely a blessed relief from the horrors of the medieval torture chamber. The confessions of witches to absurd crimes, such as stealing men's penises and having intercourse with the devil, would have added further to popular mythology about the depraved and monstrous nature of woman's sexual appetites. Witches were also forced to 'confess' the minute details of their sexual acts with the devil, including information about the size of his member, its texture and shape.

THE WITCH IN FILM

I have discussed the history of the witch in some detail because the image of the witch is one which continues to play an important role in the discourses of popular culture – particularly in children's fairy stories and in the horror film. Another discourse which seeks to explore the significance of the witch is that of psychoanalytic theory; here woman as witch is positioned as the oral sadistic mother and the phallic woman (Campbell, 1976, 73). In the horror film, the representation of the witch continues to foreground her essentially sexual nature. She is usually depicted as a monstrous figure with supernatural powers and a desire for evil. Her other social functions as healer and seer have largely been omitted from contemporary portrayals.

The witch is defined as an abject figure in that she is represented within patriarchal discourses as an implacable enemy of the symbolic order. She is thought to be dangerous and wily, capable of drawing on her evil powers to wreak destruction on the community. The witch sets out to unsettle boundaries between the rational and irrational, symbolic and imaginary. Her evil powers are seen as part of her 'feminine' nature; she is closer to nature than man and can control forces in nature such as tempests, hurricanes and storms. In those societies which lack centralized institutions of power, a rigid separation of the sexes is enforced through ritual. In such societies the two sexes are in constant conflict. Women are regarded as 'baleful schemers', the feminine is seen as 'synonymous with a radical evil that is to be suppressed' (Kristeva, 1982, 70). Irrational, scheming, evil – these are the words used to define the witch. The witch is also associated with a range of abject things: filth, decay, spiders, bats, cobwebs, brews, potions and even cannibalism.

In *Black Sunday*, Barbara Steele plays Asa, a witch who swears vengeance on the descendants of the men who executed her hundreds of years ago. She was a Moldavian princess accused by the Inquisition of practising witchcraft and worshipping Satan. The Grand Inquisitor is her own brother who watches while the mask of Satan, lined with sharp spikes, is placed upon her face. She will die when the spikes penetrate her brain. Two centuries later her coffin is discovered and the mask is accidentally removed, revealing her face, which is still miraculously preserved. The dead woman awakens and, although unable to move, is able to orchestrate her bloody revenge from the crypt. Gradually Asa begins to take over the body of her great-granddaughter Katia, who is also played by Barbara Steele. Eventually the witch is caught and consigned to the flames.

Suspiria is set in the Tam Academy of Dance in Germany. Suzie Banyon (Jessica Harper), an American student, investigates the brutal murder of a friend, unaware that the school is run by a coven of witches and that the

76

basement is the home of an ancient sorceress whose evil powers have contaminated the whole city. In the final sequence Suzie confronts the Queen Witch, Mater Suspiriorum, a grotesque, monstrous, completely hideous figure. She destroys the Queen thereby bringing about the destruction of the school and the coven. No explanation is given for the presence of the witches at the school; they simply exist and their sole purpose appears to be to wreak havoc and destruction in the world. *Suspiria* was the first of a trilogy of horror films planned by Dario Argento called *The Three Mothers*. The second is *Inferno*; the third has not yet been made. In the opening credits to *Inferno* we learn that the world is ruled by Three Mothers: Mater Suspiriorum, Mater Lacrimarum and Mater Tenebrarum who represent sorrow, tears and darkness respectively. They are witches, 'wicked step-mothers, incapable of creating life' – the voice-over at the beginning of *Inferno* tells us. The witch is an abject figure who dwells with abject things: in *Suspiria*, the mother/witches are associated with maggots, in *Inferno* with rats. Each one lives in a house where she hides her 'filthy secrets' in dark secret places which suggest the 'evil womb' of the abject mother (Tansley, 1988, 26). *Suspiria* and *Inferno*, as well as *Black Sunday*, reinforce the stereotypical image of the witch as a malevolent, destructive, monstrous figure whose constant aim is destruction of the symbolic order. Similarly both *The Evil Dead* and *Evil Dead II* reinforce this image of the witch – although with some humour.

In some horror films the witch's supernatural powers are linked to the female reproductive system – particularly menstruation. It is interesting to note that, despite the range of subjects covered in the maternal melodrama and the woman's film, menstruation is not one. It is to the horror film that we must turn for any direct reference to woman's monthly cycle. In *Carrie*, *The Exorcist* and *Omen IV: The Awakening*, the young girls who develop supernatural powers are at the threshold of puberty. In *Carrie* and *The Omen*, the girls' transformation into witch or female devil follows on from the onset of menarche. *Carrie* provides a particularly interesting representation of woman as witch and menstrual monster. Most critical articles on *Carrie* explore the way in which the film presents a critique of the family and of middle American values. In his discussion of the relationship between the horror film and its 'true milieu', the family, Robin Wood places *Carrie* in 'The Terrible Child' category (along with *It's Alive* and *Cathy's Curse*) which has connections with the category of 'Satanism, diabolic possession, the Antichrist' (Wood, 1986, 83). Wood discusses the ways in which the monster's attack is almost always related to sexual and emotional repressions within the familial context: 'The child-monsters are all shown as products of the family, whether the family itself is regarded as guilty (the "psychotic" films) or innocent' (ibid., 84). In his analysis of *Carrie*, David Pirie sees the breakdown in the adult–child relationship as a reflection of a wider collapse in social relationships. He sees the Prom apocalypse, where Carrie (Sissy Spacek) destroys the entire gathering, as the core of the film:

> The apocalypse which follows reunites the two basic strands of American horror which, as I have suggested, seem to deal either in massive, apocalyptic destruction or unnatural family relationships which themselves imply the end of society. In *Carrie*, the breakdown of relationships leads directly and concretely to the destruction of the community.
>
> (Pirie, 1977–8, 24)

The representation of Carrie as witch and menstrual monster has been largely ignored. The only critic who has, to my knowledge, drawn attention to the significance of menstrual blood in *Carrie* and *The Exorcist* is Vivian Sobchack. She points out in a footnote that the bleeding of the two female protagonists, Carrie and Regan, represents 'an apocalyptic feminine explosion of the frustrated desire to speak', a desire denied them within the patriarchal symbolic (Sobchack, 1978, 193). I agree with this comment, but their blood is also used in a wider context, specifically to construct them as figures of abjection. The symbolic function of woman's menstrual blood is of crucial importance in *Carrie*. Blood takes various forms in the film: menstrual blood, pig's blood, birth blood, the blood of sin and the blood of death. It is also blood which flows between mother and daughter and joins them together in their life-and-death struggle. The basic conflict in the film develops from Carrie's attempts to resist her mother's dominating influence. Carrie's mother, Margaret White (Piper Laurie), is a religious bigot who believes that female sexuality is inherently evil and responsible for man's fall from grace. She also believes her daughter is a witch. Not only has she declined to tell Carrie about sexuality and reproduction – in case Carrie is corrupted – she refuses to allow her to develop friendships or a relationship with a boy. Like the monstrous heroine of Brian De Palma's *Sisters*, and Norman from *Psycho*, Carrie is also a divided personality. On the one hand she is a painfully shy, withdrawn, child-like girl who just wants to be 'normal' like every other teenager, while on the other hand she has the power of telekinesis which enables her to transform into an avenging female fury.

The mother–child relationship in *Carrie*, as in *Psycho*, is depicted as abnormal and perverse. Carrie desires independence and yearns to lead her own life, yet is unable to break away from her mother's dominating influence. Although Carrie is not imbued with her mother's religious mania, she is obedient and follows her mother's orders in matters of religious observance. Even when her mother orders her into a small cupboard under the stairs to pray, Carrie obeys. She vainly tries to reason with her mother over various matters, yet is clearly bound to her by strong emotional ties. Mrs White's feelings for her daughter are more ambiguous;

her desire to control Carrie appears to stem more from a religious than a maternal sense of duty. She wants to save her daughter from the sins of womankind, specifically from the sins of the body. Mrs White is represented as the patriarchal stereotype of the sexually unfulfilled woman. As in *Psycho*, the monstrous child is ultimately depicted as a creation of the psychotic, dominating mother. This relationship constitutes one of the earliest experiences of the abject. Three scenes in *Carrie* interconnect to link her to the world of nature, blood, death and the suffocating mother: the opening shower scene and its aftermath; Prom night; and the scene of Mrs White's bloody crucifixion and Carrie's death. An analysis of each of these will enable us to see how woman's monstrousness is linked to her reproductive function.

What is perhaps most significant about Carrie's telekinetic powers is that she acquires them at the same time as her blood flows, the time of her menarche. Woman's blood is thus linked to the possession of supernatural powers, powers which historically and mythologically have been associated with the representation of woman as witch. When Carrie first bleeds, she is in the shower pleasurably massaging and stroking her body. Like Marion in *Psycho*, Carrie is shown enjoying her own body; the mood is sensual, even erotic. Soft focus, slow motion and dreamy music create a mood of gentle romanticism. Like Marion, Carrie is also cruelly punished for enjoying solitary, sensual pleasures. The romantic mood is suddenly broken as Carrie looks in horror as menstrual blood spills forth and runs freely down her legs. In panic, she runs screaming from the shower. The response of her class is swift and brutal. The girls bombard her with tampons and sanitary napkins as she cowers like a defenceless, terrified child before the savage onslaught. Apart from menstrual blood, Carrie is also associated with another form of abject matter – excrement. Prior to the shower scene, when the girls were playing sport, Carrie made a mistake and one of the girls, Chris, snarled at her, 'You eat shit.'

Carrie is rescued by the sympathetic gym teacher, Miss Collins, and sent home from school where she has to face another ordeal – her mother. Carrie tries to explain to her mother the harm she has caused by keeping her in ignorance but Mrs White refuses to listen. Instead, she raves hysterically about the sins of woman and how she and Carrie must pray for their 'woman-weak, wicked, sinning souls'. She tells Carrie that because Eve was weak and loosed the raven, or the sin of intercourse, on the world, God punished Eve, first with the 'Curse of Blood', second with the 'Curse of Childbearing', and third with the 'Curse of Murder'. Mrs White sees Carrie as one of Eve's daughters. 'And still Eve did not repent, nor all the daughters of Eve, and upon Eve did the crafty serpent found a kingdom of whoredoms and pestilences.' The sins of woman are inherited – a position also argued in *The Brood*. Finally, Mrs White forces her daughter into a small dark cupboard where she is told she must pray to God for forgiveness. Mouthing sexist religious principles, Mrs White blames all forms of human evil on woman. She believes that the curse of humanity is passed through woman's blood, from mother to daughter. Woman is the universal scapegoat, the sacrificial victim. True to the practice of ritual atonement, Carrie is literally set up as a sacrificial victim at the Prom.

Carrie is invited to the Prom by Tommy Ross, who has promised his girlfriend, Sue Snell, he will partner Carrie in order to make up for the cruelty of the girls. Sue does not know that another of the girls, Chris Hargenson, has planned a cruel trick. She has rigged the ballot for Queen of the Prom so that Carrie will win. When she is crowned, a bucket of pig's blood, perched in the rafters above, will fall on Carrie and her escort. The pig's blood is linked to woman's blood. When Chris's boyfriend, Billy Nolan, and his mates break into the piggery at night, they make jokes about women and pigs. One says: 'I went out with a girl once who was a real pig!' The scene of the pig's blood cascading over Carrie's body at the Prom echoes the earlier shower scene where her own blood runs down her body. A further parallel between Carrie and pigs is drawn when Chris tells Carrie that she eats 'shit'; pigs are stigmatized as 'dirty' creatures because of their habit of wallowing in their own excrement (if there is no mud available) to protect their extremely sensitive skins from sunburn.

Women and pigs are also linked in myth and language. In Greek and Latin the female genitals are referred to as 'pig', and the cowrie shell which clearly represents the female genitals was called 'pig'. Even today, 'sowish-ness' is used in German as a slang term for menstruation (Shuttle and Redgrove, 1978, 37). *The Exorcist* also associates woman with pigs. 'The sow is mine!' Regan screams as she tries to possess her mother sexually. Part of the problem with *Carrie* is that it plays on the debased meaning of woman's/pig's blood in order to horrify modern audiences; in so doing it also perpetuates negative views about women and menstruation. The analogy drawn between women and pigs is also central to the film's discourse on the abject. Carrie/woman is monstrous because she bleeds like 'a stuck pig', as the saying goes. But the meaning of the pig's blood is ambiguous. In their study of carnival culture, Peter Stallybrass and Allon White (1986) draw attention to the fact that the pig symbolized 'low' discourses that related to the grotesque, disgusting body. Insofar as carni-val permitted a celebration of the grotesque we can see that the drenching of Carrie's body in pig's blood represents a kind of inversion of a royal coronation. She is crowned Queen and anointed with pig's blood prior to using her demonic powers to wreak devastation on the assembly, and we are encouraged to identify with her as she carries out her terrible revenge.

By associating Carrie's supernatural powers with blood, the film draws on superstitious notions of the terrifying powers of menstrual blood. According to Pliny, 'a menstrous woman's touch could blast the fruits of the field, sour wine, cloud mirrors, rust iron, and blunt the edges of knives'

(Walker, 1983, 643). In *The Malleus Maleficarum* witches were blamed for a range of similar offences, such as turning milk sour, ruining crops and causing storms at sea. From the eighth to the eleventh centuries many churches forbade menstruating women to enter. As late as 1684 women in their 'fluxes' were ordered to remain outside (Morris, 1973, 110). In some religions, such as Judaism, menstruating women are still regarded as unclean and sexual intercourse is forbidden. Witches were also accused of vampirism and of using menstrual blood, particularly that from a girl's first bleeding, to perform magic and concoct poisonous potions. According to Robert Graves, Thessalian witches used a girl's first menstrual blood to make the world's most feared poison – 'moon-dew' (Graves, 1966, 166).

Significantly, Carrie only develops the powers of telekinesis when she first bleeds; the suggestion is that her blood is both powerful and magical. Ultimately, woman's blood is represented in the film as an abject substance and helps to construct Carrie as monstrous. When Carrie unleashes the full force of her powers, she takes on the appearance of an avenging Lamia. Standing above the crowd, her body covered in blood, her eyes bulging with fury, she wreaks destruction, transforming the night 'Among the Stars' into an orgy of death. At one point Carrie uses her powers to animate a fire hose; it writhes amongst the crowd bringing death in its wake and taking on the appearance of a giant serpent, a fitting companion for the Queen of Death. Like the witches of other horror films, Carrie has become a figure of monumental destruction sparing no one in her fury. But because she has been sadistically treated by her fellow classmates and her insane mother, Carrie is also a very sympathetic figure.

Carrie returns home to discover her house illuminated by a host of candles. Her mother is absent. Carrie takes off her bloody gown and huddles in a foetal position in the bath, where she washes away the blood and make-up, both signs of her womanhood. The bath filled with bloody water suggests a rebirth and a desire to return to the comforting dyadic relationship. As in many horror films, the pre-Oedipal mother is represented as a primary source of abjection. Unlike the young girl we first saw enjoying her body in the shower, Carrie is once again reduced to a trembling child as she was when the girls pelted her with tampons.

This movement – from child to woman and woman to child – is crucial to the film's representation of woman as abject. As Carrie attempts to break away from the maternal entity, she takes on the signs of womanhood, particularly in relation to her Prom appearance. Like a fairytale heroine, she is transformed from ugly duckling to beautiful swan. As Carrie moves back into a state of childlike dependency, she sheds these trappings (ball gown, make-up) of burgeoning independence and turns once again to her mother for protection and solace. Carrie's journey back, like her temporary escape, is symbolized by a physical change: the long nightdress and scrubbed face are those of the little girl wanting a mother. All traces of blood have been removed. As Carrie leaves the bathroom, her mother appears. She is dressed not in her customary black costume but in a white nightgown suggesting purity and innocence. Carrie falls into her arms, crying: 'You were right, Mamma!' But her mother does not understand. In her eyes Carrie has sold herself to the devil. 'Thou shalt not suffer a witch to live,' she screams.

Carrie's abortive attempt to enter the world of male–female relationships seems to awaken Mrs White's memories of her own sexual life. She embraces Carrie and begins to talk about her relationship with Carrie's father and how his sexual advances filled her with disgust. Gradually, however, the tone of her confession changes; and she tells Carrie that she liked her husband's 'filthy touching'. As the mother's tone becomes more and more impassioned, she rises up and stabs Carrie in the back. The satin nightgown takes on a new meaning – it points to the mother's role as ritual executioner – and the candles signify that a sacrificial ceremony is under way. What is most interesting about this sequence is the way in which Carrie's stabbing suggests a sexual assault by the mother. Carrie falls down the stairs and cowers in a corner as her mother dances grotesquely around her, preparing to thrust the knife into Carrie once again. Suddenly, Carrie calls on her powers of telekinesis to send a barrage of knives sailing through the air, pinning her mother to the wall. Mrs White dies in a pose which imitates that of Christ on the cross in the statue she keeps in the prayer cupboard.

There is no doubt that Carrie's knife attack has sexual connotations. As Mrs White dies she utters orgasmic moans, which suggest that her release has been brought about by a symbolic form of phallic penetration by her daughter. This scene suggests that the doomed mother–child dyad is marked by repressed sexual desire – a theme also explored in *Psycho*. Carrie pulls her mother's impaled body from the wall and returns to the womb-like closet in which her mother once entombed her, forcing her to pray to God for forgiveness that she was born female. As in the vampire film, *Carrie*'s thematic movement suggests symbolically a return to the womb; a final statement of complete surrender to the power of the maternal entity. Two scenes point to this return: Carrie's seclusion in the womb-like prayer cupboard and her blood bath in which she huddles in a foetal position as she washes away the pig's blood. The castrating mother takes back the life she once created; Carrie is locked for ever in the maternal embrace as mother and daughter die in the burning house.

The body of each woman is marked by bloody wounds; the wound is a sign of abjection in that it violates the skin which forms a border between the inside and outside of the body. As I discussed in relation to *The Brood*, a bodily wound also suggests the moment of birth in which the infant is torn away from the maternal insides. Wounds signify the abject because they point to woman's reproductive functions and her alliance with the world of nature. In *Carrie*, woman's blood also signifies maternal blood; the blood that nourishes the embryo and emphasizes woman's procreative function. In the horror genre, however, menstrual blood is constructed as a source of abjection: its powers are so great it can transform woman into any one of a number of fearful creatures: possessed child, killer and vengeful witch. Yet the film presents contradictory messages: on the one hand it redeploys ancient blood taboos and misogynistic myths; on the other, it invites sympathy for Carrie as a victim of these prejudices.

Once again we can see that woman's reproductive functions mark her as monstrous. In the horror films discussed above woman is represented as monstrous in relation to her reproductive and maternal functions. This occurs for a number of reasons: the archaic mother (*Alien*) horrifies because she threatens to cannibalize, to take back, the life forms to which she once gave birth; the possessed girl (*The Exorcist*) evokes a pleasurable disgust because she confronts us with those abject substances (blood, pus, vomit, urine) that signify a return to a state of infantile pre-socialization; the pregnant woman (*The Brood*) horrifies because her body houses an alien being – the infant/other; the female vampire (*The Hunger*) is monstrous because she draws attention to the female blood cycle and she reduces her captives to a state of embryonic dependency in which they must suckle blood in order to live; the young female witch (*Carrie*) evokes both sympathy and horror because her evil deeds are associated with puberty and menarche. The monstrous-feminine is constructed as an abject figure because she threatens the symbolic order. The monstrous-feminine draws attention to the 'frailty of the symbolic order' through her evocation of the natural, animal order and its terrifying associations with the passage all human beings must inevitably take from birth through life to death. In conclusion, I wish to re-emphasize that I regard the association of woman's maternal and reproductive functions with the abject as a construct of patriarchal ideology. (Similarly, it is man's phallic properties that are frequently *constructed* as a source of monstrosity in films dealing with the male monster.) Woman is not, by her very nature, an abject being. Her representation in popular discourses as monstrous is a function of the ideological project of the horror film – a project designed to perpetuate the belief that woman's monstrous nature is inextricably bound up with her difference as man's sexual other.

Part II

MEDUSA'S HEAD: PSYCHOANALYTIC THEORY AND THE *FEMME CASTRATRICE*

Plate 1 The egg chamber. Intra-uterine imagery, sign of the abject archaic mother, haunts the *mise-en-scène* of *Alien*.

Plate 2 The space travellers about to enter the alien ship through its monstrous vaginal portals (*Alien*).

Plate 3 Metropolis: the monstrous perfection of the female robot.

Plate 4 I Walked with a Zombie: female zombies stalk the half-light of man's nightmares (publicity poster).

Plate 5 Black Sunday: executed by a spiked demon mask, the witch (Barbara Steele) returns to vampirize the living.

Plate 6 Woman's blood is represented as a source of utmost abjection in the horror film (Sissie Spacek in *Carrie*).

Plate 7 The Wasp Woman: the monstrous wasp woman threatens a male victim with her deadly stinger! (publicity poster)

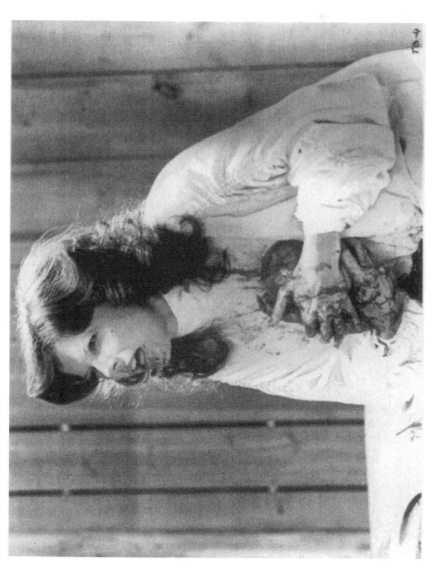

Plate 8 The horror of woman's animalistic procreative functions. Having licked away the afterbirth, woman holds her newborn infant (Samantha Eggar in *The Brood*).

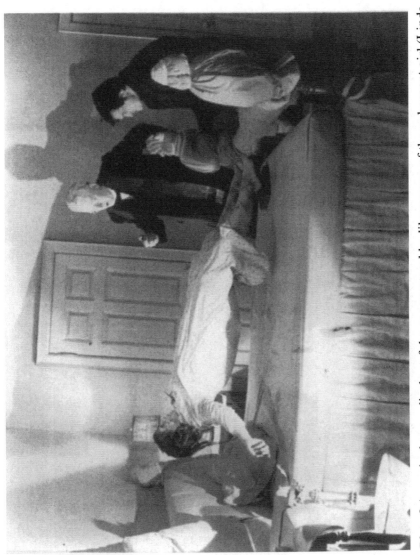

Plate 9 A carnivalesque display of the supernatural bodily powers of the pubescent girl (Linda Blair in *The Exorcist*).

Plate 10 Woman as destructive colossus in *Attack of the 50ft Woman* (publicity poster).

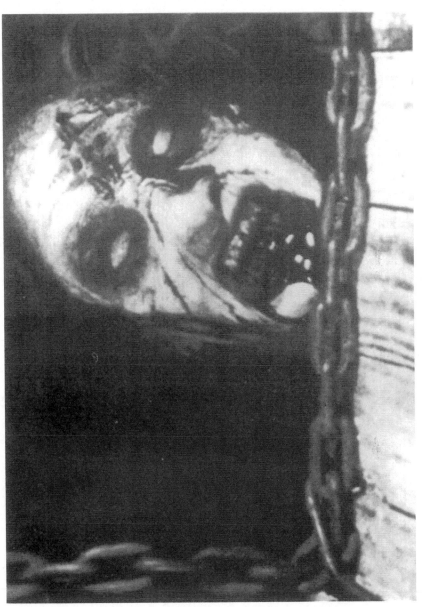

Plate 11 A witch from *The Evil Dead* sets out to terrorize her victims with a disgusting display of abject bodily horror. Reproduced courtesy of Renaissance Pictures Ltd.

Plate 12 The psychotic sister (Bernadette Gibson) of *Next of Kin* wields her deadly knife. Reproduced courtesy of Film House Pty Ltd.

PREFACE

[handwritten: capabilities]

[handwritten: Castration = impotence, women's power makes men feel powerless]

In Part II of this book I will explore a dimension of the monstrous-feminine that is not specifically related to woman's maternal and reproductive functions. Freud argued that woman terrifies because she is castrated. I will argue that woman also terrifies because man endows her with imaginary powers of castration. Because the Freudian theory of woman's castration has provided the dominant theoretical justification for analyses of woman as monster in the horror film, it is necessary to return to Freud in order to evaluate critically the origins of his theory. In the next two chapters I will present, first, a rereading of his Little Hans case history ('Analysis of a phobia in a five-year-old boy') and, second, I will examine the repression of the figure of the castrating woman in Freud's other writings and in his dream analyses. An extensive rereading of the Hans case is necessary because it is probably the most often quoted of all Freud's case studies in relation to his theory of the Oedipus complex and castration crisis. A critical rereading of Freud is also necessary because the view that woman terrifies only because she is castrated has led to a serious misunderstanding of the nature of the monstrous-feminine in critical writings on the horror film. The following critique of Freud will also provide the theoretical groundwork for the later analyses of specific faces of the monstrous-feminine: the *femme castratrice* in *Sisters* and *I Spit on Your Grave* and the castrating mother in *Psycho* and other horror films that deal with the psychotic mother. (Unless otherwise stated, all quotations of Freud's works in Chapter 7 are from 'Analysis of a phobia in a five-year-old boy'.)

[handwritten: The monstrous dwarf? The cutting blade (Han's penknife)]

7

'LITTLE HANS' RECONSIDERED: OR 'THE TALE OF MOTHER'S TERRIFYING WIDDLER'

'I tore its legs apart. Do you know why? Because there was a knife inside it belonging to Mummy. I put it [the knife] in at the place where the button squeaks, and then I tore apart its legs and it came out there.'

Freud, 'Analysis of a phobia'

In these words, Hans explains to his father the game he has been playing all morning with his indiarubber doll, Grete. The nursemaid tells his father that as Hans let the knife – a penknife belonging to his mother – drop out from between the doll's legs he would point and say: 'Look, there's its widdler!' (84). Hans seems quite definite about what the knife represents – his mother's 'missing' genitals, the widdler he has repeatedly wanted to see for himself. Although Hans is quite clear about the knife's symbolic meaning, Freud interprets it as a 'baby'. In Freud's view, Hans used this act to demonstrate 'how he imagined a birth took place'. Furthermore, 'if we look into it more closely we can see that he showed something else, that he was hinting at something which was not alluded to again in the analysis . . . that children do in fact grow inside their mother's body and are pushed out of it like a lumf' (130–1). 'Lumf' is Hans's special word for faeces.

It seems extraordinary that Freud failed to consider the meaning that Hans attached to the knife – even more extraordinary given the connection Freud himself drew between a woman's baby and her phallus. Certainly Freud placed a different interpretation on the baby/penis analogy, but the connection is there. Why not explore this area? Further – why did Hans select a knife to represent her genitals? On reading through the Little Hans case history again, I am struck by the way in which both the father and Freud manipulate Hans's childhood experiences to confirm Freud's theories of childhood sexuality. In his discussion of the Little Hans case, Erich Fromm draws attention to the way in which Hans's father suggests interpretations to him, and wonders to what extent Hans's associations are 'spontaneous' (Fromm, 1970, 96).

In my view, there is sufficient material in the Little Hans case study to open up an entirely new dimension to existing theories of childhood sexuality. It is my contention that this material suggests quite clearly that the origin of Hans's phobia was fear of the mother's genitals – her widdler – not as *castrated*, but as *castrating* organs. The material also suggests that while Hans feared his father might punish him for his desire to have his mother for himself, he also feared the mother might castrate him as a punishment for masturbation and/or for his erotic longings for her. Freud's theory that the father is the castrator is only a part of the story.

Little Hans, a five-year-old boy, suffered from a phobia which expressed itself as a fear that a white horse might bite him. This phobia later expanded to include a fear of horses falling down and of heavily laden vehicles such as carts, buses or furniture vans. Determined that Hans would not be derided or punished for his fears, the father made detailed notes of his discussions with Hans over a period of two years. These notes suggest a direct connection between the boy's phobia and his sexual desires. Hans suffered initially from anxiety hysteria; these are *'par excellence* the neuroses of childhood' (116). By subjecting himself to numerous restrictions and precautions, the child might – according to Freud – learn to overcome its anxiety but the barriers or protective structures erected in this cause will eventually manifest themselves as phobias.

The first reports date from when Hans was three years of age. At this time he developed an interest in his 'widdler'. He asked his mother if she had a widdler but his parents never explained to Hans the nature of her genitals and their difference from those of the male. At this time he also mistook a cow's teat for its widdler. 'Oh, look!' he said, 'there's milk coming out of its widdler!' When he was three and a half, Hans's mother discovered he was touching his penis. She threatened him with castration. 'If you do that, I shall send for Dr A. to cut off your widdler. And then what'll you widdle with?' Ever resourceful Hans replied, 'With my bottom' (8). Freud argues it was this event which led to Hans acquiring a fear of castration. His phobia does not develop until later. Freud does not discuss the significance of the fact that the threat is uttered by the mother. Some of Freud's associates, however, did challenge the role Freud allocated to the father in his theory of castration. In her essay 'The dread of women' Karen Horney writes that the 'prominence given to the anxiety relating to the castrating father is . . . tendentious'. She refers to Groddeck's analysis of the thumb-sucker in *Struwwelpeter*. It is 'a man who cuts off the thumb, but it is the mother who utters the threat, and the instrument with which it is carried out – the scissors – is a female symbol' (Horney, 1967, 138). Fromm also states that Freud misinterprets the case and that 'the dread of castration originates with Hans's mother' as she is the parent who utters the threat (Fromm, 1970, 92).

At the age of three and three-quarters, Hans expressed a desire to see his parents' widdlers. On one occasion he asked his father if he had a widdler because he had never seen it:

> *Hans* (aged three and three-quarters): 'Daddy, have you got a widdler too?'
> *Father*: 'Yes, of course.'
> *Hans*: 'But I've never seen it when you were undressing.' (9)

On another night, his mother asked him why he was staring at her as she undressed.

> *Hans*: 'I was only looking to see if you'd got a widdler too.'
> *Mother*: 'Of course. Didn't you know that?'
> *Hans*: 'No. I thought you were so big you'd have a widdler like a horse.' (9–10)

Given Hans's later phobia about horses, surely it is significant that he associated his mother's genitals with those of a horse? Yet Freud does not seriously consider this, merely interprets Hans's comment to mean that he is comforting himself with the thought that his own widdler will grow bigger one day. It is a 'comforting reflection' (107). Why? Hans doesn't sound as if he needs assurance. Rather, he needs to know the truth. Disappointment at not catching a glimpse of his mother's widdler appears to be his dominant mood. Freud is the one who finds the idea that the infant penis will grow a 'comforting' notion. In my view, Hans's phantasy that his mother has a huge widdler indicates the dominant role she plays in his life.

The next important event in Hans's life is the birth of his baby sister. Hans is told the stork will bring the baby. The father's notes indicate that Hans treated this idea with suspicion. Again the subject of his mother's widdler emerges. Hans pointed to the 'basins and other vessels, filled with blood and water' and commented in a surprised voice: 'But blood doesn't come out of *my* widdler' (10). Why does he imagine blood comes from his mother's widdler? Hans was jealous of his baby sister and when anyone praised her, he would comment: 'But she's not got any teeth yet' (11). This remark is important, given Hans's later phobia about being bitten by a horse. Seven days after her birth Hans commented that her widdler was 'still quite small'. He then added: 'When she grows up it'll get bigger all right' (ibid.). At this stage the two things which Hans describes about his sister as yet to grow are her widdler and teeth. Freud assumes Hans is comparing his sister's widdler to his own; it is also possible he is comparing it to his mother's imaginary widdler. Given he believes his mother's widdler is like a horse's, he knows his sister's will grow a great deal. Perhaps her teeth will also grow? When his sister was three months old, Hans again commented on her 'tiny little widdler' (14). He also examined his doll and stated that her widdler was also very tiny. Later, he plays a game with the indiarubber doll in which he imagines her widdler, represented by his mother's penknife, is held *inside* her body. Symbolically, he gives her body a cutting blade or teeth. Perhaps he thinks his baby sister lost her widdler during birth. Is this why his mother's widdler was bleeding? In Hans's phantasy life a number of things appear to have become interrelated: blood, teeth, a knife, being bitten, castration, his mother's widdler and horses' widdlers. None of these enables us to justify the conclusion that what Hans feared most was his mother as a castrated rather than castrating parent.

This brings me to a very important factor in Hans's story. Just prior to the time when Hans commented that his sister only had a 'tiny little widdler' he had occasion to see the widdler of a horse when it was urinating. His father writes: 'Hans and I walked past a horse that was micturating [sic] and he said: "the horse has got its widdler underneath like me"' (ibid.). At around the same time, Hans had drawn a sketch of a giraffe with a long widdler extended from its underbelly. It is important to note that when a gelding or stallion urinates, its widdler appears to uncoil and drop down quite a way. It would seem, then, that when comparing his mother's widdler to a horse's Hans would have been comparing her to a stallion or gelding with its widdler extended to full length. Given that a stallion or a gelding can tuck its widdler away, it is most likely that Hans imagined his mother could do the same. In other words, in his phantasy he may well have imagined that his mother, like a horse, had a widdler which was folded up inside her body; this view of female sexuality is similar to Galen's conception of the female organ as an inverted and internal version of the male organ (Bullough, 1973, 492). This is the reason why Hans refused to accept that women did not have widdlers. He knew it was there, it was large, and it was normally hidden from sight – like a horse's. This is an important point which I will take up later.

At this stage it is impossible to know *exactly* what Hans now thinks of his mother's genitals, as Hans's father does not ask any questions of this nature. At the age of four and a quarter Hans asked his mother to touch his penis. She had just finished bathing him and was powdering around his penis but taking care not to touch it. She told him she would not touch his penis because it would not be proper. Hans replied that it would, however, be 'great fun' (19).

At the age of four and three-quarters Hans began to develop a nervous disorder. He became anxious that his mother would leave him and he would have no one to 'coax' with. 'Coax' is Hans's expression for 'caress'. He was used to getting into bed with his mother in order to 'coax'. He also made a remark along these lines. The father cannot remember the exact words: 'Suppose I was to have no Mummy', or 'Suppose you were to go away.' The father expresses the view that he thinks her display of affection towards the boy is 'excessive' and that she too readily takes him to bed with her (ibid., 28). It is clear that Hans is deeply attached to his mother and wants her to himself.

The father reported two other incidents at this time. One morning Hans came into his mother's bed and recounted an event of a month earlier when his aunt watched him being bathed and said: 'He *has* got a dear little thingummy' (23). Two days later he was walking with the nursemaid when he refused to venture any further, began to cry and demanded to be taken home to 'coax' with his mother. The next day she took Hans for his walk. Again he became frightened, did not want to leave and began to cry. On the way home he reluctantly confessed to his mother that he was afraid a horse would bite him. That evening he became fearful again, and expressed a desire to be 'coaxed' with. 'I know I shall have to go for a walk again tomorrow.' And later, 'the horse'll come into the room' (24). The next day his mother warned him again about putting his hand on his widdler but he said he had continued to do so. No doubt her warning invoked for Hans a reminder of her earlier threat to castrate him.

According to Freud the above events represent the beginning of his anxiety and his phobia. The 'fundamental phenomenon' in his condition is his deep affection for his mother. His feelings for her assume a sexual note on two occasions: when he asks his mother to touch his penis when she bathes him and when he climbs into bed with her and repeats his aunt's words that he had a 'dear little' penis. According to Freud: 'It was this increased affection for his mother which turned suddenly into anxiety – which, as we should say, succumbed to repression' (25). Freud interprets Hans's anxiety as a 'repressed erotic longing' for his mother. In my view Hans's anxiety would most likely have been related to his fear that his mother would carry out her earlier threat to have Hans castrated by the doctor or even by herself *because* of his erotic longings. According to Freud, Hans dislikes streets because they represent a separation from his mother. When he is walking, he is away from her. Why then does Hans still suffer from anxiety – unsatisfied longing – when he is *with* his mother in the streets? Freud explains:

> His anxiety, then, corresponded to repressed longing. But it was not the same thing as the longing: the repression must be taken into account too. Longing can be completely transformed into satisfaction if it is presented with the object longed for. Therapy of that kind is no longer effective in dealing with anxiety. The anxiety remains even when the longing can be satisfied. It can no longer be completely retransformed into libido; there is something that keeps the libido back under repression. (26)

In a footnote, Freud adds that when the anxiety continues, despite attainment of the desired object, it becomes a 'pathological anxiety'. He also explains that Hans's anxiety, which represented his repressed longing for his mother, was characteristic of all infantile anxiety in that it is 'without an object to begin with' (25). Initially, the child does *not* know of what it is afraid. The anxiety is transformed into fear only when it finds an object.

The phobic object Hans eventually finds is the 'white horse' which will bite him. Why a horse? Freud offers several reasons: Hans has always been interested in horses' large widdlers; he thought his mother's widdler would be like a horse's. Freud however dismisses the idea that the horse might be 'merely a substitute for the mother' because this would not make sense in relation to his fear that a horse might come into his room at night. Freud does not consider that Hans might both desire and fear his mother – desire to have her for himself yet fear she might come into his room at night, when he desires her most, and cut off his widdler. Earlier she threatened to tell the doctor to castrate Hans but it is possible that Hans now believes she might cut it off with her own widdler. Perhaps he imagines his father is at risk every time he goes to bed with the mother? Perhaps he imagines this might happen to him when he is 'coaxing' in bed with his mother?

Freud makes a great deal of the fact that Hans never believed the story of the stork. We know that Hans understood that babies grow inside the mother (91) and was told that babies are pressed out of the mother like a 'lumf' (87). No doubt Hans wondered how the baby got inside his mother. He probably also knows his father has something to do with the baby's existence. He is the father; it is 'his' baby too. Freud discusses the problem of knowledge of the vagina in 'The sexual theories of children'. He argues that when the child is just about ready to 'postulate the existence of the vagina' and the role of the father's penis 'his inquiry is broken off in helpless perplexity' because he believes the mother also has a penis which is like the father's (p. 218). Perhaps, like a horse, she keeps it tucked up inside her body? As I have been arguing, we have no real justification for concluding that initially all infants believe the mother possesses a penis exactly like the father's and that they later believe she is castrated. If we remove this block, there is no reason why we cannot posit that some/many children do come to an earlier knowledge of the vagina, or baby 'box' than Freud allows.

Hans's belief that his mother kept her babies in her 'box' (78) suggests that he had some idea of the vagina. If a baby comes from an unknown place behind the mother's widdler it is possible that his whole – or part of his own – body could be taken back inside the mother, particularly if her widdler has teeth. Freud speaks of the anus being identified with a mouth (Laplanche and Pontalis, 1985, 212). If Hans has seen the labia of his little sister, which are initially very large in new babies, it is also possible that he may have imagined that these are lips. Freud dismisses the idea that the horse and its biting mouth 'is *merely* a substitute for his mother' (my emphasis) as if this explanation were too simple or obvious to take seriously; yet he presses on to demonstrate that the horse is a substitute for the father!

Another reason why Hans might associate his mother's genitals with a mouth relates to an earlier association he made between a cow's teat and a widdler. As mentioned previously, he looked at the cow and said: 'Oh, look! there's milk coming out of its widdler.' This occurred at the time he first began to ask about his mother's widdler, when he was three years of age. A parallel can be drawn between putting a teat in one's mouth and sucking milk and the act of putting the penis into a vagina where it is pulled by the vaginal walls and semen, a milky substance, is ejected. While Hans did not yet understand the nature of sexual intercourse it may well be that later, when he did consciously or unconsciously learn about coition, this early memory surfaced and momentarily filled him with terror. He may have imagined that the vagina which receives the penis also has teeth – just like his mouth when he suckled at the breast. It is also possible that Hans understood about the nature of coition between animals – perhaps horses – before he *consciously* knew about human behaviour. He apparently spent a great deal of time at the stables and playing horse games with other children on the farm where the family spent their holidays. Freud argued that children do not know of the existence of the vagina until much later which, he claimed, helps explain why children believe the mother has a penis. Not all psychoanalysts agree (Laplanche and Pontalis, 1985, 311). It is also possible that, when Hans did learn about coition, this earlier memory of mistaking a cow's teat for a breast, creating the possibility that the vagina is like a mouth with teeth, might have had a deferred effect.

Freud is determined to interpret Hans's anxiety and phobia in relation to his theory of the Oedipus complex and castration complex in which the mother is thought to be castrated. When the father suggests that the mother is the cause of Hans's neurosis because of her 'excessive display of affection' towards him, Freud invokes destiny – 'She had a predestined part to play, and her position was a hard one' (28). It appears that her part was 'predestined' – by Freud. Freud explains to the father that Hans's libido is attached to a 'wish to see his mother's widdler' and that the father should take away this desire 'by informing him that his mother and all other female beings (as he could see from Hanna) had no widdler at all' (ibid.). Again Freud not only advised a course of action based on a lie (women do have 'widdlers') but he also actively encouraged the view that women are castrated. Difference is not the same as absence. It is as if Freud himself wanted to will the disappearance of woman's genitals. Before this information is conveyed, Hans has his tonsils out and his phobia worsens. Taking tonsils from the throat through the mouth is also like a form of birth and of castration.

Hans's father recalls an important conversation in which Hans tries to convince him that horses do bite. He relates an incident which occurred when he was watching the little girl from next door about to depart in a carriage drawn by a white horse. Her father warned her not to put her finger to the white horse or it would bite. Hans tells his father that if you hold your finger to a white horse it will bite. His father then says: 'I say, it strikes me that it isn't a horse you mean, but a widdler, that one musn't put one's hand to.' Hans replies that a widdler does not bite. (Normally, Freud would interpret Hans's denial as repression.) The father persists. 'Perhaps it does, though' (30). It is possible that the father's insistence that a widdler *can bite* gave voice – and credibility – to a fear which Hans, as yet, had not consciously articulated – that woman's widdler does bite.

It is interesting to note that several days later a new maid arrived. Hans liked her very much. She would let him ride on her back when she cleaned the floor. He called her 'my horse' and would cry out – 'Gee-up' (ibid.). Freud does not comment at all on this game, despite the fact that it indicates that Hans continues to associate horses with women. He also says to the nurse/horse that if she does a certain thing she will be punished by having to undress; this will be shameful because people will see her widdler. Clearly, Hans still associates women's genitals with those of horses. By 'riding' the maid/woman/horse Hans may have been pleasurably stimulated; he is probably using a non-threatening situation to conquer his unconscious fear of woman. He is the master; woman the animal. This game takes place shortly after his father's insistence that widdlers can bite. It is also clear that the riding game is sexual.

Two weeks later Hans's father took Freud's advice and explained to Hans that women do not have widdlers. Father and son were walking together; there was very little traffic. Hans remarked: 'How sensible! God's done away with horses now.' Hans's father explained that neither little girls nor mummys had widdlers. 'Little girls and women, I said, have no widdlers: Mummy has none, Anna has none, and so on.' It is interesting that Freud did not advise the father to explain that women *do* have widdlers but they are different. Hans, however, is no fool. He asks: 'But how do little girls widdle, if they have no widdlers?' (31). Contradicting his earlier statement, the father replied that their widdlers are different, but he doesn't explain how. Hans is less anxious over the next few days but he continues to be anxious at night and when walking in the streets.

Several weeks later Hans's father took him to the zoo at Schönbrunn. He reports that Hans was terrified of all large animals such as the giraffe and elephant. He is also fearful of the pelican. Hans's father engages the boy in a discussion about large animals and their widdlers. Hans says he has seen the widdlers of horses often. Hans's father explains that big animals have big widdlers and vice versa. Hans replies: 'And every one has a widdler. And my widdler will get bigger as I get bigger; it's fixed in, of course' (34).

Why is Hans so obsessed with large horses and their widdlers? Horses, of course, were the common mode of transport so Hans would have encountered them daily. We also know that he went out of his way to observe horses. 'Yes, I went into the stable every day at Gmunden when the horses had come home' (ibid.). No doubt Hans observed horses of all sexes – mares, geldings and stallions. Yet he never asks a question about the sex of the horses. Given his interest in the widdlers of his sister and mother is it not surprising that he did not ask if the widdlers of stallions and mares were different? But perhaps it is not surprising. It is possible that Hans assumed that mares, geldings and stallions were the same and that all three possessed exceptionally long widdlers. As I mentioned earlier, Hans has seen a stallion/gelding urinating and no doubt is aware that a horse can unfold its widdler when it needs to urinate. Afterwards the gelding/stallion folds its widdler back inside itself. When he states that his widdler is 'fixed in' it may well be that he is not expressing a castration fear but a statement of fact. His widdler is fixed; he cannot extend and retract it, making it disappear, like a horse does – or, as he suspects, his mother might do. It is reasonable to assume that he believes the mother/horse folds the widdler into a space/hole between her legs. We learn that Hans later began to hold on to his faeces. The act of holding on to/letting go of faeces – which Freud argued were equivalent to the penis – also provides the child with another explanation of the nature of the mother's widdler: perhaps she can also retract and let go her widdler as if it were faeces.

The clearest evidence that Hans believes his mother's widdler is tucked away inside her body comes from his game with the indiarubber doll, Grete. As we saw earlier, Hans inserted his mother's small penknife into the doll and then tore its legs apart so that the knife dropped through. He would exclaim: 'Look, there's its widdler.' Freud claimed that the knife represented a 'baby' and that the game was about birth. I would argue that the central meaning of the game relates to a puzzle that has haunted Hans throughout his young life. What is his mother's widdler like? This enigma has led Hans to construct an elaborate phantasy about his mother's genitals in which she is terrifying not because she is castrated but because she castrates. The game therefore represents Hans's attempt to solve the riddle of Mummy's widdler. The answer he comes up with is that her widdler is phallic in shape and has a sharp, cutting blade, like teeth. Not only did she threaten him with castration when younger, he now knows she has the power to castrate him herself. Since his sister's birth, he has learnt that his mother's widdler bleeds; this terrifying fact only confirms his worst fear. Perhaps she cut his sister's widdler with her internal knife, her *vagina dentata*, during birth. He refuses to believe what his father tells him, that women, particularly mothers, do not have widdlers. Hans knows – quite rightly – that women do have widdlers but that they are different. They are retractable, mysterious and deadly.

THE MOTHER'S MUZZLE

There is another incident which also supports the above interpretation. One of the most puzzling pieces of information in the Hans jigsaw is his constant reference to the fact that he is most afraid of 'horses with a thing on their mouths'. His father asked if he meant the bit. Hans replied, 'No. They have something black on their mouths' and covered his mouth with his hand (49). His father eventually concludes that the black thing covering their mouths must have been the harness worn by dray-horses. To support his argument that Hans's fear of horses represents his fear of the castrating father, Freud interprets the black thing as representing the father's moustache. Freud tells us how he explained this to Hans. 'Finally I asked him whether by "the black round the mouth" he meant a moustache; and I then disclosed to him that he was afraid of his father, precisely because he was so fond of his mother' (42). Hans does not agree or disagree. On another occasion, when his father also suggests (tries to convince him) that the black might remind him of a moustache, Hans replies that the only similarity is the colour. On another occasion Hans plays with the idea that his father's moustache is a black 'muzzle' (53). Note that Hans does not suggest that the black thing on the horse is a moustache but a muzzle, an object which covers and encases the mouth and prevents it from opening, biting or feeding. Generally, attempts to link the black thing to Hans's father are not convincing. The mysterious 'black thing' is more easily linked with the mother. His mother's hair was black. The father at one point suggests to Hans that it was the 'black hair near her widdler' that frightened him. Hans does not deny this but says – not that she doesn't have one (a fact of which his father had previously tried to convince him) but that he has not seen her widdler. Hans still refuses to accept that his mother does not have a widdler.

In my view, the black thing on the horse's mouth which frightens Hans makes most sense if linked to the mother's black underwear, which no doubt included garters/suspender belt. Hans himself associates his mother's black underclothing with a feeling of revulsion. He says that his mother's black drawers disgust him and make him want to spit (63). There is also a parallel we can draw between a woman's garters and a horse's muzzle. Hans knows that horses bite. Given his interest in horses and their biting, Hans would probably know that a horse's harness/muzzle is designed to prevent it from biting. When he describes a muzzle to his father he covers his mouth with his hand. We know Hans associates his mother's widdler with the size of a horse's widdler. ('I thought you were so big you'd have a widdler like a horse.') It is not ridiculous to suggest that he might imagine the function of her suspender belt and/or corset could be to restrain her mysterious widdler and prevent it from biting. It is relevant to note that when horses are harnessed they also wear leather straps around

97

their back legs and near their genitals. This would reinforce in Hans's mind the association he has already made between a horse's widdler, biting teeth, black muzzle and the blood-smeared genitals of the mother.

We know that Hans was very preoccupied with his mother's 'box' where he believed she kept her babies. He refers to it as 'the stork-box' which he says is painted red. Vans or buses which are loaded with goods are 'stork-box carts' (81). Hans is also afraid of vehicles that are loaded up with goods; they appear to represent pregnancy. 'Mummy'll be loaded full up again when she has another one, when another one begins to grow, when another one's inside her' (91). He is particularly afraid of horses pulling a loaded cart and of horses falling down and making a row with their legs.

At one point Hans states that when a horse falls down it is like having a baby. It is possible that he associates the birth of his sister with these frightening images. The mother is like an overloaded horse; when she falls down and begins to kick with her legs she gives birth. We also know that Hans was jealous of his sister and did not want his mother to have another baby. Hans's phobia about streets, loaded carts and falling horses is related to – but different from – his phobia about being bitten by a horse. Clearly, the former relates to his fears about pregnancy and birth. On the basis of the knife game, it seems very likely that Hans believes his mother has a sharp instrument (teeth/knife) inside her body. He also thinks her 'stork-box' is painted red – the colour of blood – and that blood flows from his mother's widdler when she gives birth. Perhaps he believes his mother might hurt him if he places his widdler near her body when they are 'coaxing' in bed? If so, it is highly likely that once Hans realizes that the man's widdler is placed inside the mother's body he thinks that the man is in danger of being castrated. In my view, it is at this moment – the point at which the boy first learns about the vagina and the role of the penis in penetration – that he develops an acute anxiety about castration. At this point earlier memories, fears and events might have the delayed effect of reinforcing his castration anxieties as attached to the mother's body. These memories might include knowledge that the mother's genitals are bloody; memory that the girl's genitals are like lips; and oral sadistic fears associated with breast-feeding. It may well be at this point, when the boy, for the first time, comes to conscious realization that the female genitals might castrate, that he retrospectively endows the mother with a penis.

Finally, there are three dreams or phantasies which Hans has and which are relevant to my argument that his main fear is of the castrating body of the mother. The first is the dream of the two giraffes. In this he imagined there were two giraffes in his room: a big one and a crumpled one. Hans takes the crumpled one away; the big one calls out for the little one. Hans holds it in his hands and when the big one stops calling out he sits on top of it. He also states that his mother took off her chemise. Later Hans explains that his mother is the big giraffe and his sister the little one. His father disagrees with Hans's interpretation. He tells him that he, the father, is the big giraffe and its long neck reminded Hans of the father's widdler. Hans does not agree. He replies immediately that: 'Mummy has a neck like a giraffe, too. I saw, when she was washing her white neck.' In a footnote Freud states that Hans's comment 'confirmed the interpretation of the two giraffes as his father and mother, and not the sexual symbolism, according to which the giraffe itself represented the penis' (40). Once again, Freud – and the father – are so intent on interpreting Hans's situation in relation to Freud's theory of the Oedipus complex and castration crisis that they overlook crucial information offered by Hans himself.

Hans states that the big giraffe is his mother and the smaller one his sister, yet Freud insists the big one is the father and the smaller one the mother. Everything Hans says points to the fact that the giraffe with the long neck represents his mother. He even mentions that his mother's neck is 'white' – an important fact which recalls his fear of the biting white horse. Again the mother is associated symbolically with a large phallic animal. The smaller one, whom she is calling, is her child. Hans states it is his sister. Perhaps it is Hans himself – or his penis? Or his sister and Hans/his penis at the same time? The large giraffe – also associated with the mother taking off her chemise (and revealing her widdler) – calls out because Hans has taken the 'little one' away. Earlier Hans recalled the time when his aunt referred to his penis as a 'dear little thingummy'. Perhaps in his phantasy Hans imagines his mother's large widdler (long neck) now revealed (she removes her chemise); he desires her but she is too big for him. As a result his widdler is crumpled; he holds it in his hand and then hides it from view. She stops calling for his 'little one'. This phantasy may well represent Hans's fear of castration by the mother – he imagines she desires him (as he does her) but she is so big she crushes his widdler. Ashamed or perhaps fearful, he first holds it in his hand and then hides it from sight.

His second dream/phantasy concerns the plumber and the bath. In the first version of this phantasy, the plumber comes when Hans is in the bath: 'I was in the bath, and then the plumber came and unscrewed it. Then he took a big borer and stuck it into my stomach' (65). In a later dream Hans imagines that 'the plumber came; and first he took away my behind with a pair of pincers, and then gave me another, and then the same with my widdler'. Freud writes: 'Hans's father grasped the nature of this wishful phantasy, and did not hesitate a moment as to the only interpretation it could bear.' The father says: 'He gave you a *bigger* widdler and a *bigger* behind' (98). 'Yes,' says Hans.

With Hans's last phantasy the anxiety which arose from his castration complex was also overcome, and his painful expectations were given a happier turn. Yes, the Doctor (the plumber) *did* come, he *did* take

away his penis – but only to give him a bigger one in exchange for it.
(100)

Freud argues that the two phantasies are 'identical' and that both are about
castration. But the two phantasies are not identical. In the first the plumber
unscrews the 'bath' (bottom/womb) and gives him a big borer (widdler). In
the second the plumber is more aggressive; he prises Hans's bottom and
widdler from his body and gives him new ones. The first – I will argue –
involves an act of displacement (the 'bath' is inserted into his stomach); the
second phantasy an act of exchange (a new bottom and a new widdler).
Further, there is no mention of the 'big borer' in the second phantasy and
no mention of his 'widdler' in the first.

Freud's theory of castration proposes that it is the father who, as the
agent of castration, is responsible for the institution of civilization. The boy
gives up his desire for the mother in the belief that he will one day have his
own family and take up the role of the father. This belief is centred on the
fact that he will one day possess a 'bigger' penis. Yet the notion that Hans
will receive a bigger penis one day is *not even part* of Hans's phantasy. It is
the father who suggests that the plumber gives him a bigger widdler and a
bigger behind. Hans does not mention the size of his widdler in the second
phantasy. Yet, in Freud's view, the theory of the bigger widdler was 'the
only interpretation' possible. I can think of another (which Freud alluded
to but dismissed) but this involves interpreting the two phantasies separately. In my view, the first is a birth phantasy.

At this time Hans also became very interested in birth. He wants to give
birth to a little girl but he doesn't want his mother to have one (86). Freud
interprets this as jealousy but it is also possible that Hans wants to take up a
feminine or passive position in relation to his mother. She will give him a
child. He knows it is possible for him to be a mother, to have a baby,
because his father has told him babies are pressed out from the bottom like
'lumfs' – an activity he has already mastered.

When travelling to Gmunden, Hans's parents had packed a small bath
inside a large box. Hans said the bath was full of babies which he had put
there. He also said his sister was travelling in his mother's box. Freud states
in a footnote – and I agree – that to Hans a bath and a box 'represent the
space which contains the babies' (69). Presumably, Hans also associated a
bath and box with his bottom as he believed babies lived there too. Thus
Hans thinks that babies live in baths/boxes/bottoms and they are born like
a piece of 'lumf'. In his phantasy, the plumber comes along and 'unscrews
it', that is, he unscrews the bath/bottom or the place where babies live and
then sticks a big borer in Hans's stomach. What is the 'borer'? Perhaps it
represents the plumber's widdler or a baby – or both. In his game with the
penknife, which occurred at this time, Hans stated that the knife was the
doll's widdler. His father, however, insisted it was a baby. If the borer is a

phallus, the phantasy is about Hans's impregnation; if the borer is a baby the phantasy is still about his impregnation. The borer = the phallus = the baby. The plumber unscrews Hans's baby box and places the big 'borer' in his stomach. The plumber gives Hans a baby. In an interesting footnote, Freud explains that the word 'borer' ('*Bohrer*') is connected with 'born' ('*geboren*') and 'birth' ('*Geburt*'). He accepts the suggestion, made by a colleague, that Hans might have chosen this word because of these connections. 'If so, the child could have made no distinctions between "bored" [*gebohrt*] and "born" [*geboren*]' (98). It seems to me that Hans may well be using the word '*gebohrt*' or 'bored' to mean 'born'.

The third phantasy is not so much about birth as about gender identity. This time Hans is not impregnated; rather he exchanges his bottom and his widdler (not mentioned in the first plumber phantasy) for new ones, but there is no suggestion from Hans that his bottom or widdler are any bigger. His father introduces this idea. Hans agrees that his new widdler and bottom were bigger but this does not mean the father is accurate in his interpretation. Hans often agrees with his father's theories but then later utters statements which contradict them.

The crucial thing about the two phantasies is not their similarity but their difference. The first appears to be about birth while the second is not; it seems to be about an exchange. It is impossible, however, to ascertain the exact nature of the exchange because Hans's father interrupted the story and imposed his own interpretation. We know that Hans was reluctant to relate this phantasy and resisted telling the details to his father. Perhaps this is why the father took over. If Hans's father is correct in assuming that Hans was given a 'bigger' bottom and widdler in his phantasy we still need to ask about the nature of these. Perhaps the second phantasy signalled that Hans had finally relinquished his desire to have a baby; instead he has accepted his gender identity as male. The 'bigger' or new bottom and widdler indicate his desire to change and accept his masculinity. But the fact that Hans exchanged his genitals, including his bottom where he believes babies live, for a *new* set is very significant. In his interpretation, Freud seems to place more emphasis on Hans's new 'larger' widdler than on his new bottom. Perhaps Freud is not as concerned with Hans's new bottom because it is not as relevant to his castration theory?

Given Hans's belief that the bottom is the place where babies live, we should not underestimate its role in the phantasy. There are at least two possible interpretations. Either the new set is a 'male' set, suggesting Hans had finally accepted that he couldn't have babies, or the new set might be 'female', pointing to his continuing desire to have babies. Possibly Hans is still confused; he appears to believe that men can have babies. It is relevant to note that only six days prior to the second plumber dream Hans uttered his well-known statement about his desire to have children. 'Because I should so like to have children; but I don't ever want it; I shouldn't like to

101

have them' (93). Hans both wants and doesn't want children; his desire expresses perfectly the unstable nature of gender identity which Freud argued haunts the human subject throughout life. Perhaps the second plumber phantasy is about this oscillation, the desire to be one and then the other, male and female?

The other important aspect of the phantasy concerns the identity of the plumber. In Freud's view it is the doctor whom Hans's mother had said would castrate Hans if he continued to masturbate. In my view, the plumber is Hans's mother or at least her agent. She is central to the important elements of both phantasies: water, bathing, sexual pleasure, pain, babies, birth. As Freud mentions in a footnote, she always gives him his bath. She also gives Hans his enemas. She is in charge of the boy's washing routines, cleanliness, daily ablutions. He is partly frightened of her powers over him and fears she may submerge him in the water. For this reason he refuses to sit or lie in the big bath but must kneel or stand. 'I'm afraid of her letting go and my head going in' (67). Hans also cannot bear to hear his sister Hanna scream when his mother hits her on the bare bottom. No doubt Hans also received his share of smacks.

The mother is in control of Hans's body and is also a focus for his erotic desires. Hans wishes his mother would fondle his penis. He is very interested in the riddle of where babies come from. He wants to have one himself and has stated quite clearly that he wants to have a baby with her but *he* wants to have it. He will not accept that his sister belongs to his father and mother. 'No, to me. *Why not to me and Mummy?*' (87) The father explains that the baby belongs to Mummy. The mother, the parent who gives birth, constructs the 'clean and proper' body and is in charge of the bathroom, becomes the plumber who places the baby in Hans's stomach. An important aspect about this phantasy is Hans's passive positioning. This is the same position he took up in his phantasy about being bitten by an aggressive white horse which, in my view, also represents the mother. Similarly, the big borer belongs to the mother; she is the parent who, in Hans's phantasy, possesses the big widdler. If the plumber is the mother then she becomes the one who is responsible for Hans's phantasized impregnation as well as his genital castration and reconstruction. If the plumber is the doctor, her agent, she still remains in control; the parent who ultimately lays down the law. Freud never really explores the part played by Hans's mother in the origin and development of his phobia.

THE CASTRATING MOTHER

Hans's various phobias and fears all stem from his original anxiety concerning his mother's genitals. In his phobia the mother ultimately represents castration, suffocation, death, the void – themes also common to the representation of the monstrous-feminine in the horror film. This anxiety

102

developed into a phobia, and took the form it did, largely because Hans remained ignorant of the true nature of the female genitals, coition and the origin of babies. In his attempt to unravel this set of puzzling enigmas Hans constructs a series of phantasies about the mother, pregnancy and birth in which he is almost always the passive victim of his mother's frightening sexuality. She will castrate him for masturbation (her spoken threat), castrate him with her mysterious widdler (biting horse phobia), abandon him (spoken fear), drown him (his spoken fear), crush him (the crumpled giraffe dream/falling horse/overloaded cart phobia), impregnate him (first plumber phantasy), and exchange his genitals for another set (second plumber phantasy). At the same time she is also the centre of his erotic longings. He wants to see her widdler, to have her caress his widdler, to sleep with her, have her to himself, and to have a baby by her. But even the latter project is fraught with terror because he thinks a baby and blood are squeezed painfully out from his bottom like a 'lumf' falling into a chamber pot. Furthermore, Hans is not sure how babies get inside the bottom in the first place. But he does know mothers are responsible – his father told him.

Freud himself was aware that the mother is frequently viewed by children as the parent who utters the castration threat. In his study of the Wolf Man, 'From the history of an infantile neurosis', he also described the mother/nanny as the feared agent of castration:

> He therefore began to play with his penis in his Nanya's presence, and this, like so many other instances in which children do not conceal their masturbation, must be regarded as an attempt at seduction. His Nanya disillusioned him; she made a serious face, and explained that that wasn't good; children who did that, she added, got a 'wound' in the place.
>
> (p. 24)

Freud had clinical evidence that the mother is seen, by some children, as the castrator yet he insisted that it was the father who enacted this role in the family. Unable to provide a fully convincing explanation for this, in the Wolf Man case history, Freud appealed to phylogenetic reasons. 'At this point the boy had to fit into a phylogenetic pattern, and he did so, although his personal experiences may not have agreed with it.' Freud appears to have thought that the image of the father as the parental castrator constituted a kind of primal phantasy originating in 'man's prehistory' and was somehow inherited in the unconscious (86). As mentioned previously, Freud also stated that Hans's mother had 'a *predestined* part to play' in relation to her role as castrated. At no point in either case study did Freud consider that the child might also fear the mother's genitals as an agent of castration.

Hans's mother is the unattainable object of his deepest desires and the frightening parent of his nightmares. She is the mother who is terrifying *not* because she is castrated but because she castrates – in two ways. She threatens to send the doctor to castrate Hans; and her body, with its mysterious bleeding/biting widdler, also threatens to castrate. It is clear from a rereading of the Little Hans case history that we cannot use this material to justify the argument that man fears woman because she is castrated. The clinical material indicates that Hans did *not* relate to his mother as phallic and then castrated; rather, he believed she possessed phallic attributes ('a widdler like a horse') which made her powerful and terrifying. As I have argued, it is more likely that the boy endows the mother with a penis retrospectively, after he becomes consciously aware for the first time that she might castrate. Furthermore, there is no real justification for arguing, on the basis of the material available, that the biting horse represents the castrating father or that the mother is acting on behalf of the father. In an attempt to justify his argument that the father represents the agent of castration, Freud ignored clinical material in favour of an appeal to man's prehistory. Freud presupposes a state of affairs (the father signifies the parental castrator) which his clinical observations and theoretical writings should explain. If we acknowledge that there are serious problems with Freud's theory that the father is the agent of castration in the family, then we must re-evaluate Freud's theory of the Oedipus complex as the mechanism by which the symbolic order is instituted. At one point Freud states that children should be told the truth about sexuality. This is the one thing which becomes painfully clear from a rereading of the Little Hans story. To argue, however, that the story reinforces Freud's theory of woman as 'castrated' other is to back the wrong horse.

The domestic space, a space of comfort that draws youth8, then spits you out?) harms you)en

MEDUSA'S HEAD: THE *VAGINA DENTATA* AND FREUDIAN THEORY

'[My greatest sexual fear?] . . . The vagina dentata, the vagina with teeth. A story where you were making love to a woman and it just slammed shut and cut your penis off. That'd do it.'

Stephen King, *Bare Bones*

Fear of the castrating female genitals pervades the myths and legends of many cultures. It is also central to the horror film but has largely been ignored in the majority of critical writings on horror. This has led to faulty interpretations not only of individual films, such as *The Exorcist* where Regan is seen as a phallic rather than as a castrating figure, but also of entire sub-genres such as the slasher film where the heroine is also seen as phallic rather than as castrating (see Chapter 9). If we are to understand the nature of horror generated by the figure of monstrous-feminine in popular discourses such as film, it is crucial to re-evaluate other aspects of Freud's writings on male fears of woman as his views have exerted such a profound effect on critical approaches to the horror film.

Before turning to Freud, it is relevant to look at the widespread nature of myths concerning the woman as castrator. In these myths, the threatening aspect of the female genital is symbolized by the *vagina dentata* or toothed vagina. According to Barbara Walker, Yanomamo myths state that one of the first women on earth possessed a vagina that could transform into a toothed mouth which ate her lover's penis (1983, 1034). In his book *Erotic Art of the East*, Philip Rawson refers to the belief of Chinese patriarchs that a woman's genitals, apart from offering pleasure, were also 'executioners of men' (1968, 260). According to Edward Gifford, Muslim teachings stated that if a man looked into a vagina it would bite off his eye-beam and leave him blind (Gifford, 1974, 143). In *The Great Mother*, Erich Neumann refers to the terrible goddess of Melanesia who was known as Le-hev-hev and was particularly feared by the Malekulan men. Her name meant 'That which draws us to It so that It may devour us' (Neumann, 1972, 174). According to Neumann some myths represent the toothed vagina as an animal or an animal-companion of the female deity (ibid.,

105

168). Scylla the devouring whirlpool is, from the upper part of her body, a beautiful woman; the lower parts consist of three snapping hellhounds. Wolfgang Lederer states that myths of the vagina with teeth are extremely prevalent particularly in the East, India, North America, South America, Africa and Europe (Lederer, 1968, 44–52).

In *The Masks of God: Primitive Mythology*, Joseph Campbell relates various myths of the toothed vagina. One of the myths from New Mexico tells the story of how the boy hero known as Killer-of-Enemies domesticated the toothed vagina. There was once a house of vaginas where the four 'vagina girls' lived. The 'girls' were actually vaginas but had taken the form of women. Lured by stories of the vagina girls, unsuspecting men would come to the house for intercourse. Kicking Monster, father of the vagina girls, would kick the men inside to be eaten up by the vaginas who possessed exceedingly strong teeth. Outsmarting Kicking Monster, the boy hero entered the house where he convinced the four vagina girls to eat a special medicine made of sour berries. The medicine destroyed their teeth and puckered their lips so that they could no longer chew but only swallow. They found this approach far more pleasurable than the old method. In this way the toothed vagina was put to its proper use. The myths of North American Indians tell a similar story: a meat-eating fish lives in the vagina of the Terrible Mother; the hero is the one who overpowers her (Neumann, 1972, 168).

> The breaking of the vaginal teeth by the hero, accomplished in the dark and hidden depths of the vagina, is the exact equivalent of the heroic journey into the underworld and the taming of the toothy hellhound Cerberus by Herakles. Darkness, depth, death and woman – they belong together.
>
> (Lederer, 1968, 49)

The myth about woman as castrator clearly points to male fears and phantasies about the female genitals as a trap, a black hole which threatens to swallow them up and cut them into pieces. The *vagina dentata* is the mouth of hell – a terrifying symbol of woman as the 'devil's gateway'. In his February 11 Seminar, Jacques Lacan seems to imply that large women pose a greater threat: 'Queen Victoria, there's a woman . . . when one encounters a toothed vagina of such exceptional size' (cited in Heath, 1978, 61). The *vagina dentata* also points to the duplicitous nature of woman, who promises paradise in order to ensnare her victims. The notion of the devouring female genitals continues to exist in the modern world; it is apparent in popular derogatory terms for women such as 'man-eater' and 'castrating bitch'. In his *Dictionary of Obscenity, Taboo and Euphemism*, James McDonald lists a number of expressions 'which humorously disguise an element of male apprehension about the nature of the vagina'. These are: 'man trap', 'bottomless pit', 'viper', 'snapper', 'vicious circle' and 'dumb glutton' (McDonald, 1988, 44). It is also the subject of humour (see the cartoon by Leunig).

The *vagina dentata* is particularly relevant to the iconography of the horror film, which abounds with images that play on the fear of castration and dismemberment. Fear of castration can be understood in two different ways. Castration can refer to symbolic castration (loss of the mother's body, breast, loss of identity) which is experienced by both female and male, or it can refer to genital castration. The horror film offers many images of a general nature which suggest dismemberment. Victims rarely die cleanly or quickly. Rather, victims die agonizing messy deaths – flesh is cut, bodies violated, limbs torn asunder. In films like *Jaws*, *Tremors*, *Alien* and *Aliens*, where the monster is a devouring creature, victims are ripped apart and eaten alive. Where the monster is a psychopath, victims are cut, dismembered, decapitated. Instruments of death are usually knives or other sharp implements. Close-up shots of gaping jaws, sharp teeth and bloodied lips play on the spectator's fears of bloody incorporation – occasionally with humour. Sometimes the lips are only slightly parted and either a trace of blood trickles over the bottom lip or both lips are smeared with blood. Often the teeth are threateningly visible. This image is a central motif in the vampire film, particularly those which deal with the lesbian vampire. In these films (*The Vampire Lovers*, *Vampyres*, *The Hunger*) we are given close-up shots of woman's open mouth, pointed fangs and bloodied lips – a graphic image of the *vagina dentata*. The visual association between biting and bloodied lips, sexual intercourse and death provides a central motif of the vampire film.

While all images of menacing, toothed mouths – regardless of the gender of the character – suggest the *vagina dentata*, some films link this image specifically to woman. These are not always horror films. The postmodern text, *Blue Velvet*, which quotes from various film genres, including horror and *noir*, contains a scene which draws a playful connection between the heroine's sensually parted lips and an ornamental carving of a toothed vagina hanging on the hero's bedroom wall. One of the characters in *Bull Durham* jokes that men call women 'the Bermuda Triangle' because they are frightened of disappearing inside. In Ingmar Bergman's *Cries and Whispers*, a woman puts broken glass in her vagina while lying in bed awaiting her husband.

Another visual motif associated with the *vagina dentata* is that of the barred and dangerous entrance. Lederer identifies 'Briar Rose' or the 'Sleeping Beauty' story, and its variants, as providing a perfect illustration of this theme. The suitors who wish to win Briar Rose must first penetrate the hedge of thorns that bars their way. Only the prince who inspires true love is able to pass through unharmed.

The theme of the barred and dangerous entrance has many variants:

the door of the girl's house may kill all those who enter; it may be a door that quickly opens and closes of its own accord, comparable to the terrifying rocks, the Symplegades, through which the Argonauts had to pass, and which, whenever a ship attempted to pass between them, drove together and crushed it; it may be guarded by dangerous animals; or again, the symbolism may be that of gigantic bivalves which crush whoever may get caught within them.

(Lederer, 1968, 47)

The theme of the dangerous entrance or passageway is also common to the horror film: the corridor may fill with waves of blood that threaten to engulf everything (*The Shining*); or the bedroom may transform into a huge sucking hole (*Poltergeist*); or the airducts of a spacecraft may be controlled by an alien with gaping jaws and snapping teeth (*Alien*). The killer frequently hides with knife poised in a darkened doorway or at the top of a staircase. Tunnels and caves are filled with spiders, snakes or bats which attack the unwary. Giant crushing wheels threaten to bear down on victims, pulverising their entire bodies (*Batman*, *The Terminator*).

In classical art the figure of a beautiful woman was often accompanied by an animal companion with open jaws and snapping teeth; the creature represented her deadly genital trap and evil intent. In *Idols of Perversity*, Bram Dijkstra analyses the popularity of paintings that depict women and cats, tigers, lions, polar bears and grizzlies. Wild cats and other beasts, their teeth bared, are frequently positioned near a woman's genital area. Growling 'jaws suggested the *vagina dentata* which turn-of-the-century men feared they might find hidden beneath' woman's gown (Dijkstra, 1986, 294). An advertising poster for the film *Jaws*, which deals specifically with castration anxieties, uses this convention by showing an underwater view of a woman swimming with a great shark hovering immediately below her, its open mouth and teeth glistening in the dark waters. Stephen Heath has analysed *Jaws* in terms of male castration fears. He points out that, after the first female victim, 'all the victims are male and the focus is on losing legs' (Heath, 1976, 27). Heath suggests that the danger associated with female sexuality in the night-time beach scene is displaced on to the shark. The narrative sets up an opposition between the men and the shark – an opposition symbolized in the long shot of the boat seen through a pair of shark's jaws. Heath also mentions that in the novel the report of the first attack is delayed while the watchman finishes reading a story about a woman who castrates a male attacker with a knife hidden in her hair. The fairy story 'Little Red Riding Hood' also suggests symbolically the *vagina dentata* with its reference to the red riding hood/clitoris and its emphasis on the devouring jaws of the wolf/grandmother.

108

THE CASTRATING FEMALE GENITALS

Two explanations have been given for the *vagina dentata* – both stress the incorporative rather than castrating aspect of this figure. One approach interprets the *vagina dentata* as a symbolic expression of the oral sadistic mother. This is the mother feared by both female and male infants who imagine that, just as they derive pleasure from feeding/eating at the mother's breast, the mother might in turn desire to feed on them. The 'Hansel and Gretel' fairy story illustrates this infantile fear through the figure of the cannibalistic witch. The other explanation interprets the *vagina dentata* as an expression of the dyadic mother; the all-encompassing maternal figure of the pre-Oedipal period who threatens symbolically to engulf the infant, thus posing a threat of psychic obliteration. In both explanations, the image of the toothed vagina, symbolic of the all-devouring woman, is related to the subject's infantile memories of its early relation with the mother and the subsequent fear of its identity being swallowed up by the mother. In horror films such as *Psycho*, *Carrie* and *Alien*, fear of being swallowed up, of annihilation, is linked directly to the mother.

These two explanations draw connections between the notion of orality and incorporation discussed above. The *vagina dentata* is a mouth; the cannibalistic mother eats her young; the dyadic mother symbolically incorporates the infant. Fear of the *vagina dentata* and of the oral sadistic mother could be interrelated, particularly in view of the complex mythological and linguistic associations between the mouth and the female genitals (Walker, 1983, 1035). Furthermore, there may well be some contexts, such as those in *Aliens*, in which images of the oral sadistic mother are used to symbolize fear of the dyadic mother. Nevertheless, while these two female figures have much in common, they are also quite distinctive and should be separated in any discussion of the representation of the monstrous-feminine in the horror film. The toothed vagina represents an altogether different threat, that associated with the deadly genitals of woman.

To my knowledge the notion of the *vagina dentata* is not discussed by Freud. In Freudian theory, castration is posed as a threat coming from the father. The boy, who is passionately attached to his mother, begins to see the father as a rival and imagines that the father will castrate him, making him like the mother. In this way, the father is constructed as the castrator, the one who mutilates the genitals. Fear of castration by the father overcomes the boy's desire for the mother and he eventually renounces her in the knowledge that one day he will inherit the power of his father and have a woman of his own. His mother's body inspires castration fear but – according to Freud – her genitals do not threaten to castrate. It is crucial that the mother's genitals terrify from a passive perspective – terror is associated with their appearance, which indicates that something has already happened to them. As we have seen from the Little Hans story, the castration complex is seen, by Freud, as the mechanism which brings about the transmission of culture.

In his rewriting of Freud, Lacan places even greater emphasis on the notion of woman's castration. In Lacanian theory it is woman's 'lack' which produces the penis as the mark of human fullness and the phallus as symbolic presence. 'Because the penis and the phallus are (albeit illusorily) identified, women are regarded as castrated' (Grosz, 1990, 116). It is because woman is 'castrated' that she is seen to represent 'lack' in relation to the symbolic order while man inherits the right to represent this order. For Lacan 'the negativity of the feminine is a symbolic psychical necessity' (Brennan, 1989, 6). The belief that woman terrifies because her genitals appear castrated is crucial to the Freudian theory of the castration complex. The argument that woman's genitals terrify because they might castrate challenges the Freudian and Lacanian view and its association of the symbolic order with the masculine. Here I wish to examine the repression of the notion of the *vagina dentata* in some of Freud's writings. Freud put forward a number of theories to support his view that woman's genitals appear castrated rather than castrating. Viewed from a different perspective, each of these theories supports – and frequently with more validity – the argument that woman's genitals appear castrating.

MEDUSA AND THE MOTHER'S GENITALS

Freud chose the myth of Perseus and Medusa to illustrate his theory that woman is castrated. In his essay 'Medusa's head' he argued that the head with its hair of writhing snakes is a symbol of the castrated female genitals:

> We have not often attempted to interpret individual mythological themes, but an interpretation suggests itself easily in the case of the horrifying decapitated head of the Medusa . . . a representation of woman as a being who frightens and repels because she is castrated . . . [it] takes the place of a representation of the female genitals, or rather . . . it isolates their horrifying effects from their pleasure-giving ones.
>
> (pp. 273–4)

The boy's castration anxiety is first invoked when he sees the mother's genitals which, because of the pubic hair, bear an uncanny resemblance to the father's genital area, also covered in hair. The hair is very important to Freud's interpretation:

> To decapitate = to castrate. The terror of Medusa is thus a terror of castration that is linked to the sight of something. Numerous analyses have made us familiar with the occasion for this: it occurs when a boy,

110

who has hitherto been unwilling to believe the threat of castration, catches sight of the female genitals, probably those of an adult, surrounded by hair, and essentially those of the mother. . . . The hair upon Medusa's head is frequently represented in works of art in the form of snakes, and these once again are derived from the castration complex.

(ibid., 273)

Freud gives the phallic snakes/hair of the mother a double function: 'however frightening they may be in themselves, they nevertheless serve actually as a mitigation of the horror, for they replace the penis, the absence of which is the cause of the horror' (ibid.). Thus the Medusa's head serves as a classic fetish object; it confirms both the absence and presence of the mother's penis. According to the rest of the legend any man who looks upon the Medusa's head is immediately turned to stone. This is why Perseus looks at the monster's reflection in a shield before he cuts off her head. Freud interprets the 'turning to stone' as a metaphor for having an erection: 'For becoming stiff means an erection. Thus in the original situation it offers consolation to the spectator: he is still in possession of a penis, and the stiffening reassures him of the fact' (ibid.).

In presenting his argument, however, Freud has ignored a crucial aspect of the Medusa myth. With her head of writhing snakes, huge mouth, lolling tongue and boar's tusks, the Medusa is also regarded by historians of myth as a particularly nasty version of the *vagina dentata*. Erich Neumann claims that the Gorgons symbolize the mother goddess in her 'devouring aspect'. Her genitals or 'womb-gullet' are 'represented by the terrible face with its gnashing teeth' (Neumann, 1972, 169). Freud also ignores the symbolic meaning of the snake's open mouth and pointed fangs. If we stretch our imaginations, the multiplication of snake symbols on the Medusa's head may suggest a multiplication of the woman's imaginary phallus; they more clearly represent that genital in its *castrating* aspects. Representations of the snake coiled in a circle, its tail/phallus in its mouth/vagina is a ubiquitous symbol of bisexuality found in all cultures. Freud isolates the phallic and ignores the vaginal significance of the snake as a sexual symbol. To argue that the Medusa's severed head symbolizes the terrifying *castrated* female genitals, and that the snakes represent her fetishized and comforting imaginary phallus, is an act of wish fulfilment *par excellence*. Freud's interpretation masks the active, terrifying aspects of the female genitals – the fact that they might castrate. The Medusa's entire visage is alive with images of toothed vaginas, poised and waiting to strike. No wonder her male victims were rooted to the spot with fear.

MATERNAL BLEEDING

Freud argued that the male child may mistake the mother's menstrual blood as that which issues from the wound caused by her castration or from the damage inflicted on her vagina during intercourse. In 'The sexual theories of children' Freud claims that the child interprets this blood as a sign of the father's repeated sadism during coition. 'It proves to him that his father has made another similar assault on his mother during the night' (p. 222). We can, however, interpret the mother's blood differently. If the child is aware that the mother's genitals or the bedlinen are periodically bloody, he could just as easily mistake this blood for his father's. He might phantasize that the man who inserts his fragile penis into the mother's vagina is taking a great risk.

In his analysis of the crucial role of menstruation in human development, C. D. Daly stresses that the menstruation taboo is the most virulent of all taboos. He argues that the main reason for this is that sight of woman's blood confirmed man's fear of being eaten and castrated by the female genitals. Unlike Freud, Daly attaches importance to what he sees as the terrifying aspects of the olfactory stimulus in relation to menstruation:

> In the menstruation trauma the visual evidence of the mother's bleeding occasions the deepest horror and loathing. The bleeding confirms the fear of castration and of being eaten, whilst the smell (here negative and repulsive), partly because of its association with putrefaction, also conveys the deeper idea of death to the unconscious. This negative odour is not to be confused with the positive, attractive, pre-menstruation and mid-cycle odours, but belongs to the repulsive attributes of the complex and plays an important part in the formation of the incest barrier.
>
> (Daly, 1943, 160)

Daly concludes that the menstruation complex lies at the heart of castration anxiety. 'It is my contention that the menstruation aspect in particular is at the root of the extreme horror of the female genital which Freud attributed to the castration fear, though he was not satisfied that this fully explained it' (ibid., 165).

ORAL SADISM

One reason why the child might mistakenly imagine that the female genital lips open up into a mouth is the importance of the oral stage of development in the child's early years. In his 'Three essays on the theory of sexuality' Freud emphasized the importance of all activities associated with eating and sucking. The relationship of the child as suckling to the nursing mother provides the model for all other relationships during this period; it is characterized by the concepts of eating and being eaten.

The threat of incorporation issuing from the maternal body is most likely to be concentrated on the two areas associated with incorporation: the mother's facial mouth and her genital mouth. Freud claimed that children commonly identify the *anal* cavity with a mouth. Myth, legend and the history of taboos make it clear that the vagina is similarly identified. Freud, in fact, argued that the young child is unaware of the existence of the vagina – a point which according to Laplanche and Pontalis (1985, 311) is contested by psychoanalysts such as Karen Horney, Melanie Klein and Ernst Jones.

Sexual pleasure is also bound up with excitation of the mouth and lips and continues in this form into adult life. It is the connection between orality and sexuality which is of particular relevance to a discussion of the child's understanding of the nature of female genitals. According to Freud, the subject's experience and understanding of desire and satisfaction, including sexual satisfaction, are based on its early oral experiences, which represent the first stage in the infant's sexual life. The child's early experiences of the world are *all* marked by oral influences. If the child in any way sees the mother as castrating figure, her presence will always invoke a degree of anxiety. How much more terrifying her presence, then, if the male child – either consciously or unconsciously – has projected an image of a mouth on to her labia and genital area. Little Hans's association of the cow's teat with a penis ('Oh look! There's milk coming out of its widdler') suggests a parallel between the breast being sucked/bitten when in the mouth and the penis similarly being sucked/bitten in the vagina.

GLIMPSING THE FEMALE GENITALS

Freud's account of the boy's first glimpse of the female genitals is worth noting in that the boy's response differs in terms of the kind of female he is looking at – young girl or adult woman. In 'Medusa's head' Freud refers to the 'terrible fright' the boy experiences when he sees the *mother's* genitals. In 'The infantile genital organisation' Freud describes the response of the boy when he first glimpses the genitals of a *young girl* as indifferent. Freud does not explore the significance of these two different responses. There is an implication in the second instance that the boy's age is a factor influencing his response. It is strange that Freud does not consider the difference between the genitals of a young girl and a woman, because the differences between the two are striking. The genitals of the latter are covered in pubic hair making it impossible to see the labia beneath, whereas the genitals of the small girl are smooth, symmetrical and clearly in the shape of lips. In fact, the younger the girl the more pronounced the outer lips, which are extremely swollen in the first months after birth. Furthermore, there is no suggestion that the girl's genitals have been 'mutilated'. The skin is smooth and unmarked, the lips clearly formed and usually pronounced. If the boy's first glimpse is of the genitals of a girl he would be very much aware of the labia. On later seeing the mother's genitals, he would naturally be aware of the lips hidden behind her pubic hair.

If the boy's first glimpse of the female genitals is of the mother's, he is more likely to imagine she is castrated. Her pubic hair would tend to make the mother's genital area look, on first glance, more like the father's – but without a penis. In this situation, the boy may well be justified in imagining that the mother is castrated. The possibility of making such a mistake upon glancing at a small girl's hairless genitals is less likely. Freud never analyses these different responses. If the former experience (seeing the mother's genitals first) is most likely to lead to a fear of woman as castrated, then the latter (seeing a young girl's genital lips) seems most likely to lead to a fear of woman as incorporator/castrator. While both experiences may have the same effect of transforming woman's body into a source of castration anxiety for the male, the forms of this anxiety are different and that difference is crucial to our understanding of the representation of women within patriarchal culture.

THE MUTILATED CREATURE

Freud claims, in 'The sexual theories of children', that little boys are extremely resistant to the idea that girls do not have a penis. When the boy first sees his sister's genitals, he either does not show any particular interest, he sees nothing or disavows what he has seen. 'He does not comment on the absence of a penis, but *invariably* says, as though by way of consolation and to put things right: "Her _____'s still quite small. But when she gets bigger it'll grow all right"' (p. 216). Eventually, the boy comes to understand that the little girl does not have a penis. Freud's account of the boy's earlier response to his observation of the girl's genitals is worth noting:

> It is not until later, when some threat of castration has obtained a hold upon him, that the observation becomes important to him: if he then recollects or repeats it, it arouses a terrible storm of emotion in him and forces him to believe in the reality of the threat which he has hitherto laughed at.
>
> ('Some psychical consequences', 252)

Freud claims that the boy's acceptance of woman as *castrated* other and his consequent fear of castration for himself leads him to adopt one of two responses:

This combination of circumstances leads to two reactions, which may

114

become fixed and will in that case, whether separately or together or in conjunction with other factors, permanently determine the boy's relations to women: horror of the mutilated creature or triumphant contempt for her.

(ibid.)

Why has Freud omitted to describe the boy's immediate feelings about/ towards his penis? Why has he omitted what would appear to be the most important factor in this situation? Given that the boy has been forced to accept, for the first time, the possibility of his castration, destruction of part of his body, one would expect that he would immediately fear for his penis, imagine what might happen to it, construct a phantasy surrounding it. In 'The taboo of virginity' Freud stressed the wound to her narcissism which a girl experiences when her hymen is broken. How much greater must the wound be to the boy's narcissism when he realizes the constant vulnerability of his entire organ?

Perhaps there is a description of the boy's feelings hidden in Freud's account. Doesn't the statement also make sense if read 'against the grain' as a description of how the boy imagines the woman might feel ('triumphant contempt') after she has castrated him ('the mutilated creature')? If we treat Freud's statement as an instance of displacement – understandable given the threatening nature of the topic – we can understand him to be talking about woman, not as castrated, but as the castrator with the male as her victim. Certainly, the phantasy of a mutilated male creature is central to representations of the male monster in myth, legend, fairy story, the horror film and Gothic literature. It lies behind the figures of the Hunchback, the Phantom, the Beast, Dr Jekyll and Mr Hyde, the werewolf transformations and all of the other bestial metamorphoses.

Freud concludes 'The infantile genital organisation' with a definition of proper forms of femininity and masculinity. 'Maleness combines [the factors of] subject, activity and possession of the penis; femaleness takes over [those of] object and passivity. The vagina is now valued as a place of shelter for the penis; it enters into the heritage of the womb' (p. 145). Given Freud's landmark efforts in uncovering the secrets of the unconscious; the darker side of human desire; the incredible phantasies the human subject constructs around sexuality and the 'other'; given his theories about repression, transference and displacement – given all of these factors, how can Freud possibly expect us to accept that the 'normal' construction of the vagina is 'a place of shelter' – 'home sweet home'?

FETISHISM

Freud's theory of fetishism is interesting in the context of this discussion because it holds equally true for either proposition – that woman is

115

castrated or that woman is castrating. On first realizing that the mother is without a penis, the boy is horrified. If woman has been castrated then his own genitals are in danger. He responds in one of two ways. He either accepts symbolically the possibility of castration or he refuses this knowledge. In the latter situation, the shock of seeing the female genitals – proof that castration can occur – is too great and the child sets up a fetish object which stands in for the missing penis of the mother. In his essay 'Fetishism' Freud writes: 'Yes, in his mind the woman *has* got a penis, in spite of everything; but the penis is no longer the same as it was before. Something else has taken its place, has been appointed its substitute, as it were, and now inherits the interest which was formerly directed to its predecessor' (p. 154). The fetish object may be a penis-symbol, but not necessarily. The object most likely to be created as a fetish, or substitute for the missing female phallus, is that which the subject *last* glanced upon before seeing the woman's genitals – underwear, for instance.

> it is as though the last impression before the uncanny and traumatic one is retained as a fetish. Thus the foot or shoe owes its preference as a fetish – or a part of it – to the circumstances that the inquisitive boy peered at the woman's genitals from below, from her legs up; fur and velvet – as has long been suspected – are a fixation of the sight of the pubic hair . . . pieces of underclothing, which are so often chosen as a fetish, crystallize the moment of undressing . . .
>
> (ibid., 155)

Thus in soft-porn magazines we find the image of woman fetishistically draped in a fur coat, her long legs and high-heeled shoes on display. Sometimes she is adorned with phallic objects and may be dressed in leather, carrying a whip or gun, and sitting astride a motorbike. The phallic woman is created in response to the fetishist's refusal to believe that woman does not possess a penis. Freud recommends a study of fetishism for anyone who doubts 'the existence of the castration complex or who can still believe that fright at the sight of the female genital has some other ground' (ibid.).

The phantasy of woman as castrator is as terrifying as – if not more terrifying than – that of the castrated woman. It can also be used to explain why the male might desire to create a fetish, to want to continue to believe that woman is like himself, that she has a phallus rather than a vagina. In this context, the fetish stands in for the *vagina dentata* – the castrating female organ that the male wishes to disavow. It is possible that he might hold these opposing beliefs about woman alternately or even together. The image of woman as castrator and castrated is represented repeatedly in the mythology of all patriarchal cultures. She is either the tamed, domesticated, passive woman or else the savage, destructive, aggressive woman. The phallic woman is the fetishized woman – an image designed to deny the existence of both these figures (woman as castrated/castrating). By enlarging the grounds for the male castration anxiety, we in no way invalidate Freud's theory of fetishism. In his neglect of the *actively* terrifying face of woman, evident also from his analysis of the Medusa myth, Freud left untouched a crucial area of male castration anxieties.

TEETH DREAMS

In 'The interpretation of dreams', Freud describes dreams about teeth as 'typical' because 'they occur in large numbers of people and with very similar content'. They appear to be as common as dreams of flying and falling (p. 37). Almost always the dreams are of teeth falling out or being extracted. The common factor in these dreams is that the dreamer, usually male, is in possession of a large tooth which is eventually pulled out. There is often reference to a set of teeth, the mouth and throat. In dreams where there is a dentist, the dentist appears to be male but as Freud writes elsewhere the true identity of the parental figure is frequently displaced so that the male actually represents the mother.

Freud argues that tooth dreams usually have a sexual meaning. 'It may, however, puzzle us to discover how "dental stimuli" have come to have this meaning. But I should like to draw attention to the frequency with which sexual repression makes use of transpositions from a lower to an upper part of the body' ('Interpretation', 387). He interprets these dreams in two ways, giving preference to the latter. The 'pulling' of the tooth can refer to the act of 'pulling' the penis in masturbation, or 'a tooth being pulled out by someone else in a dream is as a rule to be interpreted as castration' (ibid.). Freud, however, does not explore these dreams in any depth.

The following dream, quoted by Freud, provides an interesting and fairly typical example of a tooth dream which I would interpret as a dream about castration.

> Scherner reports a dream of two rows of pretty, fair-haired boys standing opposite each other on a bridge, and of their attacking each other and then going back to their original position, till at last the dreamer saw himself sitting down on a bridge and pulling a long tooth out of his jaw.
>
> (ibid., 227)

The 'two rows of pretty, fair-haired boys' which stand 'opposite each other' and then attack before resuming their 'original position' provide an extremely apt description of a set of teeth as they open and close. The outcome of this biting activity is that the dreamer loses his 'long tooth'. This dream could represent the dreamer's fears of castration during either oral or vaginal sex. The teeth are associated with feminine qualities ('pretty', 'fair-haired') although they are symbolically male ('boys') and of a phallic nature ('attacking'). The teeth could be those of a man or woman.

117

Significantly, Freud interprets these as castration dreams but he never mentions the dreamer's partner. Who is the castrator? How is it accomplished? If we accept Freud's argument that in these dreams the lower part of the body is frequently transposed to the upper, it is most likely that the mouth refers to the vagina and the rows of teeth which open and close to a phantasy about castrating vaginal teeth.

In his discussion of Scherner's work on dreams, Freud repeats Scherner's view that 'an entrance-hall with a high, vaulted roof corresponds to the oral cavity and a staircase to the descent from the throat to the oesophagus' (ibid., 225). Elsewhere in 'The interpretation of dreams', Freud argues that a house almost always symbolizes the human body and passageways the vagina. In the teeth dreams he quotes there is often reference to rooms and passageways; however, he does not draw a connection between these and the vagina. In my view, a dream about teeth with reference to a staircase leading to a cavernous room is most likely to refer to the vagina as the entrance to the uterus. Using Freud's transposition hypothesis, that in dreams of a sexual nature the lower parts of the body are transposed on to the upper, we can interpret teeth dreams in the following way. The mouth and lips represent the vagina and labia, the rows of teeth represent the vaginal teeth and the dreamer's long tooth which is pulled out is the penis. Possibly the dreamer imagines his penis as a 'more powerful tooth' in order to lessen the threat posed by the mouth and its teeth. The 'rows' of teeth are not always mentioned – although frequently they are. In another dream, the teeth are symbolized by two 'rows of drawers' which, like teeth, also open and shut. All of these dreams, however, almost always refer to the 'mouth' and a 'passageway' of some kind. Reference to other teeth is not necessary in order to construct the vagina as a place of castration. The image of a mouth – the gaping maw of nightmares and horror scenarios – is probably enough on its own to instil dread into the dreamer. The comedy-horror film, *The Little Shop of Horrors*, plays on all of these images; some of its most memorable moments involve Audrey Jr, a man-eating plant, and a sadistic dentist.

In many of the dreams that Freud describes, the long tooth comes out (of the mouth/vagina) easily and without pain, much to the astonishment of the dreamer. For instance: 'He then seized it with a forceps and pulled it out with an effortless ease that excited my astonishment' ('Interpretation', 388). These dreams all seem to begin with the dreamer in a state of anxiety, expecting pain, but in the end finding the experience painless and usually accompanied by ejaculation which, according to Freud, 'in a dream accompanies the act of pulling out a tooth' (ibid., 391). Freud emphasizes the connection between the act of 'pulling' the penis in masturbation and of 'pulling' a tooth. 'In our part of the world the act of masturbation is vulgarly described as "sich einen ausreissen" or "sich einen herunterreissen" [literally, "pulling one out" or "pulling one down"]' (ibid., 388). I would argue that the act of 'pulling' the 'tooth' has a triple meaning: it is the penis which the dreamer fears might be 'pulled out' or castrated once inside the toothed vagina; it is the penis which is pleasurably 'pulled' by the walls of the vagina during coition – or masturbation; and it is the penis which is safely 'pulled out' from the vagina after coition. The tooth/penis is castrated and not castrated. Before coition the dreamer is in a state of anxiety; afterwards he realizes his fears have been groundless.

THE TABOO OF VIRGINITY

In 'The taboo of virginity' Freud sets out to explain the anomaly whereby so-called civilized societies value virginity while 'primitive' peoples have made the defloration of virgins the subject of a taboo. Freud uses this discussion to launch his theory of penis envy and frigidity in women. In some primitive cultures the defloration of girls is performed outside marriage and before the first act of sexual intercourse takes place. Defloration is performed by someone other than the prospective husband: the bride's father, the priest, an old woman, or a professional. Freud gives various explanations for this ritual practice: fear of first events, fear of women's blood, fear of women.

The first explanation is that primitive man associates all new or threshold events, such as defloration, with the unknown and the uncanny. He uses ritual to ward off any unexpected dangers. The second explanation holds that some people believed that woman bleeds periodically because of the presence in her vagina of a biting spirit animal; hence the vagina is a dangerous place: 'Menstruation, especially its first appearance, is interpreted as the bite of some spirit-animal' ('Taboo', 197). Many cultures believe it is a snake that lives in the vagina. Woman's blood is viewed as highly dangerous, even fatal. Consequently, women are subject to rigorous taboos when they menstruate and when they are deflowered. 'It is quite clear that the intention underlying this taboo is that of *denying or sparing precisely the future husband* something which cannot be dissociated from the first sexual act' (ibid., 199–200). Freud, however, does not consider this view.

It is the third reason in which he is most interested:

> woman is different from man, for ever incomprehensible and myster-
> ious, strange and therefore apparently hostile. The man is afraid of
> being weakened by the woman, infected with her femininity and of
> then showing himself incapable. The effect which coitus has of dis-
> charging tensions and causing flaccidity may be the prototype of what
> man fears.
>
> (ibid., 198–9)

In the process of coition, man is reminded of the possibility of his own castration. To my knowledge this is the closest Freud ever comes to broaching the subject of man's fear of the vagina as an agent of castration. But Freud does not explore this area at all. He acknowledges that man has erected a series of taboos against woman, all of which relate to her sexual functions: menstruation, pregnancy, childbirth, lying-in and, most importantly, sexual intercourse itself. But he looks elsewhere to explain the peculiar sense of dread associated with the first act of sexual intercourse and the attempt to spare the husband from some unknown horror.

Freud argues that primitive man uses the taboo of virginity to defend himself against 'a correctly sensed, although psychical, danger' (ibid., 201) coming from woman. Why does woman resent man so deeply, he asks? There are many factors: the first act of intercourse is frequently a disappointment for her; defloration causes pain; destruction of the hymen represents a narcissistic injury; loss of virginity results in a lessening of sexual value; and the husband is only a substitute for the woman's true love object – usually her father. All of these reasons, Freud concludes, frequently lead to frigidity in married women. (Given this list of woes, frigidity seems a small price to pay!) There is, however, another and more important reason why the husband should fear the woman's hostility.

> There is another motive, reaching down into still deeper layers, which can be shown to bear the chief blame for the paradoxical reaction towards the man. . . . The first act of intercourse activates in a woman other impulses of long standing as well as those already described, and these are in complete opposition to her womanly role and function.
>
> (ibid., 204)

Here, Freud turns to the comforting image of woman as castrated in order to explain man's fears. The crucial reasons for woman's paradoxical reaction are her feelings of penis envy which give rise to: 'woman's hostile bitterness against the man, which never completely disappears in the relations between the sexes, and which is clearly indicated in the strivings and in the literary productions of "emancipated" women' (ibid., 205). Freud uses all of the above reasons to conclude that woman's sexuality is 'immature' and based on a deep-seated hostility towards men, particularly the one who deflowers her. She may even wish to castrate him. This is particularly true of the virgin who, according to Freud, may wish to take 'vengeance for her defloration'. Such desires exist even in 'the mental life of civilised women' (ibid., 206).

Freud illustrates his theory of woman as castration threat with reference to dreams and literary works. He refers in particular to Friedrich Hebbel's tragedy, *Judith and Holofernes*. This concerns the biblical heroine, Judith, whose story was very popular with visual artists and writers in the nineteenth and early twentieth centuries, and was sometimes presented with feminist overtones. (It is also the subject of D. W. Griffith's *Judith of Bethulia*, 1913.) In Hebbel's version, Judith's virginity is protected by a taboo. Although married, her first husband has never dared to touch her; on their first night together he was 'paralysed . . . by a mysterious anxiety' ('Taboo', 207). Judith decides to use her beauty to destroy the Assyrian leader who has captured the city. After Holofernes has deflowered her, she cuts off his head. According to Freud: 'Beheading is well known to us as a symbolic substitute for castrating; Judith is accordingly the woman who castrates the man who has deflowered her' (ibid.). Woman is dangerous because it is her 'wish' to castrate man; it is the virgin's hostility, arising from penis envy, which man should justifiably fear. Freud does not consider the other possibility that it is man who constructs woman as a castrator and that he has displaced his anxiety on to woman – a crucial point also discussed by Mary Jacobus in *Reading Woman* (1986).

Throughout this essay, Freud avoids confronting the possibility that man's fear of sexual intercourse with woman is based on irrational fears about the deadly powers of the vagina, especially the bleeding vagina. Rather than consider man's dread of the imaginary castrating woman, Freud takes refuge in his theory of woman's castration. While he acknowledges that it is man's 'generalized dread of women' that leads to the setting up of taboos, he concludes that this dread has nothing to do with woman's possible powers – real or imagined. Instead he explains man's fears in terms of woman's lack of power. Perhaps one should conclude that acceptance of the notion of 'woman the castrator' rather than 'woman the castrated' is not only threatening to Freud as a man but also damaging to his theories of penis envy in women, the castration crisis and the role he assigns to the father in the transmission of culture.

THE *FEMME CASTRATRICE*:
I SPIT ON YOUR GRAVE, *SISTERS*

Classical theory has it that the boy fears castration by the father as punishment for his sexual interest in the mother. This is *not* verified by my clinical experience. . . . Throughout life, the man fears the woman as castrator, not the man.

Joseph Rheingold, *The Fear of Being a Woman*

Male castration anxiety has given rise to two of the most powerful representations of the monstrous-feminine in the horror film: woman as castrator and woman as castrated. Woman is represented as castrated either literally or symbolically. Her literal castration is depicted in films in which she is usually a victim, such as the slasher film, where her body is repeatedly knifed until it resembles a bleeding wound. In other horror films, woman is transformed into a psychotic monster because she has been symbolically castrated, that is, she feels she has been robbed unjustly of her rightful destiny. In *Fatal Attraction*, the heroine (an unmarried career woman) is transformed into a monster because she is unable to fulfil her need for husband and family. In a number of recent – and very popular – films about female psychotics, the killer is an outsider, a lone woman who murders to possess what has been denied her: family, husband, lover, child. In *The Hand That Rocks the Cradle*, she kills in order to possess a baby. The psychopath of *Single White Female*, who wants her room mate to take the place of her dead twin sister not only cannibalizes her friend's personality, appearance and mannerisms but also tries to murder any man who stands in her way. *Poison Ivy*'s eponymous heroine sets out to eliminate a mother and daughter in order to possess the husband. In these films, woman's violent destructive urges arise from her failure to lead a 'normal' life in possession of friends and family. This version of the female psychopath represents a more conventional view of female monstrosity in that woman transforms into a monster when she is sexually and emotionally unfulfilled. She seeks revenge on society, particularly the heterosexual nuclear family, because of her lack, her symbolic castration.

Whereas the castrated female monster is inevitably punished for her

122

transgressions, the castrating woman – usually a sympathetic figure – is rarely punished. She assumes two forms: the castrating female psychotic (*Sisters, Play Misty for Me, Repulsion, Basic Instinct*) and the woman who seeks revenge on men who have raped or abused her in some way. The group of horror films which most clearly represent woman in this light is the woman's revenge film. Films of this genre include: *Rape Squad, Lipstick, Death Weekend, I Spit On Your Grave, Mother's Day, Ms 45, Savage Streets, Naked Vengeance, Violated, Fair Game*. Usually the heroine takes revenge because either she – or a friend – has been raped and/or murdered by a single male or a group of men. In some films, woman takes revenge for causes other than rape: the reason, however, is almost always linked to some form of male exploitation. Newman sees the successful *Last House on the Left*, based on Ingmar Bergman's *The Virgin Spring*, as the American forerunner of the rape-revenge films. Directed by Wes Craven, *The Last House on the Left* prompted a series of remakes and imitations – among the latter are a number of films in which the female victims take their own revenge. Some involve a graphic castration scene, particularly *I Spit on Your Grave*, which I will shortly discuss in some detail.

One of the best known of the rape-revenge films is *Ms 45* (1981). The heroine, Thana, is a seamstress working in New York. On her way home one night she is raped, only to find a robber in her flat who also attempts to rape her. She manages to kill him and then cuts up his body, later depositing his body parts around the town. Seeking revenge against all potential rapists, Thana walks the streets at night, enticing men to her, then shooting them. The film carefully avoids the sensational; the attacks on Thana are not filmed in order to encourage the audience to identify with the rapist; nor are her acts of vengeance filmed so as to invite audience pleasure in scenes of blood and gore. *Violated* (1985) presents a most unusual example of a rape-revenge film. Banding together, a group of women who are victims of rape decide to take action against rapists who have been let out of prison and who rape again. The group consists of women from a range of professions and includes a police officer and a surgeon. The former is able to gain access to the names and whereabouts of men who are repeated rapists. The women approach their victims in bars, slip sleeping pills into their drinks and smuggle them back to the home of the surgeon, who has set up an operating theatre in her basement. (The surgeon's young daughter was raped and murdered by a man let out of prison after an earlier offence.) The surgeon surgically castrates the men, who wake up next morning in a bar or park unable to recall what has happened to them. The police have little sympathy with the men's requests for help and even make jokes about whether they should record the complaint as 'assault' or 'robbery'. As with most other films in this sub-genre, the women are not punished; rather, they are shown to be justified in their actions.

Basic Instinct (1992), an enormous success at the box office, opens with a gruesome scene in which a woman stabs a man to death with an ice-pick after reaching orgasm. He is tied to the bed; she is on top. All of the four leading women in the film are either bisexual or lesbian, suggesting that women's sexual interests are, by nature, ambivalent. The central female character is beautiful, alluring, intelligent. *Basic Instinct* suggests that all women are potential killers and that having sex with women is an extremely dangerous business. The final sequence depicts a couple making love; the last shot reveals an ice pick under the bed, suggesting metaphorically her deadly *vagina dentata*. *Basic Instinct* is not a conventional revenge film in that the narrative does not explain or justify woman's desire to kill man. Nor does it attribute the murderous game of the female psychotic to the embrace of a suffocating mother as do films dealing with the male psychotic. It seems that the desire for revenge is always present in women. The message of the film appears to be that for the unsuspecting man, caught in the throes of orgasm, death may come at any time.

THE SLASHER FILM AND THE FEMALE CASTRATOR

Although the slasher film appears to concentrate more on woman as victim, this popular sub-genre is also relevant to a discussion of woman as castrator. The typical slasher/stalker film emerged in 1978 with the release of John Carpenter's *Halloween* and continued to enjoy remarkable popularity, particularly with young audiences, over the following decade. Examples of films from this period include: *Halloween, Prom Night, Hell Night, My Bloody Valentine, Happy Birthday to Me, The Texas Chainsaw Massacre, Sisters, Friday the 13th* and *Nightmare on Elm Street*. The last two films mentioned proved so popular that each has given birth to an entire series. However, the slasher film did not just suddenly appear; its origins can be located in earlier films such as *The Lodger, The Leopard Man, Night Must Fall, Peeping Tom, Fanatic, The Nanny* and *Psycho* as well as the ripper sub-genre which dealt with the story of the infamous Jack the Ripper. In general, the term 'slasher' is used to define those films in which a psychotic killer murders a large number of people, usually with a knife or other instrument of mutilation. In the contemporary slasher film the life-and-death struggle is usually between an unknown killer and a group of young people who seem to spend most of their time looking for a place to have sex away from the searching eyes of adults. The killer, who is usually – but not necessarily – male, stalks and kills relentlessly; his powers seem almost superhuman. His weapons are sharp instruments such as knives, pokers, axes, needles, razors. His bloodbath is finally brought to an end by one of the group – usually a woman. Intelligent, resourceful and usually not sexually active, she tends to stand apart from the others.

A high level of replication, in terms of narrative structure and *mise-en-*

scène is an important feature of the slasher film. It is also marked by the recurrent use of the point of view or subjective shot taken from the perspective of the killer. This is not followed by a typical reverse shot; the identity of the killer frequently remains unknown until the very end. As Roger Ebert points out, the influence of the slasher film has led to an increasing use of the subjective camera to encourage the spectator to identify with the viewpoint of the anonymous killer which Ebert describes as 'a nonspecific male killing force' (1981, 56).

In her excellent study of the slasher film, 'Her body, himself: gender in the slasher film', Carol J. Clover writes that in most slasher films made since 1978, the year of *Halloween*'s release, men and women who indulge in illicit sex die. The difference is that more women die and the scenes of their death are more graphic.

> But even in films in which males and females are killed in roughly
> even numbers, the lingering images are inevitably female. The death
> of a male is always swift . . . [and is] more likely than the death of a
> female to be viewed from a distance, or viewed only dimly (because
> of the darkness or fog, for example), or indeed to happen offscreen
> and not be viewed at all. The murders of women, on the other hand,
> are filmed at closer range, in more graphic detail, and at greater
> length.
>
> (Clover, 1989, 105)

In Clover's view, women are chosen more often as victims because they are permitted a greater range of emotional expression. 'Angry displays of force may belong to the male, but crying, cowering, screaming, fainting, trembling, begging for mercy belong to the female. Abject terror, in short, is gendered feminine' (ibid., 117). According to Royal Brown the slasher film 'grows out of the severest, most strongly anti-female aspects of a very American brand of the Judaeo-Christian mythology' in which woman, because of her sexual appetites, is held responsible for man's fall from innocence (1980, 172). Woman is victimized because she is blamed for the human condition.

The slasher film deals specifically with castration anxieties, particularly with the male fear of castration. The image of woman's cut and bleeding body is a convention of the genre (see Dika, 1987). Freud drew attention to the way in which some men enact on woman's body a symbolic form of castration. For instance, the fetishist might cut off a woman's hair 'to carry out the castration which he disavows' ('Fetishism', 157). Symbolic castration appears to be part of the ideological project of the slasher film. Due to the development of special effects, it is now possible to show woman's symbolic castration in graphic detail. According to Freud, woman terrifies because she appears to be castrated. The terror she invokes is linked to the sight of something. Laura Mulvey drew attention to the horrifying aspects

125

of the castrated female form in film in her article on visual pleasure when she referred to woman as 'the bearer of the bleeding wound' (Mulvey, 1989, 14). It is this sight – the spectacle of woman as 'bleeding wound' – which is central to the representation of the victim in the slasher film. The slashed and mutilated female body terrifies mainly in relation to the spectacle of horror it presents. Scenes of male mutilation no doubt also give rise to castration anxiety, particularly in those texts where the castrator is female.

Very little critical attention has been given to the female castrator of the slasher film. Woman is represented as castrator in two contexts: as slasher and as heroine. There are a number of films which portray a female slasher – *Play Misty for Me*, *Hands of the Ripper*, *Friday the 13th*, *Don't Look Now*, *Sisters*. These films differ from the rape-revenge category in that the female slasher is always represented as psychotic. In some films the slasher appears to be female but is actually a male masquerading as a woman (*Psycho*, *A Reflection of Fear*, *Dressed to Kill*). In *Friday the 13th*, the castrating mother slashes both male and female victims; her victims are mutilated/murdered because they engage in sexual activities. The mother is avenging the death of her son, Jason, who drowned because a group of young people were having sex instead of minding him properly. Like Norman Bates in *Psycho*, she is also a sexually ambiguous figure. She takes on the identity of her son, speaking in a male voice to herself as she wreaks her vengeance.

The heroine of the slasher film is also represented as a castrating figure – a crucial point which is largely ignored in critical discussions of the genre. Clover emphasizes the savage nature of her revenge. In dispatching the killer, the heroine frequently engages in castration, symbolic or literal. 'His eyes may be put out, his hand severed, his body impaled or shot, his belly gashed, or his genitals sliced away or bitten off' (Clover, 1989, 115). This litany of horrific deeds enacted on the male slasher's body reads like a passage from an ancient myth or legend about the fate of the wandering hero who was foolish enough to arouse the anger of the female monster – the Bacchae, Furies, Sirens, Gorgons or Kali herself. Using a Freudian psychoanalytic framework, Clover, however, does not allow the heroine – whom she calls 'the Final Girl' – to be defined as castrating. She argues that the slasher film phallicizes the heroine. For instance, the heroine's usually boyish name (Laurie/*Halloween*, Marti/*Hell Night*, Stretch/*Texas Chainsaw II*) suggests she is not a typically 'feminine' figure:

Figuratively seen, the Final Girl is a male surrogate in things oedipal, a homoerotic stand-in, the audience incorporate; to the extent that she 'means' girl at all, it is only for the purposes of signifying phallic lack. . . . The discourse is wholly masculine, and females figure in it only insofar as they 'read' some aspect of male experience. To applaud the Final Girl as a feminist development . . . is, in the light of her figurative meaning, a particularly grotesque expression of wishful thinking.

(Clover, 1989, 119)

But because the heroine is represented as resourceful, intelligent and dangerous it does not follow that she should be seen as a pseudo man. Furthermore, there are many heroines of the slasher film who do not have boyish names: Jennifer (*I Spit on Your Grave*), Alice (*Friday the 13th*), Valerie (*Slumber Party Massacre*). In the last of these, one of the few slasher films scripted and directed by women (Rita Mae Brown and Amy Jones respectively) the heroine attacks the killer with a machete before she cuts off his hand and impales him. The particularly resourceful heroines of the *Elm Street* series are called Nancy, Kirsten, Alice and Maggie. As I have shown, the phallic woman and castrating woman are different figures. The avenging heroine of the slasher film is *not* the Freudian phallic woman whose image is designed to allay castration anxiety (we encounter her mainly in pornography and *film noir*) but the deadly *femme castratrice*, a female figure who exists in the discourses of myth, legend, religion and art but whose image has been repressed in Freudian psychoanalytic theory largely because it challenges Freud's view that man fears woman because she is castrated.

Clover argues that the slasher film resolves man's castration anxiety either by 'eliminating the woman (earlier victims) or reconstituting her as masculine' that is by phallicizing the heroine so that she can defeat the monster (Clover, 1989, 117). But the slasher film does not, as Clover suggests, simply 'eliminate the woman'. Specific female victims may disappear but the place of one victim is quickly taken by another – sometimes male – who is also cut and bleeding. Nor do these films seek to resolve castration anxiety. Clover herself demonstrates that scenes of woman's mutilation and death are shown in great detail. Furthermore, the large number of mutilated victims helps to keep this anxiety alive. This is hardly designed to allay castration anxieties. The slasher film actively seeks to arouse castration anxiety in relation to the issue of whether or not woman is castrated. It does this primarily by representing woman in the *twin* roles of castrated and castrator, and it is the latter image which dominates the ending in almost all of these films. Significantly, in his attack on the contemporary slasher film, Ebert began by deploring the victimization of women but concluded on a very different, somewhat defensive, note: 'These movies may still be exorcizing demons, but the identity of the demons has changed. Now the "victim" is the poor, put-upon, traumatized male in the audience. And the demons are the women on the screen' (Ebert, 1981, 56). Ebert's lament suggests that horror films which deal with the female castrator are either reinforcing a view that woman is deadly and dangerous and/or they are playing on the spectator's fascination with the relationship between sex and death – particularly for the male.

THE *FEMME CASTRATRICE* IN FILM

Two films which present interesting and different representations of the *femme castratrice* are *I Spit on Your Grave* and *Sisters*. The former belongs to the rape-revenge category, the latter to the psychotic slasher cycle. In *I Spit on Your Grave* the heroine literally castrates. In *Sisters* the female protagonist does not seek revenge for rape; rather she is depicted as psychotic, a madwoman who wishes to avenge herself against the whole male sex. In both films the scenes of castration and murder are presented as sensual, erotic moments characterized by a marked degree of male masochism. Why is it that male directors are interested in making films, *albeit* horror films, about male castration? Why is the *femme castratrice*, one of the more deadly personae adopted by the monstrous-feminine, almost always represented as fulfilling a stereotypical image of female beauty? For she clearly comes across as a modern-day version of the ancient Sirens, those mythological figures who lured sailors to their doom through the beauty of their song. The Sirens, of course, were images of female castrators *par excellence*. The myth resounds with images of castration anxiety: jagged rocks, cannibalism, death and dismemberment.

I Spit on Your Grave belongs to that category of rape-revenge films which presents a direct representation of the *femme castratrice*. There is no attempt to represent woman as castrator by implication or through filmic devices such as substitution or symbolism – as in *Misery*. Woman castrates her male victim literally. *I Spit on Your Grave* tells the story of Jennifer Hills (Camille Keaton), a teacher from New York, who rents a house in the country for the summer. She plans to write a book about a fictional character called Mary Selby. At the petrol station she talks to the attendant who turns out to be Johnny, the leader of a pack of local hoodlums. The other group members are Stanley, Andy and Matthew – the latter is a hanger-on who is mildly retarded and works as a delivery boy at the supermarket. The four hoodlums viciously brutalize and rape Jennifer before leaving her for dead. She recovers and enacts a deadly revenge on each of the men.

Critics have been sharply divided in their response to the film. Some focus on the rape scenes and argue that the film encourages violence against women; it is frequently singled out in debates on censorship as an example of a 'video nasty'. Others argue that the film is more likely to militate against violence. Phil Hardy has presented one of the more thoughtful responses. He argues that the men are so repulsive, the rapes so harrowing and horrifying, it is difficult to imagine that male spectators would identify with the rapists, particularly as the narrative action is presented from the woman's point of view. 'Further, there is no suggestion that "she asked for it" or enjoyed it, except, of course, in the rapists' own perceptions, from which the film is careful to distance itself.' Hardy, however, is critical of the way in which the heroine changes into an avenging fury:

> by allowing her to lapse into an almost catatonic, silent obsessive, the film distances the viewer from her, making her seem like a mere cipher and pushing her dangerously close to that negative female stereotype, the all-destructive *femme castratrice* (quite literally, as it happens, in this case).
>
> (Hardy, 1986, 329)

Jennifer's revenge is terrible, exact and executed in perfect style. She is transformed from a friendly, likeable but ordinary woman into a deadly and powerful killer. There is no suggestion that she will fail in the execution of her plans. From the moment she picks up her gun, dresses in black and asks God for forgiveness for what she is about to do, we know she – like the hero of the western – will hunt down each man and wipe him from the face of the earth. Filled with a terrible but perfectly justifiable wrath, Jennifer becomes the all-powerful, all-destructive, deadly *femme castratrice*. She appears to win, not lose, audience sympathy. Although her revenge might appear monstrous, woman is not implicated in guilt for what she has done in the way that the protagonists of the male revenge film are. Clint Eastwood in the *Dirty Harry* films is, as the title suggests, contaminated along with the criminals he pursues.

Nevertheless, *I Spit on Your Grave* is still misogynistic in its representation of woman. It is important to note that the scenes in which Jennifer carries out her revenge are deliberately eroticized. Woman is monstrous because she castrates, or kills, the male during coition. The first killing, which sets the scene for the later murders, is clearly in the mode of a sacrificial rite. Jennifer is dressed in the garb of a priestess or nymph. She lures her victim into the woods with the promise of sexual bliss. The victim dies, strangled in her noose, just as he achieves orgasm. Woman signifies sex and death. Her second killing is imbued with an even more ritualistic quality. She lures her victim into a bath where she first cleanses his body and then brings him to the point of orgasm before castrating him. As he dies, his blood streams forth to the strains of classical music. Woman, pleasure and death are intimately related in these scenes. The castrations are imbued with a sense of ritual: Jennifer takes a religious pledge prior to the deaths, she wears white robes and appears to have acquired super-human powers. The iconography of these scenes has a ritualistic quality: white robes, water, classical music; the shedding of blood as a form of atonement; the clear connection between sexual pleasure and death. Although these are scenes of revenge, it seems clear that they serve other functions as well. They offer the spectator the promise of an erotic pleasure associated with a desire for death and non-differentiation. In this context, the *femme castratrice* becomes an ambiguous figure. She arouses a fear of castration and death while simultaneously playing on a masochistic desire for death, pleasure and oblivion.

In her discussion of male castration anxiety, Karen Horney writes that the 'masculine dread of woman (the mother) . . . weighs more heavily . . . than the dread of the man (father), and the endeavour to find the penis in women represents first and foremost a convulsive attempt to deny the existence of the sinister female genital'. She then poses the interesting question as to whether or not the male dread of women might be understood for men in terms of love and death:

Is any light shed upon it by the state of lethargy – even the death – after mating, which occurs frequently in male animals? Are love and death more closely bound up with one another for the male than the female, in whom sexual union potentially produces a new life? Does man feel, side by side with his desire to conquer, a secret longing for extinction in the act of reunion with the woman (mother)? Is it perhaps this longing that underlies the 'death-instinct'?

(Horney, 1967, 138–9)

It is significant that the three rape scenes in the first half of *I Spit on Your Grave* are filmed in a completely different way from the revenge scenes of the second half. Whereas woman-as-victim is represented as an abject thing, man-as-victim is not similarly degraded and humiliated. If anything, the death scenes of the male victims offer a form of masochistic pleasure to the viewer because of the way they associate death with pleasure. (I am not suggesting, for a moment, that this inequality should be addressed by eroticizing the rape scenes.) The main reason for this difference stems from the film's ideological purpose – to represent woman as monstrous because she castrates.

The rape scenes are filmed in such a way that woman becomes a complete and total victim. She is hunted down, degraded, humiliated and tortured. The men subject her to vaginal, anal and oral rape and rape with a penis and beer bottle. She is beaten, kicked and punched. Her creative work is even derided and desecrated. Furthermore, her humiliation and subjugation are dwelt on and drawn-out. On two occasions the gang release her only to capture her again later. On each occasion their attacks grow more violent. Rarely are the rape fantasies of even hard-core pornography represented in such a brutal, horrific manner. *I Spit on Your Grave* clearly illustrates Lurie's argument, discussed earlier, that woman is 'constructed' as castrated in many films precisely because man fears that she is *not* castrated.

It seems clear that woman is actually being punished because, by her very nature, she represents the threat of castration. When one of the rapists assaults her with a beer bottle, he calls her a 'bitch' and says what he likes in a woman is 'total submission'. In this context 'total' submission could mean only one thing: he likes his women dead or nearly dead. If the scenes of castration and killing in *I Spit on Your Grave* had been filmed first and the rape scenes presented last, the extreme violence of the rapes might be more understandable. As the film stands, the rape scenes at the beginning can really only be understood retrospectively as the actions of a group of men who are terrified of women. They hunt her down in a pack and they hold her down during the rapes. She is so badly beaten there is no possibility that she might fight back. She has been symbolically and literally transformed into a battered, bleeding wound. The sadistic nature of the attack can only be seen as an attempt to rob woman of her terrifying – but imaginary – powers before she can use them.

Sisters, an off-beat thriller in which Brian De Palma pays tribute to *Psycho*, *Rear Window* and *The Cabinet of Dr Caligari*, has over the years acquired a cult status. It tells the story of a psychotic female slasher, Danielle Blanchion, who is invaded by the murderous personality of her dead Siamese twin, Dominique. Both roles are played by Margot Kidder. Whenever Danielle is attracted to a man, Dominique takes over, slashes his genitals, and then murders him. Danielle's ex-husband, Emile (William Finley) is the doctor who carried out the operation to separate the twins. He keeps Danielle drugged in order to prevent the 'return' of Dominique. When Grace (Jennifer Salt), a reporter, witnesses the murder of Philip, a man Danielle met at a quiz show in which both were participants, she brings in the police; the problem is that Philip's body has disappeared. Grace decides to investigate the murder, and the history of the twins, for herself.

Sisters has been described as a 'witty portrait of schizophrenia and sexual madness' (Hogan, 1986, 262); as yet another Brian De Palma film in which he links what is unassimilable and unknown in our culture to the female or the 'feminine energy of the inner self' and then destroys this threatening element (Waller, 1987, 141); and as an 'analysis of the way women are oppressed within patriarchal society' (Wood, 1986, 151). None of the critics who have written on *Sisters* draws attention to the horrific scenes of male castration in relation to the figure of the *femme castratrice*. Drawing on Freudian theory, Robin Wood argues that the film is primarily a study of the *castrated* woman. While the film certainly does examine this notion, its full subject is a study of the castrated/castrating woman in which the latter is represented as the central figure of female monstrosity.

The motif of identical twin sisters, one good, the other evil, is a popular structure of the woman's film (*Dead Ringers*, *Dark Mirror*, *A Stolen Life*). The representation of twins in the horror genre follows a similar pattern. The twins always look alike but are essentially different. In *Dark Mirror* one twin has committed a murder; the other hides her crime. As Mary Ann Doane points out, because the twins are identical, 'a psychiatrist is needed to *see* through the surface exterior to the interior truths of the two sisters' (Doane, 1987, 43). *Sisters* is no exception; Emile plays the double role of husband/doctor. Although the ideological issues are similar, the conventions of the horror genre allow the differences between the two sisters to be expressed in a more extreme and violent form than in the woman's film: the Danielle figure is castrated, as suggested by the scar on her side; the Dominique figure castrates – literally.

There are at least three major castration scenes in *Sisters*. These are: the mutilation/castration of Philip; Grace's hallucination/flashback in which she is drugged by Emile and forced to relive the separation of Danielle and Dominique; and the castration and death of Emile. While man's castration is genital, woman's castration is depicted as a separation from part of her own self and/or separation from another woman, her sister. In this scenario a part, but not all, of woman dies. This part constitutes woman's active, aggressive, phallic self. The self that survives is represented as symbolically castrated through the image of the scar.

The film presents its notion of the castrated/castrating woman in relation to social and sexual definitions of what constitutes the proper feminine role for woman. For instance, Grace's mother refuses to take her daughter's career seriously; she calls it her 'little job', something to do before she settles down to the serious business of marriage and family. Emile falls in love with Danielle rather than Dominique presumably because she is, as we learn in the film from the director of the hospital: 'So sweet, so responsive, so normal as opposed to her sister.' The film's representation of Grace emphasizes the sexist treatment of women in society. Her editor gives her ridiculous assignments; the police refuse to listen to her; her mother trivializes her work; the private detective she hires dismisses her suggestions; Emile drugs her in order to destroy her knowledge of the truth; and finally she ends up at home with her elderly parents where she is surrounded by toys and patronized like a child.

The hallucination sequence is crucial to our understanding of the representation of the castrated/castrating woman. The entire hallucination/flashback is presented from Grace's viewpoint. At the time, she is lying on a hospital bed next to Danielle. She has been caught by the hospital staff, drugged and hypnotized by Emile who tells her that, if she wants to know all their 'secrets', he will share them with her. He then pulls back Danielle's clothes and shows Grace the scar that covers her side, a visible reminder of her separation from her twin. When Danielle asks who Grace is he replies: 'Don't you remember? She was always here.' Emile then takes Grace back to the time when the twins were young. Emile verbally directs Grace's hallucination but it is impossible to tell which events actually happened. Not only does Grace weave her own memories into the hallucination, it is clear that Emile is somewhat demented. Extreme close-up shots of Grace's eye repeatedly fill the screen as Emile moves Grace's hallucination in new directions. Grace is now 'Dominique'. We hear Danielle's voice recalling events. The hallucination/flashback is in three parts: the picnic of freaks; the primal scene; the operation/castration of the twins. It is interrupted at least twice, when we return to the present.

The first part of Grace's hallucination/flashback follows the form of the documentary film on the Blanchion twins which Grace viewed when she began to investigate the murder. It commences with the scene from the film in which the Director of the Institute explains that Danielle is the sweet, responsive twin and Dominique is her opposite. In Grace's hallucination, however, he is now walking away from the camera as he talks. He repeats the same information but his speech now echoes through the long corridors; this creates an eerie effect as well as re-emphasizing his explanation about the diametrically opposed personalities of the twins. It is significant that Grace, who has taken Dominique's place, has chosen to recall the episode from the film in which 'her' negative qualities are stressed. Grace/Dominique 'remembers' a special party for the inmates of the Institute. She 'remembers' that she and her sister were called 'freaks'; at this point she sees her own mother, who regards her as a 'freak of womanhood', taking her photograph. When we return to the present, Emile makes Danielle recall that she cannot have a husband or a home.

Part two involves a lovemaking episode between Emile and Danielle. Grace watches herself/Dominique being put to sleep as Emile makes love to Danielle. The memory is like a bizarre primal scene in which woman is depicted as a 'double' figure, only capable of sex if her twin selves are split from each other. The man is the aggressor who deliberately silences woman's critical self in order to appeal to her 'desire' to be a wife and mother. At this point the film cuts to a wide-angle shot and we see a figure in the foreground writing on a pad as the film of the seduction scene continues. In her hallucination, Grace imagines herself taking notes as she did when first viewing the film about the Siamese twins. The difference is that Grace is now playing a double role: she is both the reporter carrying out her investigations and one of the subjects under investigation. Grace is woman investigating herself – a privileged position in patriarchal culture. In the end, however, Grace is punished for her temerity; she is denied all opportunity to reveal the truth because Emile makes her 'forget' what she has discovered.

When Emile brings Grace back to the present he makes Danielle recall an episode in which she and Dominique were walking together in the garden and Dominique tried to kill her unborn baby with a pair of garden shears. Reference to the garden shears recalls an earlier scene, when Grace broke into the Institute and encountered one of the patients in the garden menacingly pruning plants with a large pair of shears. As she left, he snapped the shears at her as if warding off an evil demon. The shears have now been incorporated into Grace's hallucination. Danielle then cries out that she is going to lose her 'baby'. It is impossible to establish the status of this scene. Did it actually occur – as Robin Wood suggests in his analysis of the film? (Wood, 1986, 153). Or is it only part of Grace's hallucination? Regardless of its status in relation to actuality, the 'baby' appears to represent Danielle's desire for normality and proper womanhood. It is this desire which Dominique has destroyed and which, by extension, Grace wishes to destroy.

Part three represents the operation to separate the twins. Grace/ Dominique and Danielle are lying on an operating table with an audience in attendance. Members of the audience include the man who made the documentary film, the detective, a pair of identical male twins, and two nursing nuns who also look like twins in their identical uniforms. The figure of the double haunts the *mise-en-scène*, invoking an uncanny atmosphere. Emile prepares to operate. He tells Danielle that she has lost the baby and is now bleeding badly. If she is to live, she must be separated from Dominique. It is Grace, however, who is lying beside her. The camera reveals a large meat cleaver lying next to the table; the cleaver is picked up by the detective whom Grace hired. He passes it to a member of the audience and finally to Emile. He raises the cleaver and brings it down swiftly in order to cut through the flesh of the hip where the twins are joined. Grace wakes up screaming hysterically. Danielle falls to the floor where she cries out for Dominique. Emile tells her that Dominique is dead.

Grace is Dominique, that is, Grace represents the female castrator, the woman who refuses to adopt the proper feminine role. This pairing is reinforced by the fact that Grace becomes Dominique in the hallucination sequence. When Emile wants to make love to Danielle, he must put her 'other self', the one which is dangerous to man, to sleep. This is the price that Danielle must pay if she is to conform to the proper feminine role. She must not listen to her 'sister'; she must permit herself to be cut off, symbolically and literally, from other women. Dominique/Grace refuses castration; Danielle has accepted castration in order to become a proper woman living within a patriarchal culture. Nevertheless, Danielle is still potentially dangerous and Emile keeps her drugged in order to prevent the return of Dominique. When Dominique takes over, Danielle becomes the *femme castratrice*.

Emile appears to be fully aware of the price Danielle must pay, yet seems to believe the sacrifice necessary and worthwhile. When Grace wakes up screaming from her hallucination, Danielle calls out for Dominique. Danielle says her sister will come back and kill Emile. In a scene of perverse desire, Emile fondles Danielle's breasts as he talks. He is clearly aroused by the danger of his situation. 'Dominique never died for you. You kept her alive in your mind. Sometimes you became her. . . .

Every time I made love to you, Dominique came back and took control of you. It was all I could do to keep you sedated until Dominique went away. Dominique is dangerous to both of us. To Dominique any man who makes love to you is me, Emile. Danielle I love you.' Danielle escapes from his embrace. He corners her and commands her to look at the knife with which she killed Philip. It is still covered with blood. 'Look at this knife! You killed a man with this knife!'

When Emile holds the bloody knife up to Danielle, he appears deliberately to awaken her castration desires, those desires which he has previously kept under control with drugs. As Emile struggles to control Danielle, who reaches for a razor, we know that he will be her next victim. Why has Emile kept the bloody knife? Why has he precipitated a situation that could lead to his own death? Not only did he arrange for Grace to play the role of Dominique by placing her on the bed beside Danielle, he guided Grace during her hallucination/flashback in such as way that she was made to relive Dominique's separation/castration from Danielle. This brutal act alone is enough to awaken Danielle's murderous desire for revenge. Emile then parades the past before Danielle, deliberately provoking her. Did he hope finally to purge Danielle of the past or was his motive related more to his own perverse sexual desires for woman as deadly 'other'? His relationship with Danielle, a woman so dangerous she had to be kept permanently drugged, was obviously fraught with danger. He says that every time he made love to Danielle, Dominique came back. For Emile, lovemaking is literally a matter of life and death.

As Danielle/Dominique grasps for the razor, she pretends to be in a stupor and recalls details from the previous castration and murder scene; she also refers to the birthday cake that Philip brought her (see illustration) and mentions making a 'wish'. Was this a wish for revenge – revenge for the loss of her sister, her other self? At this moment she finally grasps the razor, and slashes Emile across the genitals several times in the same way that she slashed Philip. Emile staggers across the room after her, clinging to her back as if trying to penetrate her from behind in a frenzy of blood. Just as he made Grace touch Danielle's wound, he now makes Danielle touch his slashed and bleeding genitals. Emile dies, clasping Danielle's hand in his own. The image of their two hands locked together, both covered with Emile's blood, points to man's fatal attraction to woman and his masochistic desire to surrender to death.

Sisters explores the representation of woman as castrated/castrator while simultaneously playing on man's inability to tell the difference. Is woman castrated or does she castrate? Does she use one persona to disguise her hidden and deadly face? What lies behind the veil? Robin Wood has described *Sisters* as 'the definitive feminist horror film . . . among the most complete and rigorous analyses of the oppression of women under patriarchal culture in the whole of patriarchal cinema' (Wood, 1986, 76). While I am in sympathy with Wood's general ideological approach, I cannot agree with his conclusion – that the monster is women's liberation and 'the subject of *Sisters* is the oppression (castration) of women under patriarchy' (ibid., 157). There are at least two monsters in *Sisters* – Emile and Dominique – and the film, while presenting an analysis of 'the oppression of women', is also about man's fear of woman as deadly castrator.

Wood claims that:

> Danielle/Dominique function both literally and symbolically; literally, as freaks whom normality has no place for, must cure, hence destroy; symbolically, as a composite image of all that must be repressed under patriarchy (Dominique) in order to create the nice, wholesome, submissive female (Danielle).
>
> (ibid., 153)

I would argue that the composite image of Danielle (castrated/proper woman) and Dominique (castrator/deviant woman) is not something that needs to be repressed in order to ensure the workings of patriarchal ideology. On the contrary, such a composite image, in which woman's nature is represented as deceptive and unknowable, is essential to the proper functioning of such an ideology. It is represented continually within different signifying practices such as film, art, religion, pornography, literature, jokes and colloquial speech. It is interesting, however, to note that the majority of critical and theoretical writings on sexual difference in the cinema have kept alive the image of the castrated woman while ignoring her *alter ego*, the castrating woman.

Sisters presents a contradictory message about the role of women in patriarchy. On the one hand, the film sets out to terrify the spectator with an image of woman as psychotic castrator. On the other hand, it presents an interesting explanation of woman's oppression within patriarchy. In *Sisters* woman's desire to castrate man is related directly to her own earlier mutilation, separation and the death of her active self. The self which survives, represented by Danielle, is the one that is passive, compliant, pliable. However, man's attempt to castrate woman symbolically and repress her active self is represented as a failure. This self, represented by Dominique, is easily aroused and man must remain forever vigilant if he is to survive. However, in *Sisters*, man's attempt to overcome his deep-seated fear of woman's castrating desires also fails. At the end, Emile appears deliberately to call forth Danielle's repressed self as he surrenders to her deadly embrace. In each sex it is the repressed aspect which emerges victorious – man's masochistic and woman's sadistic self. The film's underlying critique of subjectivity and repression – specifically in relation to gender – is perhaps its most interesting feature. *Sisters* depicts both castrators – Emile and Dominique – as monstrous. Emile becomes monstrous in the hallucination scene when we see him separate the twins with a meat cleaver. It is, however, the image of woman as castrator that constitutes the dominant figure of monstrosity in the text, partly because of the more 'realistic' status assigned to the scenes of male castration.

Emile is clearly presented as a monster in the hallucination scene. However, the entire scene is part of Grace's hallucination/flashback, which is composed partly of Grace's own memories and partly of the images Emile conjures up by his narration, while she is under hypnosis. It is relevant to consider the function of the flashback in the classic Hollywood text. Doane presents an interesting discussion of the flashback in the woman's film. Drawing on Marc Vernet's observation that Freud's 'talking cure' is represented as one brought about by the power of sight (Doane, 1987, 46–7), she argues that the flashback in film is similarly used as the means whereby the patient is able to see the past more clearly and understand the nature of her problems. This process, whereby seeing brings about a cure, is represented in films such as *Lady in the Dark* and *The Snake Pit*. But, as Doane points out, 'Psychoanalysis and the cinema alike present the woman with a very carefully constructed relation to enunciation' (ibid., 54). She argues that woman's narration is almost always interpreted and is 'therapeutic only when constrained and regulated by the purposeful ear of the listening doctor' so her narration 'is granted a limited validity' only (ibid.). The doctor elicits her enunciation with a drug or interrupts to interpret the events as she recalls them.

In *Sisters*, Emile not only injects Grace with a drug; he also hypnotizes her and then narrates the events she experiences. Grace experiences the flashback but its status as a 'truthful' account of events is completely undermined. As it stands, the sequence exhibits instabilities usually associated with a dream, or in this case a nightmare. What Grace 'sees' represents, to some extent, her own experience of living in a world hostile to the independent woman. Her hallucination is peopled with figures she knows, such as her mother, who continually attempt to deny her a voice. She experiences this as a brutal attack in which she is cut off from her 'sister', forced to live out the caricature of aggressive womanhood that is Dominique.

In contrast with woman's 'castration', the two scenes of male genital castration take place in the 'real' and by comparison are bloody and gruesome. They are not narrated through a flashback and hence do not exhibit the instabilities associated with that structure. The scenes of male castration are filmed in the present and take on the reality effect of the dominant discourse. Compared with Emile, a rather pathetic figure, Danielle/Dominique is terrifying precisely because she is a borderline personality, her normal exterior hiding a demented female fury. Nevertheless, *Sisters* is interesting in the way in which it locates the forces of repression in the dictates of patriarchal ideology. Furthermore, through the figure of Grace, it presents woman's inferior status as a result of socially induced forms of control and repression rather than as a result of penis envy – the reason Freud gave for woman's supposed desire to castrate man (see pp. 119–21). *Sisters* also openly explores male castration – a factor which has been totally ignored in its critical reception.

In the final sequence, Grace is transformed into a state of infantile dependency on her parents and Danielle/Dominique is arrested for Emile's murder. As she is taken away, she says, as all good monsters do: 'But I wouldn't hurt anyone.' The final shot reveals the private detective strapped, in an erect pose, to a phallic telegraph pole as he spies through his binoculars on the couch containing Philip's mutilated body, now abandoned at a country station. In its attempt to fortify the power of the phallus, the image conveys – intentionally – a slightly absurd, even surreal, impression. The threatening power of woman lingers in the final shot, pointing to the insecurity of the male imagination. Man must be ever on the alert, poised in phallic anticipation whenever signs of the deadly *femme castratrice* are present.

10

THE CASTRATING MOTHER: *PSYCHO*

'Go on, go tell her she'll not be appeasing her ugly appetite with my food or my son. Or do I have to tell her because you don't have the guts? Huh, boy? Do you have the guts, boy?'

Mrs Bates, in *Psycho*

In recent years, feminist film theory has increasingly focused on the representation of the mother–child relationship, particularly in the woman's film and maternal melodrama. Issues explored include repression (*The Old Maid*), sacrifice (*Stella Dallas*), incestuous desire (*Mildred Pierce*) and maternal incorporation (*Now Voyager*). Relationships in the maternal melodrama are almost always between mother and daughter; it is to the horror film we must turn for an exploration of mother–son relationships. The latter are usually represented in terms of repressed Oedipal desire, fear of the castrating mother and psychosis. Given the nature of the horror genre – its preoccupation with monstrosity, abjection and horrific familial scenarios – the issues surrounding the mother–child dyad are generally presented in a more extreme and terrifying manner. However, E. Ann Kaplan's analysis of *Now Voyager* and *Marnie*, which draws on Kristeva's theory of the abject mother, makes it clear that in some instances the woman's film can also represent the mother as a terrifying figure, a 'phobic object' who inspires 'awesome fear' (Kaplan, 1990, 133).

The monstrous mother is central to a number of horror texts. Her perversity is almost always grounded in possessive, dominant behaviour towards her offspring, particularly the male child. *Psycho*, *Fanatic* and *Friday the 13th* represent the over-possessive mother as a dangerous psychotic. In all three, the child is a son. *Psycho*, *The Psychopath*, *Twisted Nerve*, *The Fiend*, *The House That Screamed* and *Mother's Day* all to some extent represent the psychotic killer son as the product of an over-possessive mother. The mother as a dominating religious fanatic and bigot who destroys her daughter is explored in *Carrie*. The female psychotic of the extremely successful *Fatal Attraction* is ultimately shown as mad because of her voracious need to possess a child and husband. The castrating mother is central to Dario Argento's *Deep Red*. She is introduced in the credits sequence where we hear a child's nursery rhyme set against a Christmas tree. Shadows thrown on to the wall behind the tree reveal two people engaged in a life-and-death struggle. One of the figures appears to be fatally stabbed with a large knife. The bloody weapon is isolated to the left of the frame as a child's feet walk into view, indicating that the child has watched the horrifying murder. The original scene – the murder of the father – is evoked throughout the narrative when the strains of the child's song are heard just prior to each new murder. In the final sequence, the murderer, whom we have been encouraged to think is male, is identified as the mother. Throughout the narrative the son, Carlo, who is homosexual, has covered up for his deranged mother. There is a suggestion that his fear of women is linked to his childhood memory of the knife-wielding, castrating mother.

Psycho, one of the most influential horror films ever made, provides us with an exemplary study of the horror that ensues when the son feels threatened, physically and psychically, by the maternal figure. Norman Bates's desire to become the mother is motivated not by love but by fear: he wants to become the mother in order to prevent his own castration – to castrate rather than be castrated. Tania Modleski refers to *Psycho* as the 'quintessential' horror film (1988, 102). This is largely because it explores the figure of the mother as the punishing castrating parent. It is this notion of the maternal figure that seems to have inspired Little Hans's phobias and fears (see Chapter 7). Once we become aware of the prevalence of the image of woman as castrator in the horror film, we can more easily recognize the signs of her presence – cruel appraising eyes, knives, water, blood, the 'haunted' house. It is illuminating to reread *Psycho* from this perspective. Through its representation of Marion, the younger woman, *Psycho* also explores the notion that woman is castrated but this latter image is not as terrifying as that presented by the maternal castrator. Horror is further intensified through the representation of the female figure as abject in relation to images of woman's blood, the mother's entrails, the female corpse.

In 'Psychosis, neurosis, perversion' Raymond Bellour argues for the importance of Marion's and Norman's stories; he claims that the film 'contains two narratives, slipping one under the other, one into the other' (1979, 107). One is the story of Marion, the other Norman's story. In my view, there is another narrative just as important as the two mentioned by Bellour. This is the story of the mother. We can trace her story – fill in the gaps – in relation to both Norman and Marion's stories. Freud said that the story of the child's early history with the mother was 'difficult to grasp . . . grey with age and shadowy' ('Female sexuality', 373). Although similarly difficult to detect, the mother's story in *Psycho* is crucial to our understanding of the representation of monstrosity in the text. The mother's story,

140

Woman as castrator - the presence of knives

which is really about her 'fate' as a mother within a phallocentric culture, is interwoven with that of Marion, the younger woman. Both stories are related intimately with the son's story and his problem with the body of woman – is she castrated or does she castrate? In this sense the mother's story is not really 'hers'; it is ultimately the son's story. Perhaps this is why Freud found the mother's story so difficult to detect – hers is always part of another story, the son's story.

The opening sequence of *Psycho*, in which Marion (Janet Leigh) meets her lover Sam (John Gavin) in a hotel room during her lunch hour, emphasizes the power of the mother as the moral guardian of family values. Marion says she would like them to meet at her place with her mother's picture on the mantel. Sam counters her stated desire with the question: 'And after the steak do we send Sister to the movies, turn Mamma's picture to the wall?' The mother stands for social and familial respectability. It is interesting to note the way in which attention is indirectly drawn to the mother's look. It is as if she is able to watch everything from her position in the picture frame. Throughout *Psycho* woman is associated with eyes that stare and appraise. It is the maternal gaze that Norman most fears, the look that will lay bare his innermost secret desires, particularly his sexual ones; it is this aspect of the mother, her probing gaze, that he tries to 'kill' in other women.

The role of the mother as moral watchdog is again emphasized when Marion arrives at the Bates motel, where she plans to spend the night before driving on to Fairvale and giving Sam the money she has stolen from her place of work. Norman Bates (Anthony Perkins) offers to prepare a late supper for Marion. While unpacking, Marion hears Norman's mother reprimanding him for wanting to share a meal with an unknown girl.

> *Mrs Bates*: 'No! I tell you, No! I won't have you bringing strange young girls in for supper. By candlelight, I suppose. In the cheap erotic fashion of young men with cheap erotic minds.'
> *Norman*: 'Mother, please!'
> *Mrs Bates*: 'And then what? After supper – music, whispers?'
> *Norman*: 'Mother, she's just a stranger. She's hungry and it's raining out.'
> *Mrs Bates*: (*mimics him*) 'Mother, she's just a stranger. As if men don't desire strangers. Oh! I refuse to speak of disgusting things because they disgust me. Do you understand, boy? Go on, go tell her she'll not be appeasing her ugly appetite with my food or my son. Or do I have to tell her because you don't have the guts? Huh, boy? Do you have the guts, boy?'
> *Norman*: 'Shut up! Shut up!'

Mrs Bates spells out what was left unsaid in the earlier conversation between Sam and Marion at the hotel. Mrs Bates knows what Marion's mother would have seen if she had looked out from her photograph – a 'cheap, erotic' scene. She knows that 'after supper' (Sam used a similar phrase) when mother is not looking, the couple will feed their 'ugly appetite'. Mrs Bates knows that men enjoy impersonal sex, even sex with a 'stranger'. Like Marion's mother, Mrs Bates is the enculturating mother, the parent who actively discourages any form of illicit sexual desire. Mrs Bates, however, is represented as tyrannical in the extreme; she still calls Norman 'boy', indicating that in her mind he will never grow up, never be responsible for his own moral conduct. Mrs Bates is, in a sense, still toilet training her son, that is, teaching him about the clean and unclean areas of the body and mind. Visually, the contrast between respectable and unrespectable sex is reinforced by the juxtaposition of motel and house – two key symbols in the film. The house, domain of the mother, looms up behind the motel as if trying to oversee the activities that take place below, in the motel, a place associated with impersonal casual sex.

Marion agrees to have supper with him in the parlour behind the office. Significantly, Norman makes her a meal of sandwiches and milk – the kind of snack associated with a young boy – the 'mother's boy'. Hitchcock draws a number of parallels between Norman and Marion: both desire their mothers' approval; both are caught in traps of their own making. Norman's parlour is filled with stuffed birds perched menacingly on their stands. He explains his hobby to Marion: 'My hobby is stuffing things. You know, taxidermy . . . I think only birds look well stuffed because, well because they are kind of *passive* to begin with. . . . It's not as expensive as you think. It's cheap really. You know, needles, threads, sawdust. The chemicals are the only thing that, that cost anything.' The horrific import of this discussion only later becomes clear when we learn that Norman killed, cleaned out and stitched up his mother in the same manner. Norman draws the analogy between bird and mother himself when he says, 'But she's as harmless as one of those stuffed birds.'

The psychiatrist later explains that Norman preserved his mother, after murdering her, because he couldn't accept the horror of his crime; he wanted to bring her back to life. It is also possible that Norman murdered and mummified his mother because he wanted her dead and that his murderous desires were not motivated by Oedipal jealousy alone. Mrs Bates is a harsh moralist, a castrating maternal figure. Norman explains to Marion that he doesn't like stuffing dogs or cats because they are 'not passive to begin with'. What does Norman mean by 'passive'? The birds in his parlour are birds of prey; they hover menacingly overhead as if about to pounce on their victims. Norman has frozen them in time at the very moment when they are most dangerous, most threatening – the moment when they are poised, motionless, just prior to the kill. This form of passivity is not associated with a lack of will as one might expect, but with the opposite, with the power and aggressivity of a killer ready to strike.

142

Norman associates his mother with the deadly passivity of a monstrous bird of prey probably because she was the parent who hovered over him, watching his every move, threatening to pounce when he committed a mistake. She ridicules him for his lack of guts – as she probably did when alive. In retaliation, he has removed her guts, the entrails of his mother. (Hitchcock did describe *Psycho* as a 'black comedy'.) By mummifying her, Norman can freeze her aggressive, castrating demeanour, and still her prying eye.

In deciding about the true nature of Norman's mother, however, we must remember that all we have to go on is Norman's representation of her. We have no way of learning what she was like in reality; this is the son's story. In terms of Norman's portrayal of his mother, we learn that she controlled all aspects of his life. He presents her as a castrating figure, a mother who did not trust her son, particularly in relation to his sexual desires. To Norman, Mother is both the beloved and hated parent. The extent of her domination is made clear when he says to Marion, 'A boy's best friend is his mother.' As if intuitively grasping Marion's situation, and by way of describing his own, he suddenly says, 'You know what I think. I think we are all in our private traps. Clamped in them and none of us can ever get out. We scratch and claw, but only at the air, only at each other, and for all of it we never budge an inch.' Norman's private trap is his relationship with his mother.

Marion's suggestion that he go away is met with strong resistance. 'I couldn't do that. Who'd look after her? She'd be alone up there. The fire would go out. It would be cold and damp like a grave. If you love someone you don't do that to them, even if you hate them. You understand, I don't hate her. I hate what she's become. I hate the illness.' Marion suggests he 'put her some place'. Norman is now framed in a close-up. The music takes on a menacing note. Here Norman delivers a speech about the 'madhouse'. 'You mean an institution? A madhouse. People always call a madhouse *some place*, don't they. Put her in *some place*. . . . Have you ever seen the inside of those places?' Norman asks, 'The laughing and the tears and the cruel eyes studying you. My mother there!' Then in the next breath he adds, 'But she's harmless – she's as harmless as one of those stuffed birds.' The parallel Norman draws between the birds and his mother, and her tyrannical control of him, suggests that the 'madhouse' is his own internal state, his own 'private trap' and that the 'cruel eyes' that scrutinize his every action are ultimately those of the mother. Even though Norman has attempted to still her prying eye, Mrs Bates, like the stuffed birds hovering motionless overhead, continues to 'watch' over him from somewhere inside his own head.

The association of the mother with birds of prey who attack children is not unique to *Psycho*. In classical mythology, the striges were women with the bodies of birds and the clawed feet of vultures; they flew out at night to suck the blood of children and eat their flesh. Another fearful image of the monstrous-feminine in classical mythology is that of the harpy, a bird of prey with a woman's head and breasts, a large beak, hooked nails, a vile odour and an insatiable appetite. Harpies abducted children and carried them into the underworld. The term is still in current usage. Hitchcock draws connections between women and birds in a later film, *The Birds*, in which the birds may also be understood as fetish-objects, not of the castrated/phallic, but of the castrating mother.

Norman stutters when he tries to explain to Marion how much birds eat. 'You – you eat like a bird. . . . Anyway, I hear the expression "eats like a bird" -it-it's really a fals-fals-fals-falsity. Because birds really eat a tremendous lot.' Although Norman intends to convey the idea that Marion pecks daintily at her food, he then corrects his comment and tells Marion that birds actually eat a 'tremendous lot'. Like birds, women appear to peck daintily but in reality they are voracious consumers. It is the oral mother, the incorporating, devouring mother who threatens the son. Like that of a bird, woman's appetite is deceptive; it is this 'appetite' which Norman obliterates when he kills his mother. By poisoning her, Norman saves himself; similarly, he gives all of the meal to Marion, whom he later murders – he saves none of it for himself. Woman as monstrous is associated with bodily appetites, cruel eyes, a pecking beak.

The stuffed birds are represented as more and more menacing. A shadow cast by the beak of the black crow is projected on to the wall to look like a weapon. As pointed out by Raymond Bellour: 'Next to the painting, in the same shot, the menacing shadow of the crow is projected onto the wall, penetrating the picture like a knifeblade or a penis' (Bellour, 1979, 115). But a beak is somewhat different from a blade or a penis. A beak can penetrate the flesh like a blade, but it is also a mouth which, as Norman points out, devours much more than one imagines. Insofar as Norman associates his mother/other women with his stuffed birds and their devouring beaks, the beak should also be seen as a sign of the castrating mother – the mother who threatens to incorporate the child both psychically and physically. In this context, the beaks and the knife 'Mrs Bates' wields become a sign of her function as the castrating parent, the mother whom Norman becomes and whose power he assumes.

Marion's surname – Crane – also associates women and birds and further emphasizes the theme of the watchful mother; the crane is a bird with an extremely long neck which enables it to command a clear view of its habitat. Bellour points out that Marion's name also associates her with the cinema (ibid., 125). A crane is part of the cinematic apparatus; a mechanism which enables the camera to adopt an omniscient view of the set, peering down from its lofty perch. The association between woman and the camera, the mother and moral sight, is further developed through language. Marion comes from Phoenix – the name of a bird associated in mythology with rebirth. The two women represent death, watchfulness and forms of rebirth; Mrs Bates is dead but lives on in Norman's mind as his *alter ego*: Marion is associated with a mythological return which is made concrete through the intervention of the sister who bears a striking resemblance to Marion and who ultimately learns the truth, 'sees' everything.

What is it that the mother sees? Of what terrible crime does she accuse her child? In Norman's case, it would appear that she sees into his heart and uncovers his guilty secret, his sexual desires. The scene in which Marion overhears Norman/Mrs Bates denounce the individual's need for sexuality as 'filthy appetite' makes it clear that Mrs Bates represents the mother of sexual repression. Unable to accept his mother's harsh attacks and her rejection of him for another male, Norman murders his mother and her lover. Significantly, he gives them rat poison. To the extent that Norman has internalized his mother's attitude to sex, rat poison would seem an appropriate punishment for a mother who is privately indulging in the very behaviour which she publicly condemns in her son. He feeds her 'ugly appetite' with poison. Earlier Norman stumbled over the word 'falsity' when describing birds' appetites to Marion. But it is not just the appetite of birds he is talking about; the other 'fals-fals-fals-falsity' relates to the nature of sexual desire – the desire of his mother. While she appears to be a harsh moralist, she obviously does not veto sexual passion for herself – only for her son. After all, she has taken a lover. By killing and stuffing birds – and his mother – Norman puts a stop to her need for food/sex, the need she denies in him.

But what does Norman do to satisfy his own sexual needs? He tells Marion that he doesn't have any friends of his own. His mother is his 'best friend' even though a 'son is a poor substitute for a lover'. As soon as Marion returns to her room we learn that Norman is a peeping Tom, a voyeur. He has drilled a hole into one of the motel rooms so that he can spy on its occupants. The hole is covered with a painting which depicts a scene from classical mythology of a woman's sexual victimization. In the air surrounding the secret hole, several stuffed birds hang, poised, as if ready to strike. After her conversation with Norman, Marion returns to her room, where she resolves to return the money. Norman watches her through his secret hole. Norman's eye is filmed in extreme close-up, drawing attention to the activity of voyeurism. A reverse shot shows us that he is watching Marion undressing. As Norman watches Marion, we are reminded of his phrase, 'the cruel eyes studying you', a phrase he used to refer to the experience of being trapped in a madhouse – one's own private trap – and appeared to refer to the watchful eyes of his mother. Now Norman controls the look.

Most critical analyses of this scene refer to the way in which Hitchcock draws attention to the voyeurism, not just of Norman, but also of the spectator in the cinema. William Rothman links Norman's voyeurism to that of the director as well as the audience: 'But if this is Norman's eye, it equally stands in for our eye and Hitchcock's eye intently engaged in the act of viewing' (1982, 289). David J. Hogan considers our voyeurism in a moral context: 'Hitchcock has already made voyeurs of us, so how can we be presumptuous enough to condemn Norman for similar behaviour?' (1986, 186). In his analysis, Raymond Bellour links Norman's 'bulging eye' with the look of the camera and the deadly knife: 'This is the point of maximal identification between the character and the instance of the *mise-en-scène*; it can only be surpassed by its own excess, when the camera-eye becomes a body-knife, entering the field of its object and attempting in vain to coincide with it' (Bellour, 1979, 118). While critical writings associate Norman's voyeurism with that of the audience, virtually no attention has been given to the relationship between Norman's voyeurism and his sexual desires. Voyeurism is specifically associated with masturbation, particularly in relation to male spectatorship and pornographic images of women. The details of the *mise-en-scène* appear to have been arranged to emphasize this connection.

The painting which Norman has placed over his spy hole is that of *Susanna and the Elders*, a fictional story set during the Jewish Exile in Babylon; it is particularly interesting in relation to voyeurism. Two elders conceive a passion for Susanna whom they spy on when she bathes in the garden. When she refuses to have intercourse with them they denounce her, claiming they watched her as she lay with a young man. Eventually, they are caught out because their testimonies do not match. The painting depicts the moment where they apprehend her, trying to hold her semi-naked struggling body. *Susanna and the Elders* points to man's voyeurism and desire to punish woman for her supposed sexual sins. Before removing it from the wall, Norman stares for a moment at this painting, as if the scene it portrayed matched his own private phantasy. He spies through a hole drilled in the wall. Directly in his line of vision we see Marion undressing; behind her is the bathroom. Like the elders, Norman secretly spies on a woman when she imagines she is alone, bathing herself in a moment of solitary pleasure. In the shadows on the wall are paintings of birds – sign of the punishing mother. Norman replaces the painting and returns to the house, where he halts at the foot of the stairs that lead to the bedrooms. He then turns and we see him in long shot as he sits at the kitchen table as if waiting for something to happen.

Back in her room Marion sits at a desk making calculations. She flushes the torn paper, on which she has been writing, down the toilet bowl and turns on the shower taps. The camera asks us to identify with Marion through a series of subjective shots taken from her viewpoint as she looks up at the shower head. Marion is clearly enjoying the cleansing hot water as it streams down her body. Suddenly, we see a shadowy figure enter the bathroom. As the shower curtain is pulled back, the music erupts into shrill bird-like sounds signalling the presence of the beaked mother. 'Mrs Bates' stands there, a large knife in her upraised hand. She stabs brutally at Marion's defenceless body, cutting open her flesh. Norman, masquerading as Mother, punishes Marion, mutilates her flesh, transforming her body into a bleeding wound.

The shower scene murder has traditionally been interpreted in one of two ways: as representative of the desire of the 'Mother' to eliminate Marion as a dangerous rival for her son's affections; and as a symbolic form of rape enacted by Norman. Neither explanation is entirely satisfactory. The first – the explanation given by the psychiatrist at the end – argues that Norman is acting out the role he has *attributed* to his mother; he imagines she is jealous and wants to eliminate her rivals. The psychiatrist explains: 'Because he was so pathologically jealous of her, he assumed that she was as jealous of him. Therefore, if he felt a strong attraction to any other woman, the mother-side of him would go wild.' The psychiatrist interprets the shower scene murder as one of jealous revenge. Norman-as-mother murders women who arouse his desires and threaten to take him away from 'her'. In his discussion of *Psycho*, Robin Wood criticizes the psychiatrist's account as 'glib', an explanation that 'ignores as much as it explains'. One of the things it ignores is the murder as 'symbolic rape' (Wood, 1970, 132). Bellour also interprets the knife attack as a form of symbolic rape enacted by the phallic mother – the mother-as-a-fetish-figure of and for the son. In his analysis of doubling in the text, Bellour links Sam with Norman. He also parallels the hotel lovemaking scene with that of the shower murder. In the former, man's aggression towards woman is disguised: in the latter it erupts in a murderous attack. Through a relay of symbols, the knife is associated with the phallus – 'phallus-bird-fetish-mother-eye-knife-camera' (Bellour, 1979, 119). Adopting the 'classical dialectic – as described by Freud and Lacan – of the phallus and castration', Bellour interprets the mother as fetishized figure. 'The mother's body fetishized to death, so to speak, becomes the body that murders' (ibid.). According to Bellour:

> Through the incredible incorporation of a metaphor-become-reality, Norman's fascinated look carries within it that phallus immemorially attributed to the mother. But he can acknowledge it in himself only on condition that he ceaselessly encounter it in his mirror-image, namely in the body/look of woman (which engenders the mirage), and as an absolute threat to which he must respond.
>
> (ibid., 119–20)

Bellour's interpretation depends upon an acceptance of the Freudian argument that the infant believes the mother is phallic until that moment when he understands she is different and interprets that difference as castration; in other words, he imagines she has lost her phallus/penis. But, as I have argued, man also fears the mother because she castrates.

147

The notion that man fears the mother because she is the punishing, castrating parent provides us with another way of interpreting the shower-scene murder. The 'Mother' who attacks Marion in the shower is the castrating parent. The knife does not just represent a phantasm, the phallus 'immemorially attributed to the mother'; it also represents an actual threat posed by the mother – the threat of castration which she poses directly through her actions. Norman 'becomes' mother largely to turn the tables on mother, to ensure his own survival – to castrate rather than be castrated. 'Mrs Bates' punishes/mutilates Marion for taking pleasure in her body in the shower – a punishment Mrs Bates no doubt threatened Norman with for his own illicit practices. As suggested earlier, Norman's predilection for voyeurism suggests that his own sexual pleasures, like those of the elders who spied on Susanna, were masturbatory in nature.

Although they do not link this to the 'mother's' punishing attack, various critics have suggested that Marion is masturbating in the shower. Bellour argues that the shower scene shows us what was only intimated in the earlier scene which represented Norman as a peeping Tom. He argues that Marion's pleasure 'goes well beyond all diegetic motivation'. He refers particularly to the way 'close-up shots of her naked body alternate with shots of gushing water' and the way 'she leans into the stream, opens her mouth, smiles, and closes her eyes in a rapture'. Bellour sees this scene as answering the earlier lovemaking scene with Sam in the hotel but here we see the pleasure that Marion did not show earlier. Her pleasure is 'made all the more intense because it contrasts with the horror that is to come' (Bellour, 1979, 121). William Rothman also interprets this scene as one in which Marion is clearly experiencing sexual pleasure. 'Marion's shower is a love scene, with the shower head her imaginary partner' (Rothman, 1982, 292). In his tribute to this scene in the films *Carrie* and *Dressed to Kill*, Brian De Palma does show the female protagonists engaged in the act of masturbation. The shower murder is horrific because it presents us with a graphic, explicit, disturbing image of the mother carrying out the law, enforcing retribution. This scene awakens in the spectator an infantile fear of the castrating, punishing parent.

Most critics single out the shower scene as the most horrifying in the film – even in the history of the cinema. Ivan Butler states that: 'Nothing in the remainder of the film approaches this sequence in horror, though there is plenty of nightmare to come' (120). Fredric Jameson refers to it as 'the most horrific and immediate scene in motion picture history' (1982, 35). Robin Wood states that 'the shower-bath murder [is] probably the most horrific incident in any fiction film' (Wood, 1970, 128). In their analyses of this scene, most critics concentrate on its horror in relation to the victim, the brutal stabbing of Marion, and the way in which it was filmed and edited. According to Donald Spoto, it has 'evoked more study, elicited more comment, and generated more shot-for-shot analysis from a technical viewpoint than any other in the history of cinema' (Spoto, 1983, 419). But, as I have argued, one of the main reasons for this excess of critical attention is probably that the shower-scene murder awakens our unconscious fears of the mother as parental castrator. 'Mrs Bates' appears without warning, just at the moment when Marion is most enjoying the sensual pleasures of her body. In the Little Hans case study, Hans felt most vulnerable in relation to his mother at bath time and developed an anxiety that she might drown him in the bath. Children no doubt feel particularly vulnerable at this time not only because they are naked but also because this is the moment when they are likely to explore their body and/or engage in masturbation. *Psycho* clearly plays on this anxiety. With her severe bun, austere dress and sudden appearance, 'Mrs Bates' is a grim, frightening figure.

It is significant that in at least two of his case histories, Little Hans and the Wolf Man, Freud discovered it was the mother who threatened to castrate as a punishment for sexual activity. As discussed in Chapter 7, Freud had clinical evidence that the mother is seen, by some children, as the castrator yet he insisted that it was the father who enacted this role in the family. Unable to provide a fully convincing explanation for this, Freud appealed to 'a phylogenetic pattern' into which the boy had to fit. *Psycho* appears to me to provide an exemplary text in which the mother is represented as the feared castrator. 'Mrs Bates' castrates her boy in a number of ways: she lashes him with her tongue; watches him with her cruel eye; forbids him to have sexual relations with anyone; refuses to let him grow up. Symbolically, her castrating role is represented by a beaked bird of prey and a knife. Finally, whenever we see Norman as Mother, he is not only wearing her clothes but also carrying her knife, the sign of her castrating function.

In relation to the shower murder, it is important to note, however, that it is woman who is punished most graphically by the mother and it is probably the gaze of the female spectator that is more directly repelled as she watches her cinematic counterpart brutally assaulted. Tania Modleski notes that the sexism inherent in Hitchcock's celebrated scene is almost never discussed. 'Critics frequently point to *Psycho* as a film which punishes audiences for their illicit voyeuristic desires, but they ignore the fact that within the film not only are women objects of the male gaze, they [Marion and the girls in the swamp] are also recipients of most of the punishment' (Modleski, 1988, 14). The private detective, Arbogast, is also stabbed to death by 'Mrs Bates' but, as discussed in relation to the slasher film (Chapter 9), his death – as that of the male in general – is not depicted in as much detail as the deaths of women.

The cellar scene, perhaps even more than the shower scene, emphasizes the all-pervasive presence and indestructible power of the mother as the controlling, castrating parent. When Lila enters the cellar to escape from

149

Norman, she spies the figure of Mrs Bates sitting on a rocking chair, her back turned to the doorway. As she approaches the chair, Lila calls out her name. She reaches out and gently touches Mrs Bates's shoulder. The chair slowly swings round. Suddenly, Lila is confronted with a grotesque, grinning skull. It fills the screen, huge black eye sockets stare out from the head as if still able to control everything in their line of vision. Norman must have encountered this look daily as he 'lived' with his mother. We know he 'played out' scenes in which he, as 'mother', pronounced judgment on himself as the terrible son. Roger Dadoun isolates this moment as the most terrible in the film, primarily because it reinforces the all-pervasive presence of the mother, a presence which continues to haunt the subject even after the mother's death. 'The most horrific moment of the film, the scene that is the fantasmatic and emotional pivot of the whole story, is the one where the mother is everywhere, occupying the whole screen from one edge of the frame to the other' (Dadoun, 1989, 50–1).

In the penultimate scene of the film the seemingly indestructible nature of the power of the mother is made clear once and for all. The mother's hideous skull-face, with its open jaws and jagged teeth, is superimposed on her son's grinning face. Once again Mrs Bates's eye sockets appear animated as she stares directly at the audience, a bizarre grin forming on her lips. Mother continues to see everything, even beyond the grave. Poison, burial, mummification – all efforts to destroy her power have failed. She stares out through Norman's eyes, her grin infusing his face with wicked delight. The grotesque image points symbolically to the kind of power the mother exerts over her son. In Norman's case she is so powerful that he gives up his own identity. She is not an external, separate entity; she is part of the child's inner self, the interior voice of the maternal authority. It is this dimension of the mother – her enculturating, moral function – that has generally been neglected in critical approaches to *Psycho*, despite the fact that a major part of the film's ideological and sexist project seems to be to demonstrate that, when left without a husband, the 'true' representative of the law, the mother is incapable of exercising authority wisely. In *Psycho*, all boundaries that mark out the speaking subject as separate from the other have collapsed, giving rise to the terror of the abject self. In order to confront this terror, Norman becomes the parent he both loves and fears – the castrating mother of infancy. When Norman says to Marion: 'Mother . . . isn't quite herself today', he was dead right. She was not. She was someone else. Her mad son – Norman.

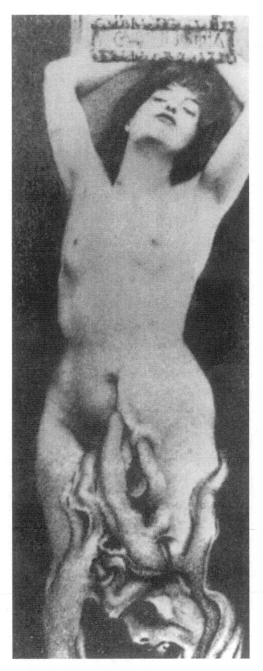

Plate 13 Istar: a Medusan nightmare. A vivid portrayal of the deadly *vagina dentata* in *fin-de-siècle* art.

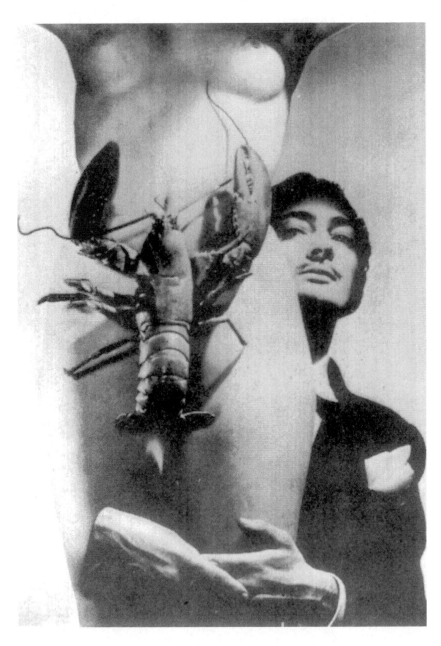

Plate 14 Once bitten, twice shy. Salvadore Dali keeps a wary eye on his version of the dentata.

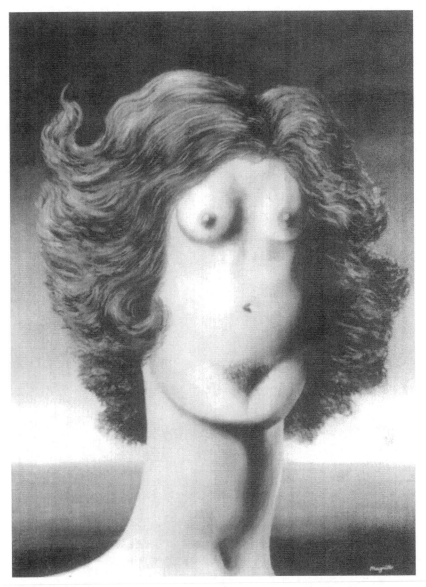

Plate 15 Woman's hidden genital mouth. A surreal displacement in
Magritte's *The Rape*, © ADAGP, Paris and DACS, London 1993.

Plate 16 Process of Enlightenment: the intellectual woman is truly a maneater. Cartoonist Leunig's humorous comment on man's fear of woman. Reproduced by kind permission of Michael Leunig.

Plate 17 A vaginal nightmare. The cannibalistic nightmare mouth of the crazed female vampire (Amanda Bearse in *Fright Night*).

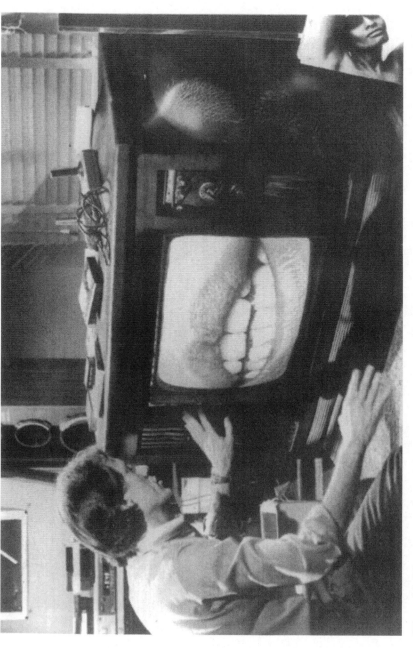

Plate 18 Electronic dentata. Man (James Woods) recoils from woman's parted lips – the entrance to a terrifying world of sado-masochistic sex in *Videodrome*.

Plate 19 Aquatic dentata. In *Jaws* woman and shark are closely linked through image and narrative (publicity poster).

Plate 20 The psychotic twin (Margot Kidder) of *Sisters* makes a birthday wish and lunges at her male victim before castrating him.

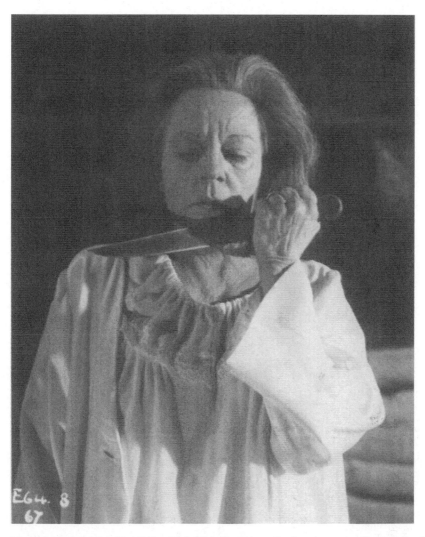

Plate 21 Mad Mrs Trefoile (Talullah Bankhead), the demented mother of *Fanatic*, contemplates her deadly blade – sign of the castrating mother.

Plate 22 Cat People: like a jungle cat, the untamed woman is always ready to strike, to tear man apart with claw and fang (publicity poster).

Plate 23 The lascivious snake woman (Jacqueline Pearce) of *The Reptile*, her deadly claw and fangs hidden from view.

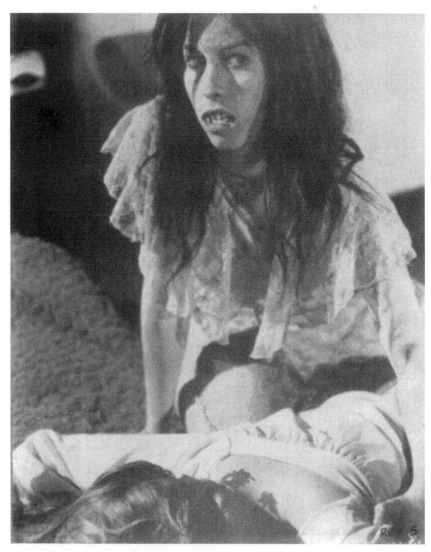

Plate 24 The lesbian vampire's deadly bite. A metaphor for the insatiable sexual desires of woman in *The Return of Count Yorga*.

11

THE MEDUSA'S GAZE

> from a feminine locus nothing can be articulated without a question-
> ing of the symbolic itself.
>
> Luce Irigaray, *This Sex Which Is Not One*

Wife, mother, daughter, virgin, whore, career woman, *femme fatale* –
these are the most popular stereotypes of woman that have been addressed
by feminist theorists in their writings on popular cinema. Very little has
been written on woman as monster. As with the more critically popular
images of woman, those which represent woman as monstrous also define
her primarily in relation to her sexuality, specifically the abject nature of
her maternal and reproductive functions. As I have shown, the monstrous-
feminine constitutes an important and complex stereotype which can be
broken down into a number of different figures of female horror: woman as
archaic mother, monstrous womb, vampire, possessed monster, *femme
castratrice*, witch, castrating mother. The representation of the monstrous-
feminine in patriarchal signifying practices has a number of consequences
for psychoanalytically based theories of sexual difference. On the one
hand, those images which define woman as monstrous in relation to her
reproductive functions work to reinforce the phallocentric notion that
female sexuality is abject. On the other hand, the notion of the monstrous-
feminine challenges the view that femininity, by definition, constitutes
passivity. Furthermore, the phantasy of the castrating mother undermines
Freud's theories that woman terrifies because she is castrated and that it is
the father who alone represents the agent of castration within the family.

The image of the castrating woman is complex and multi-faceted.
Representations of woman as an agent of castration take various forms in
the horror film: oral sadistic mother (the vampire film); *femme castratrice*
(the woman's revenge film); castrating mother (family horror). Recurring
images and motifs associated with woman as castrator include knives, axes,
ice picks, spiked instruments, teeth, yawning chasms, jagged rocks, the
deadly *vagina dentata*. In comparison with other genres, the horror genre
does not attempt to soothe castration anxiety. The spectator is confronted

with images of woman as symbolically castrated (for example, the muti-lated female victims of the slasher film) and as an agent of castration (the woman's revenge film). Significantly, the horror film does not attempt to construct male and female in a totally different relation to castration – both are represented (man literally/woman symbolically) as castrated and as agents of castration. However, this factor is not usually recognized in critical writings on horror; it is the male who is almost always described as the monster and the agent of castration, woman as his victim. The exist-ence of the monstrous-feminine in the horror film also has important consequences for the way in which we situate popular cinema. It may be that the horror genre is more directly responsive to questions of sexual difference, more willing to explore male and female anxieties about the 'other', than film texts which belong to mainstream genres such as the detective, suspense thriller, comedy and romance films.

THE MONSTROUS-FEMININE AND SPECTATORSHIP

Why has the concept of woman as monster been neglected in feminist theory? A major reason is that the majority of feminist articles on the cinema have addressed genres such as the melodrama, *film noir* and the woman's film which, at first glance, appear to be more directly concerned with questions of female desire and phallocentric representations of female sexuality. A study of horror reveals that this genre also is intimately bound up with questions of sexuality and the way in which woman's abjection helps to found the patriarchal symbolic order. Why has the image of woman as castrator, a major archetype of female monstrosity, been ignored? A central reason for this relates to the Freudian basis of much feminist psychoanalytic criticism. Because the notion of the castrating woman is repressed in Freud's writings, it has similarly been neglected in feminist film theory. As I have shown, Freud not only repressed the concept of the castrating woman in his theories of infantile sexuality, his analysis of dreams, myths and legends, but also in his case history of Little Hans – specifically the second plumber phantasy – which is frequently invoked to justify the theory of the castration complex.

Drawing on the Lacanian rereading of Freud, feminist theory has con-centrated on the representation of woman as lack and absence. Laura Mulvey's pioneering article, 'Visual pleasure and narrative cinema', pub-lished in 1975, best expresses the way in which the representation of woman has generally been viewed: 'The paradox of phallocentrism in all its manifestations is that it depends on the image of the castrated woman to give order and meaning to its world' (1989, 14). While this image does give 'order and meaning' to the patriarchal symbolic and to the representation of woman in many film genres, it does not explain the representation of male fears in the horror film which are *not* alleviated or repudiated either

152

by the textual processes of fetishization or the narrative processes that reinforce the controlling power of the male protagonist. Nor does it explain those texts in which the castrated male body, not the female body, represents lack and absence. In these texts it is the mutilated male form that evokes castration anxiety while the heroine is represented as the avenging castrator, the central protagonist with whom the spectator is encouraged to identify. The *femme castratrice* controls the sadistic gaze: the male victim is her object.

In her use of the masochistic aesthetic, Gaylyn Studlar has presented an important critique of the dominant Freudian–Lacanian model of spectatorship. She argues that the 'female in the masochistic aesthetic is more than the passive object of the male's desire for possession. She is also a figure of identification, the mother of plenitude whose gaze meets the infant's as it asserts her presence and her power' (Studlar, 1984, 273). Although Studlar's model opens up a space in which to re-evaluate theories of spectatorship, it does not account for the figure of the monstrous-feminine who is very different from the 'mother of plenitude'. Clearly existing theories of spectatorship are inadequate: they do not help us to theorize the presence of woman as active monster in the horror text, her relationship to the characters in the diegesis, or the relationship of the spectators – male and female – in the cinema.

Elizabeth Cowie's article, 'Fantasia', in which she draws on Freud's theory of the primal phantasies, proposes a model for viewing which is particularly relevant to the experience of watching horror films. Cowie argues that forms of identification in the cinema are extremely fluid and are not restricted by considerations of gender that position woman as object and man as controller of the gaze. To support her argument, Cowie draws upon Laplanche and Pontalis's definition of phantasy as the setting or *mise-en-scène* of desire. In 'Fantasy and the origins of sexuality' they write that phantasy is not 'the object of desire, but its setting. In fantasy the subject does not pursue the object or its sign: he appears caught up himself in the sequence of images' (Laplanche and Pontalis, 1985, 26). Cowie argues that phantasy, as the setting of desire, is found not only in daydreams but also in public forms of phantasy such as novels and films. She applies her theory to various texts drawn from the woman's film.

The horror film also provides a rich source for constructing the settings upon which phantasy is attendant. It continually draws upon the three primal phantasies (see Chapter 2) – birth, seduction, castration – in order to construct its scenarios of horror. Like the primal phantasies, horror narratives are particularly concerned with origins: origin of the subject; origin of desire; origin of sexual difference. Compared with other genres, however, the horror film represents these phantasies in a *mise-en-scène* which is marked by horror and the abject. The subject is frequently born from a strange union (human/alien/animal) and in a dark terrifying place

153

(the monstrous womb/pit/cellar); desire is for the unknowable terrifying other; knowledge of sexual difference invokes fear of castration and death. Constructions of the primal phantasies in horror narratives involve images associated with weapons, bodily disintegration in one form or another, blood, an array of abject bodily wastes, pain and terror. The horror film is, by definition, obsessively concerned with death; death is so crucial that it constitutes a fourth primal phantasy which should rank in importance with the three other phantasies stipulated by Freud. The end can also be seen as a beginning, the origin of a new journey. What happens after death? Does the individual subject live on in a different form? These questions are central to the horror film – specifically the vampire, zombie, ghoul, ghost and possession films. Where did I come from? Where am I going? To a terrible place, the horror film knowingly, and sometimes mockingly, replies. In these texts, the setting or sequence of images in which the subject is caught up, denotes a desire to encounter the unthinkable, the abject, the other. It is a *mise-en-scène* of desire – in which desire is for the abject. It is in relation to this abject scene that the subject, and by extension the viewer, is caught up.

According to Laplanche and Pontalis the subject does not take up a 'fixed place' in relation to phantasy but is free to adopt a number of subject positions – regardless of gender. 'As a result, the subject, although always present in the fantasy, may be so in a desubjectivised form, that is to say, in the very syntax of the sequence in question' (1985, 15). The subject positions with which the horror film most frequently encourages the spectator to identify oscillate between those of victim and monster but with greater emphasis on the former. In this respect, the horror film sets out to explore the perverse, masochistic aspects of the gaze.

When the spectator is encouraged to identify with the victim, an extreme form of masochistic looking is invoked; here the look is confronted by horrific images signifying extreme terror, pain, death. Whereas the classic horror film tends to affirm the controlling gaze at the moment of narrative closure (the monster is defeated/life is affirmed) the contemporary horror film frequently asserts the primacy of the masochistic look in its moment of closure (the monster lives/death reigns). Both forms, classic and modern, draw on the masochistic look throughout the unfolding of the narrative. As discussed in Chapter 2, the extreme moment of masochistic viewing seems to occur when the viewing subject, male and female, is forced to look away. The scene of horror is so terrifying, abject and confronting that the spectator cannot bear to look at all. Not even the look of the camera, which may have attempted to freeze the horrific image through fetishization or control it by maintaining a voyeuristic distance, is enough to entice the terrified viewer into snatching another terrified glance.

In those films where the male is the victim of the monstrous-feminine in one of her many guises – witch, vampire, creature, abject mother, castrator, psychotic – the male spectator, who identifies with his screen surrogate, is clearly placed in a powerless situation. Through the figure of the monstrous-feminine, the horror film plays on his possible fears of menstrual blood, incorporation, domination, castration and death. One of the most salient features of the horror film is that it does allow for an explicit representation of man's castration anxieties in relation to his own body. In the slasher sub-genre these fears are displaced on to woman but in other films man must face this threat alone. In films like *Sisters*, *I Spit on Your Grave* and *Basic Instinct* male castration fear is aligned with a masochistic desire for death. Mulvey's theory of the sadistic male gaze, which seems to describe so well the structure of spectatorial relations in other genres, does not explain the very different structure of looks that is constructed in the horror film.

What is the appeal of the horror film to the female spectator? Does she recognize herself in the figure of the monstrous-feminine? To what extent might the female spectator feel empowered when identifying with the female castrator? Does she derive a form of sadistic pleasure in seeing her sexual other humiliated and punished? The answers to these questions are complex and vary from text to text. For instance, the female spectator might feel empowerment from identifying with the castrating heroine of the slasher film when the latter finally destroys the male killer. She may also feel empowerment from identifying with the castrating heroine of the rape-revenge film when the latter takes revenge on the male rapist. But the psychotic castrating heroine of films like *Sisters* does not actively encourage spectator identification in that she is depicted as insane. Nor does the castrating mother figure of *Psycho* or *Friday the 13th* encourage sympathetic identification – particularly when her victims are female. This does not, however, mean that the female spectator does not identify with these figures of feminine horror. Given that the horror film speaks to our deepest fears and most terrifying fantasies it is – as I have argued – most likely that identificatory processes are extremely fluid and allow the spectator to switch identification between victim and monster depending on the degree to which the spectator wishes to be terrified and/or to terrify and depending on the power of the various filmic codes (subjective camera, close-up images, music) designed to encourage certain modes of identification above others.

One response to the castrating heroine of the horror film is to argue that she is actually a phallicized heroine, that is, she has been reconstituted as masculine. If female spectators derive pleasure from identifying with an aggressive or violent heroine it is because they have been contaminated by patriarchy. It is only the phallic male spectator who is empowered by identifying with an aggressive hero figure in the diegesis. This view appears to be based on the argument that only phallic masculinity is violent and that femininity is never violent – not even in the imagination. This argument is essentialist, that is, it assumes that if women lived outside patriarchy they would never, as spectators, derive pleasure from identifying with acts of aggression on the screen. The feminine imagination is seen as essentially non-violent, peaceful, unaggressive. This is the very argument that patriar-chal ideology has used for the past 2,000 years to control women – it is precisely because women by definition are 'pure' creatures that they need men to 'guide' them through life's stormy passage. This is one of the arguments used by the Reverend Don Wildman, Jerry Faldwell and other members of the moral majority who want to tighten current censorship laws in the United States.

It may be objected that most horror films are made by men and that the only pleasures/terrors on offer are male-defined. (This argument, of course, applies to the majority of mainstream cinematic genres.) But I do not believe the unconscious is subject to the strictures of gender socializa-tion and it is to the unconscious that the horror film speaks, revealing – perhaps more than any other genre – the unconscious fears and desires of both the human subject (pain, bodily attack, disintegration, death) and the gendered subject (male fears of woman's reproductive role and of cas-tration and woman's fears of phallic aggressivity and rape). No doubt if women made horror films, the latter area would be explored more fully. The reason women do not make horror films is not that the 'female' unconscious is fearless, without its monsters, but because women still lack access to the means of production in a system which continues to be male-dominated in all key areas.

The presence of monstrous-feminine also undermines the view that the male spectator invariably takes up a sadistic position because the monster is always male. The male spectator is frequently asked to identify with a male monster that is feminized. He is feminized via the body; he bleeds, gives birth, is penetrated, and generally undergoes abject bodily changes associated with the feminine. Furthermore, male victims are frequently placed in a masochistic position via the female monster. Further work needs to be undertaken in the area of spectatorship and questions of audience identification in relation to the construction of the monstrous in the horror film and other popular fictions.

THE PHALLIC AND CASTRATING WOMAN

The presence of the female castrator in the horror film also raises problems for the Freudian theory of fetishization and the phallic woman. The notion of the castrating woman has sometimes been confused with that of the phallic woman. According to Laplanche and Pontalis, the image of the phallic woman has two forms: the woman either has a phallus or phallic attribute or she has retained the male's phallus inside herself (1985, 311). In their discussion of problems of definition, they state that the term

156

'phallic woman' is often used 'in a loose way as a description of a woman with allegedly masculine character-traits – e.g. authoritarianism – even when it is not known what the underlying phantasies are' (ibid., 312). This confusion is particularly marked in relation to the so-called phallic/ castrating woman. Freud argued that children of both sexes, influenced by their own phallic stage of development, believe in the phallic mother. She is the mother who exists prior to the child's knowledge of castration and sexual difference. The boy imagines the mother is like himself; the girl believes that her penis will eventually grow to be like the mother's. The deadly *femme fatale* of *film noir*, the woman who carries a gun in her purse, is regarded as a classic example of the phallic woman. In the horror film and pornography she is sometimes given a penis/dildo. Like the castrated woman she, too, is another manifestation of the representation of female sexuality in relation to the phallus. Her image is also informed by the workings of patriarchal ideology. Janey Place argues that the 'ideological operation of the myth (the absolute necessity of controlling the strong, sexual woman) is thus achieved by first demonstrating her dangerous power and its frightening results, then destroying it' (Place, 1980, 45).

When film critics draw attention to the notion of woman as powerful and dangerous they usually invoke the concept of the phallic woman, frequently referring to her as if she were the same figure as the castrating woman. The following description of the mother in *Psycho* is a fairly typical example of the way in which the two concepts are collapsed together: 'An essential aspect, as specified in Freud's analysis of fetishism, is the way she appears as a phallic woman, as woman with a penis, a murderous, all-devouring or castrating mother' (Dadoun, 1989, 50). This description of Regan from *The Exorcist* also links these two notions: 'Regan-as-Devil becomes the phallic, castrating woman (she seizes the psychiatrist, who invokes her, by the testicles), and is endowed with a parodying perversion of "masculine" characteristics – bass voice, violence, sexual aggressiveness, unladylike language' (Britton, 1979, 51). In her description of the heroine of the slasher film, Clover also describes her castrating aspects in terms of phallicization (Clover, 1989, 116). But as I have shown, man's fear that woman might castrate him either symbolically or literally is *not* necessarily related to his infantile belief that she is phallic. The penis, as such, is not an instrument of incorporation or castration but of penetration. In representations of the penis as an instrument of violence, it doesn't threaten to castrate but rather to penetrate and split open, explode, tear apart. It is the mythical *vagina dentata* which threatens to devour, to castrate via incorporation. Critical neglect of the monstrous-feminine in her role as castrator has led to a serious misunderstanding of the nature of the monstrous woman in the horror film and other popular genres such as *film noir* and science fiction.

The archetypes of the phallic and castrating woman are quite different and should not be confused; the former ultimately represents a comforting phantasy of sexual sameness, and the latter a terrifying phantasy of sexual difference. The notion of the phallic woman is crucial to Freud's theory of castration; if the child did not initially believe the mother was phallic, it could not later construct her as castrated. In Lacanian terms, woman could not be seen as representing 'lack' and 'absence'. According to Freud, the importance of the penis for both sexes is a corollary of the fact that the child is unaware of the existence of the vagina and its proper function until the tenth or eleventh year – a theory I questioned in relation to the Little Hans case study. Even before he turned five, Little Hans was aware of his mother's 'baby box', and the fact that she had a place somewhere behind her navel that she kept her 'knife'. At this stage, according to Freud, the child is aware of only two possibilities – the difference between having the phallus and being castrated. Yet Hans's extreme fear of the biting white horse indicates that he knew, consciously or otherwise, that his mother's widdler was very different from his own.

Is she or isn't she castrated? This was the question that so troubled Freud. It is this question that enabled him to erect his theory of fetishism around the disturbing sight/site of the female genitalia. As I have argued, however, the question could have been posed differently. Is woman castrated or does she castrate? This question seemed to lie behind the game Little Hans played with his doll when he let his mother's knife drop from between her legs. The concept of the castrating mother also enables one to construct a theory of fetishism in relation to the sight of the female genitalia. In this version, the fetishist disavows the horrifying thought that the vagina might be a site of castration by erecting a fetish in its place. Arguing that man fears woman's vagina as a site of castration, rather than a castrated genital, in no way alters the *principle* behind the theory of fetishism. The fetish object denies the horrifying aspects of the female genitals – the *way* in which the genitals might horrify is open to interpretation. The important point is that the process is marked by the structure of disavowal. In Freud's theory, the protest is stated in these terms: 'I know woman isn't castrated, but. . . '. The proposition could also be: 'I know woman doesn't castrate, but. . . '.

THE MATERNAL CASTRATOR

Why did Freud dismiss the possibility that man might fear woman as castrator? We know he considered the idea. Along with a number of his contemporaries, Freud had clinical evidence that the mother, or her substitutes, is frequently feared by the male child as the parental castrator. In the Wolf Man case history, Freud addressed the problem directly:

Although the threats or hints of castration which had come his way had emanated from women, this could not hold up the final result for long. In spite of everything it was his father from whom in the end he came to fear castration. In this respect heredity triumphed over accidental experience; in man's prehistory it was unquestionably the father who practised castration as a punishment and who later softened it down into circumcision.

('From the history of an infantile neurosis', 86)

Freud invoked the notion of 'heredity' and 'prehistory' to explain castration, which he saw as a harsher form of circumcision for at least two main reasons. First, this enabled him to position the workings of castration as a 'law', a mechanism that operates regardless of the individual history of the subject. The law of castration enabled Freud to explain the Oedipus complex in more 'scientific' terms. According to Juliet Mitchell (1975), Freud fine-tuned his theory of castration during the second phase of his writings, commencing after 1920. By defining the castration complex as a law, Freud was also able to deal with a problem that affected his earlier version of the Oedipus complex – that the complex was presented as a 'passing developmental stage' which somehow 'dissolved naturally'. As a law, the castration complex provides an explanation for the origins of the human order which does not leave things up to chance or human nature. Mitchell emphasizes the crucial importance of this:

Together with the organising role of the Oedipus complex in relation to desire, the castration complex governs the position of each person in the triangle of father, mother and child; in the way it does this, it embodies the law that founds the human order itself. Thus the question of castration, of sexual difference as the product of a division, and the concept of an historical and symbolic order, all began, tentatively, to come together.

(Mitchell and Rose, 1982, 14)

Second, the notion of castration as a law enabled Freud to propose a theory of sexual difference which was not based on any pre-given or biologist notion of male and female. The father represents a principle – 'the third term'. Freud's theory of castration also explains the patriarchal nature of the human order. According to Mitchell:

To Freud, if psychoanalysis is phallocentric, it is because the human social order that it perceives refracted through the individual human subject is patrocentric. To date, the father stands in the position of the third term that must break the asocial dyadic unit of mother and child.

(ibid., 23)

There is, however, a problem with Freud's position. He is arguing that

Patriarchy!

because we live in a patriarchal world, the phallus *must* be the primary signifier. If woman exercises power, for instance if she threatens to castrate, her authority is 'borrowed'. Yet, as I have shown, Freud's justification for stating that the phallus is the primary signifier is not his clinical material; it is a sociological observation. It is only by ignoring clinical evidence and establishing the father, not the mother, as the one who represents the threat of castration and as a consequence the law that Freud is able to provide an explanation for the patriarchal nature of the symbolic – although, of course, he is still unable to explain how patriarchy came into existence in the first place.

The question of what constitutes the difference between the sexes is central to Jacques Lacan's rereading of Freud's theory of the castration complex. Although Lacan makes it clear that *both* women and men are subject to castration, he also ultimately positions the father as representative of the symbolic order and attempts to lock the father into this role in a more decisive way than Freud achieved. Like Freud, Lacan also sees the father's role as fixed, unchanging. 'It is in the name of the father that we must recognize the support of the Symbolic function which, from the dawn of history, has identified his person with the figure of the law' (Lacan, 1968, 41). Like Freud, Lacan also appeals to a quasi-sociological concept – 'the dawn of history' – to justify a psychic operation.

By analysing Freudian theory in terms of modern structural linguistics, Jacques Lacan tried to circumvent the charge frequently laid against Freud that his theory of castration ultimately does confuse the psychic and the biological. He makes Freud's theories of castration and the phallus central to the formation of subjectivity and sexual difference. Whereas Freud used the term 'phallus' to refer to the 'symbolic function' of the penis, Lacan reorientated psychoanalytic theory 'around the idea of the phallus as the "signifier of desire" ' (Laplanche and Pontalis, 1985, 312–14). According to Lacan, desire is to be understood in a double sense – the child both desires the mother and desires to be the object of the mother's desire, the phallus. According to Jacqueline Rose: 'Castration means first of all this – that the child's desire for the mother does not refer to her but beyond her, to an object, the phallus, whose status is first imaginary (the object presumed to satisfy her desire) and then symbolic (recognition that desire cannot be satisfied)' (Rose, 1982, 38). As a signifier no one has a privileged relation to the phallus. 'The basic structure of desire would follow from the law of the signifier, in that it signifies something only in relation to another signifier, so desire is always desire for *another* thing' (Benvenuto and Kennedy, 1986, 13).

In Lacan's rewriting of Freudian theory, castration is meant to represent the child's acknowledgement of the law and its willingness to renounce its desire to be the object (the phallus) of the mother's desire. The threat of castration is not something enacted in the real; it is *always* symbolic.

Castration may derive support from *privation*, that is to say, from the apprehension in the Real of the absence of the penis in women – but even this supposes a symbolization of an object, since the Real is full and lacks nothing. In so far as one finds castration in the genesis of neurosis, it is never real but symbolic and is aimed at an imaginary object.

(cited in Grosz, 1990, 71)

Lacan claims that the child, male or female, can only enter the symbolic order through its acknowledgement of castration and privation.

The problem with the Lacanian theory of castration is that it continues to construct the symbolic order as a patriarchal one. 'Assuming that it is true that psychosis is the alternative to the symbolic, this need not of itself be an unsurpassable obstacle, providing one can conceive of a symbolic that is not patriarchal. The real problem is that Lacan's symbolic makes patriarchy seem inevitable' (Brennan, 1989, 3). A major reason for this relates to the atture and status of the phallus in Lacanian theory. The phallus is a supposedly neutral term that signifies the 'lack' which leads to the constitution of subjectivity and speech. Elizabeth Grosz argues it is 'thus simultaneously and indissolubly the mark of sexual difference (and identity), the signifier of the speaking position in language, and the order governing exchange relations' (Grosz, 1990, 126). The phallus is tied to the penis – for a number of reasons. First, a parallel between the symbolic father and the phallus exists in that the former breaks up the mother–child dyad while the latter represents that separation. In the second place, insofar as the penis can represent lack – it fills woman's 'lack' – it can stand in for the supposedly neutral phallus. 'If the penis assumes the function of the phallus this is because female sexuality is considered a mutilation or castration' (Grosz, 117). In theory the phallus is a neutral term that no one, male or female, can possess; in practice the phallus is frequently aligned with the penis. Brennan emphasizes this point: 'Feminists influenced by Lacan have stressed that both sexes can take up the masculine and feminine places; these shift and slide – no one has the phallus. Yet the tie between phallus and penis exists, and persists' (Brennan, 1989, 4). For this reason alone, it is clear that the Freudian/Lacanian theory of the Oedipus complex is problematic. If we add to this the fact that Freud ignores/ represses the phantasy of the castrating mother, and the possibility that the mother can be identified with the law, it becomes clear that the theory is completely inadequate as a means of explaining the origins of human subjectivity and sexual difference.

While the phantasy of the castrating mother is repressed in Freud's writings, Lacan does discuss the notion but only in relation to the concept of homosexuality and various perversions. The castrating mother, the parent who 'lays down the law', has been given too much power by the father. On discovering that the mother has the power, the future homosexual child learns to overvalue the phallus, 'cannot tolerate its lack, and is usually horrified by female genitals'. Consequently, he seeks it in his partner (Benvenuto and Kennedy, 1986, 135). However, the phantasy of the castrating mother is too persistent and widespread to be marginalized as relevant primarily in relation to the question of so-called perversions. This phantasy not only finds expression in a wide range of cultural and artistic practices but is central to one of Freud's most important case histories as well as being repressed in many of his own writings. Furthermore, the fact that the patriarchal symbolic functions to soothe man's anxieties regarding woman's threatening nature suggests that this phantasy is dominant in helping to influence the social and political treatment of women. Patriarchal ideology works to curb the power of the mother, and by extension all women, by controlling woman's desire through a series of repressive practices which deny her autonomy over her body. The most violent of these measures include domestic assault, rape and female genital mutilation. In her documentary film, *Rites*, Penny Dedman estimates that female genital mutilation is on the increase and currently affects 75–85 million women worldwide. Fear of the clitoris as a 'barb' or tooth, dangerous in sexual intercourse, has been proposed as the reason behind the barbaric practice of female genital mutilation in African countries (Lederer, 1968, 46) – incorrectly described by Freud in 'The taboo of virginity' as 'female circumcision'. (Circumcision is the removal of skin, not an entire organ.) This practice, in which the clitoris and labia are excised, suggests a deep-seated attitude of horror towards the female genitals – an attitude which is widespread, and which consequently cannot be dismissed as belonging to the realm of 'perversions'. It also clearly indicates that those peoples who practise female genital mutilation do not regard woman's genitals as having already been castrated; their aim is, in fact, to carry out a form of castration.

But the question of woman's 'castrating' desires can never be closed down completely because of the nature of sexual intercourse. In 'The taboo of virginity' Freud drew attention to the fact that coitus reminds man of his possible castration. Freud's account of sexual intercourse provides an explanation for man's fear of the vagina as a place of pleasure and danger. 'The man is afraid of being weakened by the woman, infected with her femininity and of then showing himself incapable. The effect which coitus has of discharging tensions and causing flaccidity may be the prototype of what the man fears' (p. 198). As discussed above, Lacan's theory of the phallus – because of its association with the penis – does not resolve the problem of man's castration anxieties.

[Man] desires his 'possession' of the phallus be affirmed through the woman's desire for his penis, which is (symbolically) detachable from him and capable of being 'given' to her. She desires access to the phallus he 'owns'. Ironically, sexual relations problematize the very link between penis and phallus that she strives to affirm. Sexual intercourse is both the affirmation of his possession of the phallus and a reminder of the possibility of castration. For a moment at least, he fills the woman's 'lack' and at that moment becomes the site of lack himself.

(Grosz, 1990, 134–5)

It is the representation of man as 'site of lack' which is central to the representation of masculinity in the horror film – an area of study which is outside the scope of this book but which also challenges existing theories of sexual difference and spectatorship in the cinema (see Creed, 1993). Grosz states that it is the 'residue' of the castration threat, given a more concrete expression during intercourse, that lies behind man's 'paranoid fantasy of the *vagina dentata*' (1990, 135). To this fear, I would also add the child's fear of the castrating mother – the mother of Little Hans's nightmares and phobias.

From the above discussion, we can see that the representation of woman as the monstrous-feminine in horror – particularly the image of the castrating woman – challenges a number of psychoanalytically based theories which are central to current debates within feminism about the representation of sexual difference and spectatorship in a range of popular discourses including film, photography and pornography. These include the following: the Freudian argument that woman terrifies because she is castrated; the Freudian theories of the castration complex, the phallic/castrating woman and fetishism; the model of spectatorship which posits woman as object of the controlling male gaze; and the propositions that the father alone represents the law and that the symbolic is necessarily patriarchal.

WOMAN AND THE SYMBOLIC

As we saw in Part I, Kristeva's theory of the abject provides us with a way of opening up the debate about the mother's relation to the symbolic still further. Kristeva's theory of the abject – and the related notion of the thetic – challenges the view that the child's separation from the mother *commences* with the intervention of the father as the third term who brings about a separation of mother and child. The situation is far more complex.

Kristeva's answer is that before the full intervention of the symbolic begins, a prior state is necessary, one which will be the repressed desire and the symbolic. . . . The point is that the symbolic is not, of

163

its own accord, strong enough to ensure separation; it depends on the mother becoming abjected.

(Lechte, 1990, 159)

Kristeva uses the term, 'the thetic', to describe the bridging space between the semiotic and the symbolic. On the one hand, the semiotic refers to the unorganized and dispersed drives which are inscribed across the child's body. On the other hand, there are moments within the semiotic when there is order and structure, when the drives are given form and shape. The 'threshhold between the semiotic and the symbolic – the *thetic* – is an anticipation of the symbolic from within the semiotic, as well as the residues of the semiotic in the symbolic' (Grosz, 1990, 45). Kristeva's theories of the abject and the thetic reveal that the child's separation from the mother should be seen as a gradual process, one that stretches from the semiotic to the symbolic. In 'Revolution in poetic language', Kristeva sees castration as only the final part of a long process: 'Castration puts the finishing touches on the process of separation that posits the subject as signifiable, which is to say, separate, always confronted by another' (1986, 47).

While attempting to make a place for the maternal figure in the pre-symbolic on par with the paternal figure of the symbolic, she does not question the patriarchal base of the symbolic. In my view, we can question the so-called 'inevitable' link between patriarchy and the symbolic still further by taking into account the crucial role played by the phantasy of the maternal castrator in the development of the child's castration complex. It is possible that the child's anxiety concerning his own possible castration by the mother plays a significant role in helping to rupture the mother–child dyad. Fear of the castrating mother may also help to explain the ambivalent attitude in which women are held in patriarchal societies – an attitude which is also represented in the various stereotypes of feminine evil that exist within a range of popular discourses. The mother is the child's first love object but insofar as she threatens castration she also becomes an object of fear and dread. Clearly, the widespread phantasy of woman as castrator raises crucial problems for psychoanalytic theories of sexual difference. My intention, however, is not to try and absorb the figure of the maternal castrator into Freud's theory of the Oedipus and castration complexes but rather to point out the inadequacy of these theories in helping us to understand the origins of patriarchy.

Entry into a symbolic order is a long and gradual process in which the mother, or a number of complex reasons, plays an active central role but one that has been rendered invisible in relation to the Freudian theory of castration. The problem is that the processes whereby the infant separates itself from the mother, and the role she plays in this, are not clearly delineated. With its emphasis on law, logic and rationality,

What about materiality

the language of the symbolic order does not easily tolerate borders, boundaries and processes that interweave in complex and various ways. In relation to entry into the symbolic, the mother is represented as an essentially ambiguous figure. She teaches the child through its toilet training to separate itself from all signs of its animal origins, yet she is also associated with the world of nature – and consequently denigrated – because of her reproductive and mothering functions. She teaches the infant to abhor what she herself comes to represent within the signifying practices of the symbolic. An ideology which denigrates woman is also endorsed by woman: patriarchal ideology works in and through woman, as we saw in *Carrie*.

Psychoanalytic writings which argue that the symbolic is an order represented by the father alone can only do so by repressing and distorting the crucial role played by the mother in relation to the constitution of society and culture – albeit at this stage a patriarchal culture. The problem is not that this order is inevitable but that patriarchy, of necessity, values men and male activities above women and the traditionally female activities associated with pregnancy, childbirth and motherhood. Despite clear evidence that man fears woman as castrating, it constructs woman as a castrated creature, man's lacking other. It would appear that the symbolic order is supported by the imaginary beliefs of the male subject, specifically the view that the mother who was once phallic has been castrated. Insofar as the patriarchal symbolic is structured by a male imaginary, the crucial task becomes one of understanding differently the phantasies that inform the male imaginary – even reconstruct the male imaginary. But for 'men to make a break with their imaginary, another term would be needed – woman as symbolic' (Whitford, 1989, 119). By pointing out the inadequacies in psychoanalytic theories of sexual difference, we can begin to reevaluate and recreate.

Fifty years ago Karen Horney also argued that man fears woman because she might castrate. She listed a series of myths and legends – including that of the Sphinx – which portrayed woman as evil.

> The riddle of the Sphinx can be solved by few, and most of those who attempt it forfeit their lives. . . . The series of such instances is infinite; always, everywhere, the man strives to rid himself of his dread of women by objectifying it. 'It is not,' he says, 'that I dread her; it is that she herself is malignant, capable of any crime, a beast of prey, a vampire, a witch, insatiable in her desires. She is the very personification of what is sinister.'
>
> (Horney, 1967, 134–5)

These images of woman as monstrous-feminine are alive and well in the contemporary horror film and represented in a variety of ways: witch, archaic mother, monstrous womb, vampire, *femme castratrice*, castrating mother. They shock and repel, but they also enlighten. They provide us with a means of understanding the dark side of the patriarchal unconscious, particularly the deep-seated attitude of extreme ambivalence to the mother who nurtures but who, through a series of physical and psychic castrations associated with her body and the processes of infant socialization, also helps to bring about the most painful of all separations, necessary for the child's entry into the symbolic order. Perhaps man's ambivalence towards the maternal figure stems from his association of the mother – not the father – with his reluctant entry into the symbolic. In the horror film this ambivalence has given rise to the representation of woman as monstrous because she gives birth and 'mothers'. In this sense, every encounter with horror, in the cinema, is an encounter with the maternal body *constructed* (I am not arguing that woman is essentially abject) as non-symbolic by the signifying practices of patriarchal ideology. Woman's abjectification is crucial to the functioning of the patriarchal order. 'For without the exploitation of the body-matter of women, what would become of the symbolic process that governs society?' (Irigaray, 1985, 85). An encounter with the monstrous-feminine of the horror film takes us on an aesthetic and ideological journey, 'a descent into the foundations of the symbolic construct' (Kristeva, 1982, 18). This journey no doubt began in the realm of myth and legend and continues today in its various representations of the monstrous-feminine in film, literature, art, poetry and pornography and other popular fictions. By questioning a number of psychoanalytic theories which inform current debates within feminism on the representation of sexual difference in a range of popular fictions we can gain a more accurate picture of the fears and fantasies that dominate our cultural imaginary.

When Perseus slew the Medusa he did not – as commonly thought – put an end to her reign or destroy her terrifying powers. Afterwards, Athena embossed her shield with the Medusa's head. The writhing snakes, with their fanged gaping mouths, and the Medusa's own enormous teeth and lolling tongue were on full view. Athena's aim was simply to strike terror into the hearts of men as well as reminding them of their symbolic debt to the imaginary castrating mother. And no doubt she knew what she was doing. After all, Athena was the great Mother-Goddess of the ancient world and according to ancient legend – the daughter of Metis, the goddess of wisdom, also known as the Medusa.

BIBLIOGRAPHY

Bakhtin, Mikhail (1984) *Rabelais and His World*, trans. Helene Iswolsky, Bloomington: Indiana University Press, 1984.

Bataille, Georges (1962) *Death and Sensuality: A Study of Eroticism and the Taboo*, New York: Walker.

Bellour, Raymond (1979) 'Psychosis, neurosis, perversion', *Camera Obscura* Summer 1979: 105–32.

Benvenuto, Bice and Kennedy, Roger (1986) *The Works of Jacques Lacan: An Introduction*, London: Free Association Books.

Boss, Pete (1968) 'Vile bodies and bad medicine', *Screen* 27.1: 14–24.

Brennan, Teresa, ed. (1989) *Between Feminism and Psychoanalysis*, London: Routledge.

Briffault, Robert (1959) *The Mothers*, abridged, with an Introduction by Gordon Rattray Taylor, London: Allen & Unwin. Repr. New York: Atheneum, 1977: *The Mothers, A Study of the Origins of Sentiment and Institutions*, 3 vols, 1927.

Britton, Andrew (1979) 'The Exorcist', in Robin Wood and Richard Luppe, eds, *The American Nightmare: Essays on the Horror Film*, Toronto: Festival of Festivals, 50–3.

Brophy, Philip (1968) 'Horrality – the textuality of contemporary horror films', *Screen* 27.1: 2–13.

Brown, Frank A. (1972) 'The "clocks" timing biological rhythms', *American Scientist* Nov–Dec.: 756–66.

Brown, Royal S. (1980) '*Dressed to Kill*: myth and male fantasy in the horror/ suspense genre', *Film/Psychology Review* 4: 169–82.

Bullough, Vern L. (1973) 'Medieval medical and scientific views of women', *Viator: Medieval and Renaissance Studies* 4: 485–501.

Bundtzen, Lynda K. (1987) 'Monstrous mothers: Medusa, Grendel and now *Aliens*', *Film Quarterly* 40.3: 11–17.

Butler, Ivan (1967) *Horror in the Cinema*, London: A. Zwemmer Ltd; New York: A. S. Barnes & Co.

Campbell, Joseph (1976) *The Masks of God: Primitive Mythology*, Harmondsworth: Penguin.

Carroll, Noel (1990) *The Philosophy of Horror: Or, Paradoxes of the Heart*, New York: Routledge.

Clover, Carol J. (1989) 'Her body, himself: gender in the slasher film', in James Donald, ed., *Fantasy and the Cinema*, London: BFI, 91–133.

Cowie, Elizabeth (1984) 'Fantasia', *m/f* 9: 71–105.

Creed, Barbara (1989) 'Horror and the monstrous-feminine: an imaginary abjection', in James Donald, ed., *Fantasy and the Cinema*, London: BFI, 63–90.

Creed, Barbara (1993) 'Dark desires: male masochism in the horror film', in Steve Cohan and Ina Hark, eds, *Screening the Male*, New York: Routledge, 118–33.

Dadoun, Roger (1989) 'Fetishism in the horror film', in James Donald, ed., *Fantasy* and the Cinema, London: BFI, 39–61.

Daly, C. D. (1943) 'The role of menstruation in human phylogenesis and ontogenesis', *International Journal of Psychology* 24: 151–70.

Derry, Charles (1987) 'More dark dreams: some notes on the recent horror film', in Gregory A. Waller, ed., *American Horrors: Essays on the Modern American Horror Film*, Urbana: University of Illinois Press, 162–74.

Dervin, Daniel (1980) 'Primal conditions and conventions: the genres of comedy and science fiction', *Film/Psychology Review* 4: 115–47.

Dijkstra, Bram (1986) *Idols of Perversity: Fantasies of Feminine Evil in Fin-de-Siècle Culture*, New York: Oxford University Press.

Dika, Vera (1987) 'The stalker film, 1978–81', in Gregory A. Waller, ed., *American Horrors: Essays on the Modern American Horror Film*, Urbana: University of Illinois Press, 86–101.

Doane, Mary Ann (1987) *The Desire to Desire*, Bloomington and Indianapolis: Indiana University Press.

Douglas, Drake (1967) *Horrors*, London: John Baker.

Ebert, Roger (1981) 'Why movie audiences aren't safe anymore', *American Film* 5: 54–6.

Evans, Walter (1973) 'Monster movies: a sexual theory', *Journal of Popular Film* 2.4: 353–65.

Fisher, Lucy (1989) *Shot/Countershot: Film Tradition and the Women's Cinema*, Princeton, NJ: Princeton University Press.

Frazer, Sir James George (1922) *The Golden Bough*, London: Macmillan.

Freud, Sigmund 'A child is being beaten: a contribution to the study of the origin of sexual perversions', in *The Standard Edition of the Complete Psychological Works of Sigmund Freud*, 24 vols, trans. James Strachey, London: Hogarth, 1953–66, vol. 17, 175–204.

—— 'Analysis of a phobia in a five year old boy', in *Standard Edition*, vol. 10, 1–50.

—— 'Beyond the pleasure principle', in *Standard Edition*, vol. 18, 1–64.

—— 'Female sexuality', in *Standard Edition*, vol. 21, 221–46.

—— 'Fetishism', in *Standard Edition*, vol. 21, 147–58.

—— 'From the history of an infantile neurosis', in *Standard Edition*, vol. 17, 1–122.

—— 'The infantile genital organisation', in *Standard Edition*, vol. 19, 141–8.

—— 'Inhibitions, symptoms and anxiety', in *Standard Edition*, vol. 20, 75–172.

—— 'The interpretation of dreams', in *Standard Edition*, vols 4 and 5.

—— *Introductory Lectures on Psycho-Analysis*, in *Standard Edition*, vol. 16.

—— 'Medusa's head', in *Standard Edition*, vol. 18, 273–4.

—— 'Moses and monotheism: three essays', in *Standard Edition*, vol. 23, 1–138.

—— 'An outline of psycho-analysis', in *Standard Edition*, vol. 23, 139–208.

—— 'On the sexual theories of children', in *Standard Edition*, vol. 9, 205–26.

—— 'Some psychical consequences of the anatomical distinction between the sexes', in *Standard Edition*, vol. 19, 241–61.

—— 'The taboo of virginity. (Contributions to the psychology of love, III)', in *Standard Edition*, vol. 11, 191–208.

—— 'Three essays on the theory of sexuality', in *Standard Edition*, vol. 7, 123–230.

—— 'Totem and taboo', in *Standard Edition*, vol. 13.

—— 'The uncanny', in *Standard Edition*, vol. 17, 217–52.

Fromm, Erich (1970) *The Crisis of Psychoanalysis*, London: Jonathan Cape.

Gifford, Edward S. Jr (1974) *The Evil Eye*, New York: Quadrangle Books.

Graves, Robert (1966) *The White Goddess*, New York: Farrar, Straus & Giroux.

Greenberg, Harvey R. (1986) 'Reimagining the gargoyle: psychoanalytic notes on *Alien*', *Camera Obscura* 15: 87–111.

Greer, Germaine (1991) *The Change: Women, Ageing and the Menopause*, London: Hamish Hamilton.

Grosz, Elizabeth (1990) *Jacques Lacan: A Feminist Introduction*, Sydney: Allen & Unwin.

Gunew, Sneja (1983) 'Feminist criticism: positions and questions', in 'Forum: feminism and interpretation theory', *Southern Review* 16.1: 149–73.

Handling, Piers (1983) *The Shape of Rage: The Films of David Cronenberg*, Toronto: General.

Hardy, Phil, ed. (1986) *The Encyclopedia of Horror Movies*, New York: Harper & Row.

Harkness, John (1983) 'The word, the flesh and David Cronenberg', in Piers Handling, ed., *The Shape of Rage*, Toronto: General, 87–97.

Hays, H. R. (1963) *In the Beginnings*, New York: G. P. Putnam's Sons.

Heath, Stephen (1976) 'Jaws, ideology and film theory', *Framework* 4: 25–7.

—— (1978) 'Difference', *Screen* 19.3: 51–112.

Hogan, David J. (1986) *Dark Romance: Sexuality in the Horror Film*, Jefferson, NC: McFarland.

Hollier, Denis, ed. (1988) *The College of Sociology 1937–39*, trans. Betsy Wing. Minneapolis: University of Minnesota Press.

Horney, Karen (1967) *Feminine Psychology*, New York: W. W. Norton.

Huet, Marie-Hélène (1983) 'Living images: monstrosity and representation', *Representations* 4: 73–87.

Irigaray, Luce (1985) *This Sex Which Is Not One*, trans. Catherine Porter, New York: Cornell University Press.

Jacobus, Mary (1986) *Reading Woman: Essays in Feminist Criticism*, London: Methuen.

Jameson, Fredric (1982) 'Reading Hitchcock', *October* (Winter): 15–42.

Jones, Ernst (1972) 'On the nightmare of bloodsucking', in Roy Huss and T. J. Ross, eds, *Focus on the Horror Film*, Englewood Cliffs, NJ: Prentice-Hall, 57–62.

Kaplan, E. Ann (1990) 'Motherhood and representation: from postwar Freudian figurations to postmodernism', in E. Ann Kaplan, ed., *Psychoanalysis and Cinema*, New York: Routledge, 128–42.

Kavanaugh, James H. (1980) '"Son of a bitch": feminism, humanism, and science in *Alien*', *October* 13 (Summer): 91–100.

Kelly, Mary (1984) 'Woman–desire–image', in *Desire*, London: Institute of Contemporary Arts, 30–1.

Kinder, Marsha and Houston, Beverly (1987) 'Seeing is believing: *The Exorcist* and *Don't Look Now*', in Gregory A. Waller, ed., *American Horrors: Essays on the Modern American Horror Film*, Urbana: University of Illinois Press, 44–61.

King, Stephen (1988) *Bare Bones: Conversations on Terror with Stephen King*, eds Tim Underwood and Chuck Miller, London: New English Library.

Kramer, Heinrich and Sprenger, James (1971) *The Malleus Maleficarum*, New York: Dover edition.

Kristeva, Julia (1982) *Powers of Horror: An Essay on Abjection*, trans. Leon S. Roudiez, New York: Columbia University Press.

Kristeva, Julia (1986) 'Revolution in poetic language', in Toril Moi, ed., *The Kristeva Reader*, Oxford: Basil Blackwell.

Lacan, Jacques (1953) 'Some reflections on the ego', *The International Journal of Psychoanalysis* 24: 11–17.

—— (1968) *The Language of the Self: The Function of Language in Psychoanalysis*, trans. (with notes and commentary) Anthony Wilden, Baltimore: Johns Hopkins University Press.

—— (1977) *Ecrits: A Selection*, trans. Alan Sheridan, London: Tavistock.

—— (1978) 'Le séminaire XX', trans. Stephen Heath, 'Difference', *Screen* 19.3: 59.

Laplanche, J. and Pontalis, J. B. (1985) *The Language of Psycho-Analysis*, London: Hogarth.

Lechte, John (1990) *Julia Kristeva*, London: Routledge.

Lederer, Wolfgang (1968) *The Fear of Women*, New York: Harcourt Brace Jovanovich.

Le Fanu, J. S. (1964) 'Carmilla', in *Best Ghost Stories*, New York: Dover.

Lenne, Gérard (1979) 'Monster and victim: women in the horror film', in Patricia Erens, ed., *Sexual Stratagems: The World of Women in Film*, New York: Horizon, 31–40.

Lévi-Strauss, C. (1963) *Structural Anthropology*, trans. C. Jacobson and B. G. Schoepf, New York: Penguin.

—— (1969) *The Elementary Structures of Kinship*, trans. James Harle Bell and John Richard von Sturmer; ed. Rodney Needham, London: Eyre & Spottiswoode.

—— (1973) *From Honey to Ashes*, London: Jonathan Cape.

Lurie, Susan (1981–2) 'The construction of the "castrated woman" in psycho-analysis and cinema', *Discourse* 4: 52–74.

McDonald, James (1988) *A Dictionary of Obscenity, Taboo and Euphemism*, London: Sphere.

McNally, Raymond T. (1985) *Dracula was a Woman: In Search of the Blood Countess of Transylvania*, London: Hamlyn.

Marshack, Alexander (1972) *The Roots of Civilization*, London: Weidenfeld & Nicolson.

Melville, Herman (1851) *Moby Dick*.

Miles, Margaret R. (1989) *Carnal Knowing: Female Nakedness and Religious Meaning in the Christian West*, Boston: Beacon Press.

Mitchell, Juliet (1975) *Psychoanalysis and Feminism*, Harmondsworth: Penguin.

Mitchell, Juliet and Rose, Jacqueline, eds (1982) *Feminine Sexuality: Jacques Lacan and the école freudienne*, trans. Jacqueline Rose, London: Macmillan.

Modleski, Tania (1986) 'The terror of pleasure: the contemporary horror film and postmodern theory', in Tania Modleski, ed., *Studies in Entertainment*, Bloomington: Indiana University Press, 155–66.

—— (1988) *The Woman Who Knew Too Much: Hitchcock and Feminist Theory*, New York: Methuen.

Morris, Joan (1973) *The Lady was a Bishop*, New York: Macmillan.

Mulvey, Laura (1989) 'Visual pleasure and narrative cinema', in *Visual and Other Pleasures*, London: Macmillan.

Neale, Stephen (1980) *Genre*, London: BFI.

Neumann, Erich (1972) *The Great Mother: An Analysis of the Archetype*, trans. Ralph Manheim, Princeton, NJ: Princeton University Press.

Newman, Kim (1988) *Nightmare Movies: A Critical History of the Horror Movie from 1968–88*, London: Bloomsbury.

Pirie, David (1977–8) 'American Cinema in the '70s', *Movie* 25: 20–4.

Place, Janey (1980) 'Women in *film noir*', in E. Ann Kaplan, ed., *Women in Film Noir*, London: BFI, 35–67.

Polan, Dana B. (1984) 'Eros and syphilization: the contemporary horror film', in Barry Keith Grant, ed., *Planks of Reason: Essays on the Horror Film*, Metuchen, NJ: Scarecrow.

Prawer, S. S. (1980) *Caligari's Children: The Film as Tale of Terror*, New York: Da Capo.

Rawson, Philip (1968) *Erotic Art of the East*, New York: G. P. Putnam's Sons.

Rheingold, Joseph C. (1964) *The Fear of Being a Woman*, New York: Grune & Stratton.

Rose, Jacqueline (1982) 'Introduction' in Juliet Mitchell and Jacqueline Rose, eds, *Feminine Sexuality: Jacques Lacan and the école freudienne*, London: Macmillan.

Rothman, William (1982) *The Murderous Gaze*, Cambridge, MA: Harvard University Press.

Russell, Sharon (1984) 'The witch in film: myth and reality', in Barry Keith Grant, ed., *Planks of Reason: Essays on the Horror Film*, Metuchen, NJ: Scarecrow.

Russo, Mary (1986) 'Female grotesques: carnival and theory', in Teresa de Lauretis, ed., *Feminist Studies Critical Studies*, Bloomington: Indiana University Press.

Russo, Vito (1981) *The Celluloid Closet: Homosexuality in the Movies*, New York: Harper & Row.

Sammon, Paul (1981) 'David Cronenberg', *Cinefantastique* 10.4: 20–34.

Shuttle, Penelope and Redgrove, Peter (1978) *The Wise Wound: Eve's Curse and Everywoman*, New York: Richard Marek.

Silverman, Kaja (1988) *The Acoustic Mirror*, Bloomington: Indiana University Press.

Slater, Philip E. (1971) *The Glory of Hera: Greek Mythology and the Greek Family*, Boston: Beacon Press.

Sobchack, Vivian (1978) 'Bringing it all back home: family economy and generic exchange', in Gregory A. Waller, ed., *American Horrors: Essays on the Modern American Horror Film*, Urbana: University of Illinois Press.

Spoto, Donald (1983) *The Dark Side of Genius: The Life of Alfred Hitchcock*, London: Muller.

Stallybrass, Peter and White, Allon (1986) *The Politics and Poetics of Transgression*, London: Methuen.

Stone, Merlin (1976) *When God Was a Woman*, New York: Harcourt Brace Jovanovich.

Studlar, Gaylyn (1984) 'Masochism and the perverse pleasures of the cinema', *Quarterly Review of Film Studies* 9.4: 267–82.

Tansley, Rebecca (1988) 'Argento's Mothers: matriarchal monsters, maternal memories', unpublished diss: University of Auckland.

Tudor, Andrew (1989) *Monsters and Mad Scientists: A Cultural History of the Horror Movie*, Oxford: Basil Blackwell.

Twitchell, James B. (1985) *Dreadful Pleasures: An Anatomy of Modern Horror*, New York: Oxford University Press.

Ursini, James and Silver, Alain (1975) *The Vampire Film*, Cranbury, NJ: Barnes.

Walker, Barbara G. (1983) *The Women's Encyclopedia of Myths and Secrets*, San Francisco: Harper & Row.

Waller, Gregory A. (1987) *American Horrors: Essays on the Modern American Horror Film*, Urbana: University of Illinois Press.

Whitford, Margaret (1989) 'Rereading Irigaray', in Teresa Brennan, ed., *Between Feminism and Psychoanalysis*, London: Routledge.

Willemen, Paul (1980) 'Letter to John', *Screen* 21.2: 53–66.

Williams, Linda (1984) 'When the woman looks', in *Re-Vision*, Los Angeles: University Publications of America, 67–82.

Wood, Robin (1970) *Hitchcock's Films*, New York: Paperback Library.

—— (1983) 'Cronenberg: a dissenting view', in Piers Handling, ed., *The Shape of Rage: The Films of David Cronenberg*, Toronto: General, 115–35.

—— (1986) *Hollywood from Vietnam to Reagan*, New York: Columbia University Press.

Zimmerman, Bonnie (1984) 'Daughters of darkness: the lesbian vampire on film', in Barry Keith Grant, ed., *Planks of Reason: Essays on the Horror Film*, Metuchen, NJ: Scarecrow, 153–63.

FILMOGRAPHY

Abby (William Girdler, 1974) 31
Alien (Ridley Scott, 1979) 16–30, 50–7, 83, 107, 109
Aliens (James Cameron, 1986) 50–1, 56, 107, 109
Alien³ (David Fincher, 1992) 51–3
Alien Seed (Bob James, 1989) 56
Altered States (Ken Russell, 1980) 17
The Amityville Horror (Stuart Rosenberg, 1979) 55
Arachnophobia (Frank Marshall, 1990) 56
Audrey Rose (Robert Wise, 1977) 31–2
Basic Instinct (Paul Verhoeven, 1992) 1, 123–4, 155
Batman (Leslie Martinson, 1966) 108
The Birds (Alfred Hitchcock, 1963) 6, 12, 24
The Black Cat (Albert S. Rogell, 1941) 55
Black Sunday (Mario Bava, 1961) 73, 76–7
Blood and Roses (Roger Vadim, 1961) 60
Blood Bath (Stephanie Rothman, 1966) 62
Bloodbath at the House of Death (Pete Walker, 1984) 62
Blood Brides (Mario Bava, 1969) 62
Blood Diner (Jackie Kong, 1987) 9
The Blood Drinkers (Gerardo de Leon, 1966) 62
Blood Feast (Herschell Gordon Lewis, 1963) 9, 62
Blood for Dracula (Paul Morrissey, 1974) 62
Blood Orgy (Herschell Gordon Lewis, 1971) 62
Bloodsucking Freaks (Joel M. Reed, 1976) 11
Bloody Birthday (Ed Hunt, 1986) 62
Blue Velvet (David Lynch, 1986) 107
The Brides of Dracula (Terence Fisher, 1960) 64
The Brood (David Cronenberg, 1979) 1, 38, 43–58, 79, 82–3
A Bucket of Blood (Roger Corman, 1959) 62
Bull Durham (Ron Shelton, 1988) 107
Burn Witch Burn! (Sidney Hayers, 1962) 73
The Cabinet of Dr Caligari (Robert Wiene, 1919) 131

INDEX

abject: attraction of 13–14, 31, 37, 42,
60–1, 66, 81; and birth 41, 43–53, 58;
as bodily waste 9, 11, 13–14, 31, 38,
49, 77, 154; as border 8–11, 14, 25,
29–30, 32, 37–8, 42, 48–9, 53–4, 58,
61–2, 69, 71; as corpse 9–10, 140;
definition 9–10; as excrement 10–12,
14, 31, 79; and female sexuality 14,
31, 40; and fertile female body 7, 25,
40, 47–8, 62; and horror film 10–14;
as invaded self 32; and maternal
figure/body 11, 14, 22, 164–6, 38;
and menstrual blood 10, 12, 14, 31,
41, 59, 62, 73–8; and mother–child
dyad 82, 139–40; and narcissism 12;
in religion 9, 11, 14, 42, 48; and self
37, 150; and spectatorship 28–30; as
unsocialized body 38, 40; and
vampirism 70; and woman's blood
68–9; and womb 49–53, 77; and
women 10, 47; as wound 48, 70, 82
see also the monstrous-feminine
Andromeda 46
apocalypse 52, 78
archaic mother *see* monstrous-feminine
Athena 166

Bacchae 126
Bakhtin, Mikhail 57–8
Bataille, Georges 10, 28
Bathory, Countess Elizabeth 60, 63, 67
Bellour, Raymond 140, 144, 146–8
Benvenuto, Bice 160, 162
bible 41–2, 47
birds: as female fetish 24; as women
142–3, 144–6
birth: as grotesque 56–8 *see also* abject
blood: in film titles 62; hymenal 66;

and lesbian vampire 59–61, 70;
menstrual 63–4; and oral sex 69–70;
pig's blood 80; and vampirism 59–62
passim, 69–70 *see also* abject;
menstruation; vampire
body: as abject female 37–42; bleeding
wound 147; clean and proper body
11–13, 40, 42, 47; feminized male
body 19; as grotesque 58; as
house/womb 55; menstrual body
62–72; and mirror phase 29–30;
physical transpositions 117; in revolt
34, 40; symbolic (male) body 11, 25,
47, 49, 58, 68 *see also* abject
Boss, Pete 48
Brennan, Teresa 110
Britton, Andrew 39, 157
Brophy, Philip 48
Brown, Frank A. 64
Brown, Royal 125
Bullough, Vern L. 56–7, 91
Bundtzen, Lynda K. 51
Butler, Ivan 148

calendar: and menstrual cycle 64
Campbell, Joseph 1, 74, 106
cannibalism 2, 11, 22, 55, 67
Carmilla (Sheridan le Fanu) 60
carnivalesque 42, 80
Carroll, Noel 39
caste system 13
castrating mother *see*
monstrous-feminine
castration: anxiety 5, 12, 53–5, 74–5,
105–21, 154, 155, 162; castration of
male 2, 105–21, 122–38, 148–9, 153;
female castration complex 22;
Freudian theory of 1–9 *passim*, 87,

178

An environmentally friendly book printed and bound in England by www.printondemand-worldwide.com

#0245 - 061212 - C0 - 234/156/10 - PB